Tullio Viola
Peirce on the Uses of History

Peirceana

Edited by
Francesco Bellucci and Ahti-Veikko Pietarinen

Volume 4

Tullio Viola

Peirce on the Uses of History

—

DE GRUYTER

ISBN 978-3-11-099674-6
e-ISBN (PDF) 978-3-11-065156-0
e-ISBN (EPUB) 978-3-11-064961-1
ISSN 2698-7155

Library of Congress Control Number: 2020940741

Bibliographic information published by the Deutsche Nationalbibliothek
The Deutsche Nationalbibliothek lists this publication in the Deutsche Nationalbibliografie;
detailed bibliographic data are available on the Internet at http://dnb.dnb.de.

© 2022 Walter de Gruyter GmbH, Berlin/Boston
This volume is text- and page-identical with the hardback published in 2020.
Revised version of dissertation titled "Philosophy and History: The Legacy of Peirce's Realism";
Dept. of Philosophy, Faculty of Humanities, Humboldt University of Berlin; reviewed by
Prof. Dr. Volker Gerhardt, Prof. Dr. Jürgen Trabant and Prof. Dr. Christian Möckel; defended on
07.09.2015 under Dean Prof. Michael Seadle, PhD.
Printing and binding: CPI books GmbH, Leck

www.degruyter.com

Acknowledgments

This book is the revised version of my Ph.D. thesis. I thank my supervisors, Volker Gerhardt, Jürgen Trabant and the late John-Michael Krois, as well as Christian Möckel, for their generous guidance and advice. During the years of my doctorate, I benefited from a stipend from the Kolleg-Forschergruppe "Bildakt und Verkörperung" of the Humboldt-Universität zu Berlin, directed by Horst Bredekamp, John-Michael Krois and Jürgen Trabant. I thank them and all the friends who have worked there for a truly unique research atmosphere.

The final version of the book was completed while I was a research fellow at the Max-Weber-Kolleg für kultur- and sozialwissenschaftliche Studien in Erfurt, thanks to a research grant from the Max-Planck-Forschungspreis "Religion und Moderne: Säkularisation, gesellschaftliche und religiöse Pluralität," guided by Hans Joas. I thank him not only for the opportunity to work in Erfurt, but also for invaluable help at all stages of my research. I also thank my Max-Weber-Kolleg colleagues for having discussed parts of the manuscript with me. I am particularly grateful to Gabriel Abend, Sebastian Bandelin, Matteo Bortolini, Martin Fuchs, Petra Gümplova, Christoph Henning, Bettina Hollstein, Urs Lindner, Daniele Miano, Andreas Pettenkofer, Hartmut Rosa, Matteo Santarelli, Magnus Schlette and Emiliano Urciuoli.

My interest in Peirce, pragmatism and the philosophy of history goes back to my student's years in Pisa. I would like to thank three teachers who have changed the way I think: Alfredo Ferrarin, Aldo Gargani, Carlo Ginzburg.

Thanks to Francesco Bellucci and Ahti-Veikko Pietarinen for agreeing to include my book in the book series Peirceana. Chiara Ambrosio, Francesco Bellucci, Gabriele Gava and Mathias Girel read either the entire final manuscript or chapters thereof and provided invaluable criticism. I thank them most warmly. The director of the Peirce Edition Project, André De Tienne, has not only been an extremely helpful interlocutor over the years; he was also kind enough to let me consult a part of the forthcoming ninth volume of Peirce's *Writings*.

Over the years, I have talked with so many colleagues and friends about the ideas of this book that it would be impossible to list them all. Let me thank in particular Andrew Abbott, Lucio Biasiori, Francesco Buscemi, Daniel Cefaï, Vincent Colapietro, Franz Engel, Rossella Fabbrichesi, Roberto Frega, Sascha Freyberg, Roberto Gronda, Matthias Jung, Sybille Krämer, Marion Lauschke, Giovanni Maddalena, Sabine Marienberg, David Marshall, Helmut Pape, Moritz Queisner, Frederik Stjernfelt, Maddalena Vaglio Tanet and Amadeu Viana.

In Chapter 1, I have used some excerpts from my article, "Peirce and Iconology," in: *European Journal of Pragmatism and American Philosophy* 4. No. 1

(2012). Thanks to the journal editors for their permission to make use of this material.

Thanks to Jay Lingham for her linguistic help.

Finally, I am grateful to all the friends and family who stood by me throughout the years. And this book is for Maddalena, who was there from the start.

Berlin, March 2020

Abbreviations

CD	Whitney William Dwight (Ed.). *Century Dictionary. An Encyclopedic Lexicon of the English Language*. Edited with assistance from Benjamin Eli Smith. New York: The Century Co., 1889–1891.
CN	*Charles S. Peirce: Contributions to The Nation*. 4 vols. Kenneth L. Ketner/James E. Cook (Eds.). Lubbock: Texas Tech Press, 1975–1987.
CP	*Collected Papers of Charles S. Peirce*. 8 vols. Charles Hartshorne/Paul Weiss/Arthur W. Burks (Eds.). Cambridge/MA: The Belknap Press, 1931–1958. Cited by volume and paragraph number.
EP	*The Essential Peirce: Selected Philosophical Writings*. 2 vols. Nathan Houser/Christian Kloesel/Peirce Edition Project (Eds.). Bloomington, Indianapolis: Indiana University Press, 1992–1998.
HP	*Historical Perspectives on Peirce's Logic of Science. A History of Science*. 2 vols. Carolyn Eisele (Ed.). Berlin, New York, Amsterdam: Mouton, 1985.
NEM	*The New Elements of Mathematics*. 4 vols. Carolyn Eisele (Ed.). The Hague, Paris: Mouton, 1976.
R/RL	Charles S. Peirce Papers, Am 1632, Houghton Library, Harvard University. The manuscript numbers follow Richard Robin, *Annotated Catalogue of the Papers of Charles S. Peirce* (Amherst: University of Massachusetts Press, 1967). The abbreviation RL refers to the letters listed in the correspondence section of Robin's catalogue.
RLT	*Reasoning and the Logic of Things. The Cambridge Conferences Lectures of 1898*. Kenneth L. Ketner (Ed.). Cambridge/MA, London: Harvard University Press, 1992.
S&S	*Semiotics and Significs. The Correspondence between Charles S. Peirce and Victoria Lady Welby*. Charles S. Hardwick/James Cook (Eds.). Bloomington, London: Indiana University Press, 1977.
W	*Writings of Charles S. Peirce: A Chronological Edition*. 8 vols. Peirce Edition Project (Ed.). Bloomington, Indianapolis: Indiana University Press, 1982–.

Contents

Acknowledgments —— V

Abbreviations —— VII

Introduction —— 1

Part I

1   **The Making of a Polymath** —— 11
        Science, Religion, and Metaphysics —— 11
        First Historical Studies —— 15
        A Decisive Model: William Whewell —— 18
        1867–1869: Cartesianism versus Scholasticism —— 22
        "Metaphysical History": The Review of Berkeley —— 25
        Clear and Cloudy Nights —— 30
        Transition to a New Phase —— 35

2   **Not a Mere Wonder Book** —— 38
        Philosophy and History from 1884 on —— 38
        The Rationales for a History of Science —— 42
        The "Mutual Aid" between History and Philosophy —— 46
        A Pragmatist's History, Pragmatic History, Practical Lessons —— 48
        The Classification of the Sciences —— 52
        Natural Classes, Genealogy, Natural History —— 60
        An Alternative Approach —— 65

Part II

3   **Historicity as Process** —— 71
        An "Attraction for Living Facts" —— 71
        Early Semiotic Processualism —— 73
        Habit and the Law of Mind —— 77
        Evolution, Love, and Teleology —— 83
        The Growth of Symbols —— 88

Embodiment, Final Causation, and Genealogy —— 92
A Pragmaticist's Analysis of Time —— 96

4   **Autonomy and the Value of Experience —— 100**
Wading into the Slough —— 100
Tradition, Prejudice, Common Sense —— 104
Experience: The Outward Clash and the Little Mouse —— 109
Pragmatism, Analysis, and the A Priori —— 112
"Facts about Men": The Challenge of Psychologism —— 118
History and Ampliative Reasoning —— 123
An Exchange with Dewey —— 127

5   **Sociality, Dialogue, Disagreement —— 131**
The Problem of Peirce's Social Thought —— 131
The Guiding Thread of Dialogue —— 133
Science: A Community in History —— 137
Philosophy: The Architectonic Principle —— 143
Disagreement and Convergence —— 147
Conservatism and Sentimentalism —— 151
The Ethics of Terminology —— 155

Part III

6   **Peirce the Historian —— 161**
The Scope of Peirce's History of Science —— 161
The Origins of Science —— 163
The Laws of Growth: Evolution versus Revolutions —— 167
The Laws of Growth: Individuals versus Collectives —— 173
Looking at Art, Artifacts, Architecture —— 178
An "Extraordinary Little Book" —— 181
Observation of Lives —— 185

7   **The Logic of Historical Inquiry —— 192**
Peirce on Historical Method —— 192
Documents and Monuments of Ancient History —— 193
Three Case Studies: Aristotle, Plato, Pythagoras —— 198
Hypothesis, Explanation, Truth —— 204
Unintentional Evidence: Betraying versus Parading —— 209
The Journey of a Footnote —— 211

The Interpretation of Fellow Thinkers —— 214

Conclusion: The Legacy of a Realist —— 219

Bibliography —— 227

Index of names —— 243

Index of terms —— 246

Introduction

1

This book examines the relation between philosophy and history in the work of Charles S. Peirce. It asks, in particular, to what extent Peirce allowed history to have a bearing on philosophy. To do so, it follows two paths. It examines those philosophical arguments that deal, directly or indirectly, with the role of history. And it looks at Peirce's own historical inquiries.

It is often recalled that Peirce was a philosopher-polymath, and that his style of philosophizing cannot be understood if one does not take into account his interest in logic, mathematics, and the experimental sciences, as well as his attempt to conceive of philosophy as being contiguous with scientific inquiry. This book starts from a kindred observation: Peirce's interest in history is a fundamental component of his scientific and philosophical profile. Peirce started cultivating historical interests very early in his life, in parallel with his engagement with the experimental sciences. Later on, he started writing firsthand historical works. Though his focus was the history of science, he made some forays into other areas of historical learning as well. But how did he conceive of the link between these historical interests and his work as a philosopher? Peirce neither asked nor answered this question unambiguously. This book is devoted to spelling out the precise terms of the problem and to exploring its most significant implications.

Peirce's sensitivity to history displays two sides. On the one hand, his historical writings testify to an eager intellectual interest that cannot be discarded as the mere by-product of an eclectic mind. On the other hand, these writings are not even close to being as systematic or comprehensive as other branches of Peirce's production. Peirce was neither a fully-fledged philosopher of history nor a mature, first-rank historian. But he made excellent contributions to both fields of study. Likewise, his observations about the relation between history and philosophy are often penetrating and original. Still, they give the reader the impression of being left underdeveloped, especially when compared to the painstaking detail with which Peirce worked out other segments of his system.

I believe that this tension can be ascribed to at least three main sources. The first source is biographical. In the last three decades of his life, Peirce was an increasingly secluded scholar. His work displays the traits of the brilliant outsider, able to shed new light on difficult issues, but also idiosyncratic in his judgment and isolated from the scholarly community. This fact is reflected in the uneven quality of his historical writing.

A second source is philosophical. Peirce's style of work is characterized by a propensity to tackle philosophical issues by taking as seriously as possible the arguments on both sides. The highly sophisticated and original positions he developed on many epistemological, logical and metaphysical issues owe much to this ability.[1] But in some cases, his inclination to look at both sides of the matter stopped just short of culminating in a truly successful synthesis. The question of whether history may have a bearing on philosophy is, I believe, one such case. Peirce seems to oscillate between a more liberal and a more restrictive answer to this question, and the relation between his historical inquiries and his philosophical activity is therefore never free of tension.

Finally, a third source is Peirce's willingness to experiment with a plurality of ways in which history can become relevant to philosophy, as well as with different methodological strategies to study the human past. One such strategy is highly metaphysical and speculative. It consists in putting forth sweeping generalizations about the dynamics of historical progress. Peirce's tormented relation with Hegel is pivotal in understanding this aspect of his work, as is his complex allegiance to evolutionism. However, another methodological strategy is seemingly opposite to the first. It hinges on erudite research, on philological and archival work, on the quintessentially antiquarian love for those traces of the past that are apparently devoid of interest.[2] As Peirce himself put it in a text I shall extensively discuss: "My own historical studies [...] have been somewhat minutely critical."[3] We will see throughout the book, moreover, that these two strategies are just the poles of a complex spectrum of methodological approaches that coexist in Peirce's oeuvre.

2

This pluralism might be taken for a weakness of Peirce's philosophy. However, I am more interested in the flip side of this argument. Peirce's work is significant precisely because it offers a blueprint to investigate the complexity and ramifica-

---

[1] On Peirce's method of work, see Turrisi 2014. On metaphysics, see, e. g., Boler 1963, p. 13–14, who speaks about the dilemma of realism versus idealism: "The point of particular interest in Peirce is the way pragmatism serves to prevent each position from gravitating to its extreme." On epistemology and the theory of perception, see Haack 1994, p. 9.
[2] This oscillation is captured by Topa 2016, par. 1, when he notes that "[Peirce's] *écriture* is pervaded by an encyclopaedic and intensely curious historical consciousness that neither shies away from the consideration of minute details [...] nor from the responsibility to understand the causes of large scale historical processes."
[3] CP 6.604 (1893).

tions of the philosophy of history and historiography.[4] Moreover, his broaching the problem both from the viewpoint of the philosopher and from that of the historian enhances the significance of his reflections for different communities of scholars. Given the disciplinary focus of his writings, one such community is, quite naturally, that of historians and philosophers of science. But Peirce's ideas will turn out to be equally relevant to philosophers of history, historians, and social scientists at large.

Born a few years after the death of Hegel, Peirce lived through a period in which philosophy experienced a profound transformation. Philosophers faced new and unprecedented challenges coming from the burgeoning field of social and human sciences, but also from the revolutionary import of Darwin's theory of evolution. The epochal contribution of Hegel to the philosophy of history was soon challenged by those historicist thinkers who looked at history as an empirical, non-speculative enterprise.[5] At more or less at the same time, philosophers were negotiating the boundaries with empirical inquiries. The heated debate about psychologism, and the charges of relativism that it often brought with it, are paradigmatic in this sense.[6]

Peirce's work is not only a reaction to this intellectual scenario but a crucial component thereof. Moreover, it is the point of origin of a philosophical tradition, pragmatism, which has profoundly reshaped our understanding of philosophy's relation to both history and empirical inquiry. On the basis of my study, I hope that more precise comparisons with other pragmatist philosophies of history and historiography (John Dewey's and George H. Mead's in particular) will become possible. Also, I hope to clarify to what extent Peirce's philosophy may contribute to the study of the historicist element of pragmatist thought, and to a renewed appreciation of pragmatism's relevance to contemporary debates in the philosophy of history.[7]

3

Despite the many conceptions of history and the many uses of history that I have mentioned above, a fundamental claim of my book is that there is one specific

---

[4] On the distinction between philosophy of history and philosophy of historiography, see, e. g., Kuukkanen 2015, p. 5.
[5] See Schnädelbach 1984, Ch. 2.
[6] See Kusch 1995.
[7] Among recent studies on this topic, let me single out Brandom 2002, Introduction; Kloppenberg 2004; Koopman 2009; Joas 2016; Kuukkanen 2017; Grigoriev/Piercey 2019. See also Gronda/Viola 2016.

element that gives Peirce's philosophy of history its basic significance and its specific identity within the pragmatist family. This is its distinctive realist character. For Peirce, history is first and foremost a science, and science is the "pursuit of those who are devoured by a desire to find things out."[8] It is about learning new things about the world. How to do so in a reliable, objective manner is a problem of paramount importance to both Peirce's theory of science and his theory of history.

However, history stands out from the other sciences in that the object of its study is the past. This opens up a whole set of new problems. One commentator, in particular, has claimed that Peirce did not live up to the goal of providing a clear solution to the challenges raised by the peculiar status of the historical past. Peirce's conception of history, argues Joseph L. Esposito, oscillates between an "objectivist" and a "transcendental" conception, or between a realist and a constructionist perspective on the past.[9] While I agree with Esposito that these tensions play a role in Peirce's work, I think they also point to one important reason why Peirce the philosopher of history has something important to tell us. Peirce delineates a complex and sophisticated form of realism, which manages to stay clear of most of the drawbacks often associated with that position. Moreover, I do not think it is entirely fair to argue that the tensions in Peirce's philosophy of history are due to Peirce's devoting "little time to the study of the conditions of historical consciousness," as Esposito states.[10] That Peirce devoted much time indeed to such a study is testified to, among other things, by the text I shall focus on in the last chapter of this book, namely the lengthy treatise "On the Logic of Drawing History from Ancient Documents, Especially from Testimonies" (1901). This treatise does make clear, however, that when Peirce embarked on a systematic account of the conditions of historical consciousness, it was the realistic conception of history that gained the upper hand.

Of course, this does not settle Esposito's objections; nor does it settle the problem of how to create a coherent picture out of the plurality of Peirce's approaches to history. These problems will keep us busy throughout the book. In addition, I will point to another possible shortcoming of Peirce's realist philosophy of history. Peirce's emphasis on the epistemological continuity between history, philosophy and science may make it hard to explain some important differences between the way science and philosophy resort to historical arguments. In particular, Peirce was inclined to consider the possibility of reaching universal

---

[8] CP 1.8 (c. 1897).
[9] Esposito 1983. For a recent critique, see Colapietro 2016.
[10] Esposito 1983, p. 155.

consensus among competent researchers as a necessary condition of rationality. This may have led him to neglect the possibility that philosophers also recur to history as a way to deal with those situations in which agreement or consensus seem out of reach.

4

The study of Peirce's approach to history itself has a history. The generation of English-speaking scholars coming to maturity around the 1950s is particularly worthy of attention in this respect. That generation was instrumental in routing the study of Peirce in a rigorous philological direction. But it also emphasized the many points of contact between Peirce and the philosophy of history. Max H. Fisch, the initiator of the chronological edition of Peirce's writings, was also a scholar of Giambattista Vico. The question of the interactions between philosophy and history lies at the very center of his intellectual legacy.[11] Murray G. Murphey, the author of a pioneering monograph on *The Development of Peirce's Philosophy* (1961), went on to write two fairly influential books on the philosophy of history.[12] Philip P. Wiener, a pivotal figure in the North American history of ideas, was a prolific Peirce scholar; especially noteworthy is his book on the evolutionary background of pragmatism.[13] Finally, Walter B. Gallie, best known today for his writings on "essentially contested concepts" and on the narrative dimension of historiography, began his career as a Peirce scholar. As we will see, his work on history and contested concepts is related to this Peircean background, although in ways that are not easily perceivable at first.[14]

The title of my book is indebted to one of the first essays explicitly devoted to Peirce's philosophy of history: "Peirce on the Use of History," by Willard M. Miller (1971). I have allowed myself to take up Miller's title almost verbatim – only turning it into the plural – because that phrase seems to me to be the most precise way to refer to the problem I want to tackle.

Miller's paper gave rise to a debate with Philip P. Wiener in the pages of the *Transactions of the Charles S. Peirce Society*.[15] The debate revolved around the logical validity and the philosophical relevance of Peirce's philosophy of history. While Miller's tone was more laudatory, Wiener pointed to precisely those incon-

---

11 See Marshall 2016.
12 See Murphey [1961] 1993; Murphey 1979; Murphey 1994; Murphey 2009.
13 Wiener 1949. See also Wiener 1946; Wiener 1952.
14 Gallie 1952; Gallie 1956a; Gallie 1956b; Gallie 1964. I have examined the relation between Gallie and Peirce in Viola 2019. See Ch. 5 for more details.
15 Miller 1971; Miller 1972; Miller 1978; Wiener 1971; Wiener 1972.

sistencies and tensions between the different conceptions of history that I have mentioned above. In particular, he argued that Peirce's evolutionary approach to the history of science, far from being the result of careful empirical generalization, was instead the result of an undue application of speculative theories of evolution to the facts of human history. In this sense, Wiener was not far from his teacher, Arthur O. Lovejoy, who had looked at the pragmatist conceptions of history with a mixture of sympathy and criticism.[16]

As I have anticipated, a similar mixture of sympathy and criticism was articulated a few years later by Joseph L. Esposito. Setting out from a very insightful reading of Peirce against the background of German idealism, Esposito detected an oscillation between two conceptions of history. The first position is decidedly realist ("without a past to study there would be no historical consciousness"), while the other is more "constructionist" ("without an historical consciousness there would be no past to study").[17] Esposito argued that Peirce started with the first position but ended up lapsing into the second on many occasions, and failed to deploy the necessary tools to develop a more consistent synthesis.

Today, our appraisal of criticisms such as Esposito's or Wiener's can only gain some credibility by taking into account another milestone in the history of Peirce's scholarship, which appeared just a few years after Esposito's paper. I refer to Carolyn Eisele's edition of Peirce's most significant historical writings (1985).[18] For it is only by studying Peirce's actual, painstaking work as a historian and as a methodologist of historiography, which began to emerge with Eisele's editorial work, that one can truly appreciate the sense in which Peirce was concerned with the intellectual challenges posed by history. What's more, focusing on Peirce's historical work can also help us appreciate another crucial issue we will have to touch upon in the book, namely the link between the methodology of historiography and Peirce's epoch-making contributions to the study of inferential reasoning. In particular, his treatment of abduction, or hypothetical inference, has long attracted the attention of both philosophers and historians.[19]

---

16 See Wiener 1972, p. 193–194: "Need I pay further tribute to Peirce as an intellectual historian and methodologist than to say that my own work in the history of ideas and its methodology owes more to Peirce than to any other philosopher, save the two critical intellectual historians who were my teachers and senior colleagues, Morris R. Cohen the first editor of Peirce's papers, and Arthur O. Lovejoy, the critic of the thirteen pragmatisms." See Ch. 7 for a further discussion of Lovejoy and Wiener.
17 Esposito 1983, p. 156.
18 Throughout the book, I will refer to this edition as HP. Cf. Ketner 1982. See also Eisele 1979.
19 See, in particular, the essays collected in Eco/Sebeok 1983, to which I return in Ch. 7.

5

The book is articulated in three parts, which approach the relation between history and philosophy from slightly different perspectives. Part I (Chapters 1–2) fulfills an introductory function. It first looks at the development of Peirce's conception of the history-philosophy relation from a biographical viewpoint. Then, it examines those parts of Peirce's mature work in which this relation is the object of explicit analysis. Part II (Chapters 3–5) contains the argumentative gist of the book. Here I seek to provide a comprehensive reconstruction of the different senses in which Peirce's philosophy allows history to play a significant role. Finally, Part III (Chapters 6–7) focuses on Peirce's actual work as a historian and as a methodologist of historical inquiry. A short conclusion closes the book.

Chapter 1 is a narrative account of Peirce's early intellectual career. I describe the paths along which Peirce shaped his conception of the mutual relation between history and philosophy from his student years until the late 1880s. That conception would bear its ripest fruit in the early 1890s. In particular, the period from approximately 1891 to 1893 would turn out to be pivotal. In those years, Peirce worked assiduously on his history of science; he started developing a "classification of the sciences" in which the relation between history and philosophy was explicitly conceptualized; and he worked on an ambitious philosophy of evolution that is tightly bound up with his historical investigations. Chapter 2 follows up on this narrative and considers Peirce's explicit reflections on the relation between history and philosophy from the early 1890s on. Two main topics emerge as especially significant. The first is the variegated web of rationales through which Peirce tried to justify his work as a historian of science. The second is his classification of the sciences. The latter indicates rather precisely the basis on which philosophy and history can be expected to entertain a fruitful exchange. I will show, however, that there are good reasons not to take the classification of the sciences to be the most accurate description of the actual relation between philosophy and history in Peirce's work.

The three subsequent chapters, 3, 4 and 5, are best read as a unitary argument. In Chapter 3, I look at what I call the problem of *historicity:* to what extent does a comprehension of the past play a role in our understanding of present states of affairs? I argue that Peirce cultivated a strong conception of historicity, one that becomes most visible once we focus on the processualist nature of his semiotics, of his metaphysics, and of his theory of evolution. In Chapter 4, I look at a complementary problem: what conception of *intellectual autonomy* is harbored in Peirce's writings? Does philosophical thinking need to rely on the data of experience? Does it need to take into account the opinion of other thinkers, both present and past? Answering this question will give us an idea of the role of history in Peirce's conception of philosophical *Selbstdenken*. Finally,

Chapter 5 focuses on the issue of intersubjectivity and sociality: a particularly fruitful perspective, I will argue, to let both the strengths and the weaknesses of Peirce's conception of history emerge.

In Chapter 6, I go back to a more descriptive approach, by examining Peirce's mature work as a historian. Needless to say, I cannot pretend to offer an exhaustive interpretation of this very large segment of Peirce's production. Rather, I isolate some of the most significant themes from his historical writings. A similar approach is then pursued in Chapter 7, where I examine Peirce's thoughts on the methodological and epistemological issues raised by historiography. The aforementioned treatise, "On the Logic of Drawing History from Ancient Documents," will take center stage. But I will take into account other sources as well. Following Peirce's own strategy, this chapter combines methodological observations with a discussion of the epistemology of historical explanation and the status of historical truth.

Part I

1 The Making of a Polymath

Science, Religion, and Metaphysics

Charles S. Peirce entered his twenties at the beginning of a crucial period in American history. In 1861, the Civil War broke out. Two years before the war, another epochal event, although a very different one, had shaken the house of New England intellectuals in which he was living: Charles Darwin had published *On the Origin of Species*.[1]

During those years, Peirce received a severe intellectual education under the guidance of his father, Benjamin Peirce. Benjamin was a mathematician and one of the most authoritative figures of pre-war American science. He personally attended to the education of his son and imparted to him the notions he most cherished. These were, first of all, mathematics and natural science; but philosophy was by no means neglected. Charles studied "almost [...] by heart" Kant's first *Critique*, and combined it with other readings, such as Schiller's *Aesthetic Letters* and Richard Whately's *Elements of Logic* (1826). Peirce would later describe the encounter with Whately's book as his first contact with logic, the discipline that would stay at the center of his intellectual interests throughout his life.[2]

Finally, there was religion: Benjamin, a Unitarian Protestant, was a very devout man, close to the mysticism of Swedenborg and to the transcendentalists (Ralph Waldo Emerson was a close acquaintance).[3] He advocated a view of science as an inquiry into the will of God. In this, he concurred with another re-

---

[1] See Brent [1993] 1998, Ch. 1, for biographical information. On Peirce's own recollections of how he first learnt about Darwin's book, see EP2, p. 158 (1903), and Wiener 1946, p. 322. On the "catastrophic effect of the Darwinian theory upon the world view of American intellectuals" see Murphey 1979, p. 14. On the caesura of the Civil War in American philosophy, see Fisch 1986a, p. 110–113.

[2] See Fisch 1982, p. xviii. On Kant, I am quoting Peirce's own recollection, in CP 1.560 (c. 1905). On Peirce and Schiller, see also Barnouw 1988. I go back to Whately from a different perspective in Ch. 7.

[3] See Brent [1993] 1998, p. 34–36, 45. On Benjamin Peirce as a scientist, see Peterson 1955. Decades later, Charles Peirce would go back to the influence of transcendentalism on his thought with cautious and half-ironic words. See "The Law of Mind" (1892), W8, p. 135: "[T]he atmosphere of Cambridge held many an antiseptic against Concord transcendentalism, and I am not conscious of having contracted any of that virus. Nevertheless, it is probable that some cultured bacilli, some benignant form of the disease was implanted in my soul, unawares, and that now, after long incubation, it comes to the surface, modified by mathematical conceptions and by training in physical investigation."

nowned Cambridge scientist, as well as a close friend of his: the Swiss emigré naturalist Louis Agassiz, one of Darwin's most authoritative adversaries in America during the first period of the debate over evolutionism.[4] Agassiz championed a view of science as the study of the ideas of God that are incarnated in the world. But again, as in the case of Peirce's father, this view did not entail any significant concession as concerns the autonomy of science from religion. Agassiz vigorously asserted such an autonomy without therefore feeling that he was jeopardizing his religious faith.

Peirce had made acquaintance with Agassiz's ideas at a crucial juncture in his early years. In 1860, a moment in which he "wondered what [he] would do in life," he had studied natural history and the methods of classification under the Swiss scientist.[5] From that moment on, he would retain a very high esteem for the intellectual achievements of both Agassiz and his father. But unlike his first two mentors, he could no longer count on the immediate conception of a reason in service of faith that permeated American scientific circles prior to the Darwinian revolution. That unity of science and religion had been challenged for good; and for somebody who had been formed in its shadow, a problematic scission arose, along with the necessity of a new reconciliation.[6]

The reason I am recalling this well-known story is twofold. First, I would like to stress the role of evolutionism as a major force of Peirce's intellectual development, one that was destined to exert a profound influence on his understanding of history (see Chapter 3). Second, I aim to interpret the tension between science and religion as a crucial component in what we might call the situation of departure of Peirce's intellectual career.[7] This tension acts both as an intellectual urgency and as an argumentative pattern to which Peirce resorted repeatedly throughout the years. Moreover, the way Peirce ended up thinking about the relation between philosophy, science and history is shaped by his early reflections on the interplay between science and religion.

The texts and fragments from the late 1850s and early 1860s are very telling in this respect. They show the young philosopher at work to find an equilibrium between two different intellectual activities: "science" on the one hand, "metaphysics" or "philosophy" on the other.[8] The two activities embody opposite in-

---

[4] On Agassiz, see Irmscher 2013; Jordan 1923. On Agassiz's and Benjamin Peirce's social and political views, compromised by racism and pro-slavery beliefs, see Menand 2001.
[5] W1, p. 3. Cf. Fisch 1982, p. xv; Brent [1993] 1998, p. 38.
[6] Among the many interpreters who have insisted on the significance of the young Peirce's familiar background for his reception of Darwinism, see Murphey [1961] 1993, p. 294.
[7] On the "situation of departure" see Tonelli 1962, p. 289–290.
[8] See, in particular, W1, p. 4–9 (1853–1888); 37–43 (1859); 57–84 (1861–62); 85–90 (1861).

tellectual stances, which need to be reconciled. Science is the progressive and cumulative investigation of reality, based on observations and inductions. But it is also the faculty of exerting skepticism: of bracketing off prejudices and uncertain assumptions in order to build new knowledge on more solid foundations. Metaphysics, on the contrary, is concerned with that part of knowledge that does not come from observation. It does not add new knowledge but digs into our a priori concepts and categories. The two intellectual stances need to proceed hand in hand, so as to avoid lapsing into either dogmatism or a radical form of skepticism. Moreover, while scientists are predominantly nominalists, metaphysicians are realists and idealists. The two perspectives are both, in a sense, legitimate. Although Peirce, in this period, was still sympathetic with nominalism, as early as 1859 he jotted down that "it is not that Realism is false; but only that Realists did not advance in the spirit of the scientific age."[9]

However, the task of more precisely determining the nature of metaphysics proves a difficult one, because many definitions can be given of it, each with its own domain of validity. In the end, the definition Peirce ends up trusting more is the "logical" one, according to which metaphysics is "the analysis of conceptions."[10] But Peirce also alerts us to the possibility that this analytical operation may go astray, either by lapsing into the excesses of "rationalism,"[11] or by not recognizing that analysis is always in need of being sustained by its empirical counterpart.[12] Moreover, metaphysical beliefs are different from logical or scientific ones. Strictly speaking, metaphysics is not even a doctrine, but an activity that resembles "meditation," or the "wisdom" that comes out of the "unfolding of the mind."[13] It cannot even be put into books: "You may put suggestions towards it into books but each mind must evolve it for himself."[14] Finally, metaphysics presupposes an act of faith in the primitive conceptions that are tied up with our judgments, and which ultimately refer to the ideas of the perfect and unconditioned, the absolute, the divine. Faith and knowledge must proceed in parallel: "Wherever there is knowledge there is faith. Wherever there is Faith [...] there is Knowledge."[15] So metaphysics shows some affinity to religious atti-

---

9 R 921 (1859). See Fisch, 1984, p. xxvi n6.
10 W1, p. 58, 74.
11 W1, p. 65.
12 See W1, p. 111–112 (1863).
13 W1, p. 4.
14 W1, p. 60.
15 W1, p. 78.

tude. "All the higher life is strengthened by metaphysics. And we find metaphysicians are generally Holy Men."[16]

Peirce would gradually evolve out of these fragments a theory about the fundamental metaphysical categories of reality. These early attempts represented the first step toward what would soon become the veritable backbone of Peirce's philosophy, namely his list of three metaphysical categories, later called *Firstness*, *Secondness* and *Thirdness*. As of the late 1850s, in particular, he attempted to draw a first list of categories out of the triad of English personal pronouns, I, IT, and THOU, precisely in virtue of the simple and seemingly basal nature of these conceptions. "If conceptions which are incapable of definition are simple, I, It and Thou are so. Who could define either of these words, easy as they are to understand?"[17] This idea anticipates not only the triadic partition of the later theory, but also some of the basic traits of each metaphysical category. The I refers to the dimension of subjective immediacy; the IT to the ideas of objectivity and contrast; and the THOU to a mediation between the two, one that is based on intersubjectivity.[18]

The triadic pattern already displayed by Peirce's writings on personal pronouns can be variously interpreted. It can, for instance, be related to a broader post-Kantian tendency to rework and reconcile the dichotomies of Kantian philosophy by means of conceptual trichotomies. (Think, for instance, of Schiller's triad of form drive, sense drive and play drive in the *Aesthetic Letters*.)[19] Or it can be related to Peirce's religious background. Peirce made explicit reference to the Christian trinity as related to his three metaphysical categories.[20] In those years, moreover, Peirce abandoned his father's Unitarianism in favor of the Episcopal Church, which upheld a trinitarian doctrine.[21] But if we look more attentively at the internal development of Peirce's philosophy, we may perhaps go a step further. The categories are related to that tension between science and religion which permeates Peirce's early philosophical reflections. That tension involved the problem of a reconciliation between abstract and empirical ways of thinking,

---

[16] W1, p. 62.
[17] W1, p. 45–46 (1861). Throughout the book, I shall follow Peirce's inclination to write the pronouns in capital letters when they refer to the categories. I will go back to I, IT and THOU in Ch. 5.
[18] See W1, p. 45–46, and R 1137 (1859), quoted in Fisch 1982, p. xxviii.
[19] Peirce elsewhere cites explicitly Schiller's influence. See the note in the margin to R 1633 (W1, p. 10–12, 1857), cited in W1, p. 534. Cf. Topa 2007, Ch. 3.
[20] See, e.g., W1, p. 503 (1866).
[21] See Fisch 1982, p. xxx-xxxii. In his decision to convert to Trinitarianism, Peirce was influenced by his first wife, Melusina Fay.

or between transcendence and immanence. And in their triadic scheme, the categories offered precisely a way to think rigorously about similar conflicts. They conceptualized the contrast between immediate abstraction (the I, later Firstness) and empirical reality (the IT, later Secondness), while pointing to a mediation between them (the THOU, later Thirdness).

First Historical Studies

Metaphysical speculations were not the only intellectual interest of the young Peirce. Around 1861, the year after he had begun his study with Agassiz wondering "what he would do in life," he felt he had finally "defined [his] object" and developed a more consistent career plan.[22] On the practical side, he was appointed as an aide to the United States Coast Survey, the federal agency for geodesic measurements for which he would work for more than three decades, carrying out inquiries in disciplines as diverse as astronomy, metrology, spectroscopy and cartography. On the intellectual side, he was striving to put together the diversity of his interests around a long-term research program. First and foremost, he wished to devote himself to mathematics and the natural sciences. In turn, these inquiries were instrumental to a broadly conceived study of logic. And logic itself was the foundation of metaphysics.[23]

In the course of the 1860s, Peirce gradually transformed his intellectual plan into a more precise professional project. He came to see himself as a logician and scientist, on the lookout for a methodology that might reconcile his logical interests with both his study of mathematics and his empirical inquiries.[24] His early writings give us abundant testimony of his study of the natural sciences, and in particular of chemistry, the discipline in which he had specialized as a student.[25] However, the point to be emphasized here is that Peirce did not neglect the history of science either. The attempt to develop a sound historical consciousness constantly accompanied his scientific and philosophical preoccupations. He wanted to become an expert in the natural sciences, but one who was also competent in the history of those sciences. At the same time, he envisaged the possibility of a mutual exchange between history and metaphysical inquiries. All in all, we can therefore say that, during the 1860s, Peirce explored different ways in

---

[22] W1, p. 3.
[23] See Fisch 1982, p. xx-xxiii.
[24] See Fisch 1982, p. xxiii-xxiv.
[25] See W1, p. 50–56; 95–100.

which history could be related to his intellectual interests. Let me list three of them.

The first is a speculative philosophy of history that is directly related to his metaphysics. In a speech delivered in 1863 on "The Place of Our Age in the History of Civilization," Peirce drew a sweeping portrait of human history from a Christian perspective. The text bears the traces of German post-Kantian sources such as Schiller, Schelling, and Agassiz's mentor, Alexander von Humboldt.[26]

One goal of the text is to describe the "primary tendencies" of the nineteenth century within the broader history of human civilization. Peirce focuses, in particular, on the unbound use of reason and on the impulse to adopt a skeptical and irreverent attitude toward tradition. As he maintains, these tendencies are at work in domains as different as the history of philosophy, the arts, "political history," and so forth. In all these domains, the "Age of Reason" is clearly distinguished from the preceding "Age of the Reformation," in which the leading impulse was, indeed, more to reform tradition than to do away with it. But enlarging the gaze even more, these two ages appear as the culmination of a series of six ages that have succeeded one another "since the beginning of Christianity" at a distance of circa three centuries each, and which can be described as functions of the "central fact[s]" that characterize them: "the Rise of Christianity," "the Migrations of the Barbarians," "the Establishment of Modern Nations," and so forth.[27]

Another goal of the text, and an even more ambitious one, is to put forth a "philosophy" of this historical succession: that is, an account that elevates the historical facts to general laws. Drawing on the Schellingian idea of history as a "well-constructed play," Peirce suggests that Christianity itself is "the plot of History," that is, the main spiritual element which is then actualized and brought to a necessary conclusion in the temporal succession of human affairs. In this sense, Christianity does "follow determinate laws in its development, so that from a consideration of them we can gather where we are and whither we are tending."[28] At this juncture, Peirce resorts to his nascent theory of the categories, and more in particular to the personal pronouns, as a means of describing the general laws of historical development: "First there was the egotistical stage

---

[26] W1, p. 101–114. Cf. Peirce's own, much later retrospective remark, CP 1.563 (c. 1898): "[A]fter trying to solve the puzzle in a direct speculative, a physical, a historical, and a psychological manner, I finally concluded the only way was to attack it as Kant had done from the side of formal logic." On this point and what follows, see Topa 2016.
[27] W1, p. 101–107.
[28] W1, p. 108. Peirce never explicitly cites Schelling in this text. The parallel has been drawn by Topa 2016.

when man arbitrarily imagined perfection, now is the idistical stage when he observes it. Hereafter must be the more glorious tuistical stage when he shall be in communion with her."[29]

The way the text ends brings to the fore once again Peirce's preoccupations with the reconciliation of science and religion. In describing the future "tuistical stage" of history, Peirce first claims that it will finally put to rest one of the fundamental antinomies of the "Age of Reason," namely the conflict between materialists and idealists, each with their legitimate and complementary claims.[30] Then, he goes on to maintain that precisely this metaphysical reconciliation will help disclose the realm of "true religion," different both from the materialist or skeptical rebuttal of anything spiritual and from the idealist propensity to reduce religion to its theoretical or intimist dimension. "True religion [...] consists in more than a mere dogma, in visiting the fatherless and the widows and in keeping ourselves unspotted from the world."[31] This religion, truly anchored to the world, incarnated in the world, is part of a grand vision of harmony between science, poetry, and religion:

> [M]an will see God's wisdom and mercy, not only in every event of his own life, but in that of the gorilla, the lion, the fish, the polip, the tree, the crystal, the grain of dust, the atom. [...] The time is coming when there shall be no more poetry, for that which was poetically divined shall be scientifically known. It is true that the progress of science may die away, but then its essence will have been extracted. This cessation itself will give us time to see that cosmos, that æsthetic view of science which Humboldt prematurely conceived.[32]

A second use of history that is at play in Peirce's early writings, quite different from the speculative one that I have just examined, centers on minute philological studies. In 1864, Peirce and his Harvard colleague, John B. Noyes, published an essay in the *North American Review* on as unexpected a topic as the pronunciation of Shakespeare's English.[33] The text moves from the conviction that a study of "precisely how Shakespeare pronounced" is much more than "a curious thing." "It leads to other knowledge, highly important," such as a better understanding of the text and of the "derivation of words." This study, in turn, was to

---

29 W1, p. 113.
30 See W1, p. 111: "Human learning must fail somewhere. [...] If materialism without idealism is blind, idealism without materialism is void."
31 W1, p. 112.
32 W1, p. 114.
33 See W1, p. 117–143 (1864). Cf. the Editorial Note on p. 541–542. The English scholar Alexander John Ellis saw in this paper "[t]he first published attempt to gather the pronunciation of Shakespeare from the writing of preceding orthoepists" (Ellis 1869, p. 917n1).

be based on a variety of historical sources; and focused not so much on "rhymes, puns, misspellings," as previous authors had done, but rather on a reconstruction of the stable and permanent aspects of linguistic phenomena.[34]

Finally, a third use of history emerges out of another important step in Peirce's professional career, namely the two series of lectures on "the Logic of Science" which he was invited to deliver in 1865 (at Harvard) and 1866 (at the Lowell Institute in Boston). The lectures contain the first nucleus of many logical and semiotic doctrines. They were mainly aimed at developing a "thoroughly unpsychological" conception of logic as the science of inferences and general representations.[35] But they also reveal a keen attention to history, this time more explicitly related to its significance for science and philosophy. In one passage, for instance, Peirce describes the American people as particularly well suited for philosophy, thanks to their "love of research and especially of history, – so manifest in the great number of historians in New England." And again: "It has been truly said that history is the metropolis or capital city of philosophy; when we have once mastered it we may easily extend our conquests everywhere."[36] This plea for history, however, is not unconditioned, as it coexists with the conviction that the activity of "judging" a philosophical system is not a historical task.[37]

A Decisive Model: William Whewell

What was driving Peirce to take the role of history more and more seriously? The 1865 Harvard Lectures give the first evidence of Peirce's encounter with an author who played a crucial role in this respect, as he provided a paradigmatic model of how to hold together a disparate range of inquiries within a sound phil-

---

34 W1, p. 117–118.
35 See W1, p. 161–302 (1865); 357–504 (1866). For Peirce's "unpsychological view of logic" see, in particular, p. 164.
36 W1, p. 456. The editors of the *Writings* inform us (W1, p. 560) that Peirce first attributed this sentence to Polybius, then crossed out the reference. In fact, the sentence comes from Diodorus Siculus (1993–2002, I, 2). As regards the New England historians to which Peirce refers, he may have had in mind his acquaintance George Bancroft, who was also a good acquaintance of the Humboldt brothers, and is the author of a monumental *History of the United States of America* (Bancroft 1854-1878). See Fisch 1984, p. xxxiv. For Peirce's remarks about the intellectual character of peoples, which sometimes veers into racism, see below, Chapter 6.
37 See W1, p. 212 (1865): "the historical argument is obviously incompetent to judge any system."

osophical framework. This author is the British philosopher, theologian, scientist and historian William Whewell.[38]

In one of his Harvard Lectures, devoted to Whewell, Mill, and Comte, Peirce calls the British polymath "the most profound" among contemporary philosophers of science. He sets out, in particular, to defend Whewell's broadly Kantian view of induction and scientific inference against the more empiricist theory of John Stuart Mill.[39] As a matter of fact, Whewell and Mill had engaged in a wide-ranging and extremely influential debate on precisely this topic.[40] Whereas Mill interpreted induction as the derivation of general laws from particular observations, Whewell claimed that observation necessarily entails conceptual elements that cannot be derived from it. As Whewell says, "all facts involve ideas unconsciously; and thus the distinction of Fact and Theories is not tenable, as that of Sense and Ideas is."[41] Those unconscious ideas are "supplied by the mind itself," not as a "consequence of experience," but as "a result of the particular constitution and activity of the mind."[42] Unlike Kant, however, Whewell thought that the "fundamental ideas" on which we build scientific knowledge are not foundational of experience in general, but may be circumscribed to the domains of single sciences.[43] Moreover, these ideas do not have a merely transcendental status, but are rooted in the objective features of the world, and Whewell, who was not a Darwinian thinker,[44] went as far as to claim that they originate from the mind of God.

As Peirce remarks, a result of Whewell's constitutive intertwining of facts and ideas is a conception of scientific knowledge as resulting from two different activities. Whewell called these two activities "the explication of conceptions" and the "colligation of facts." By the explication of conceptions, ideas are "unfolded into clearness and distinctness" in the course of scientific progress.[45] By colligation, facts are "not only brought together, but seen in a new point of view." Now, the real gist of induction lies precisely in this creative act of seeing

---

38 On Peirce and Whewell, see Niiniluoto [1978] 1984; Cowles 2016; Girel 2017.
39 See W1, p. 205–211 (1865).
40 See Strong 1955; Snyder 2006.
41 Whewell 1840, p. xvii. Cf. W1, p. 205.
42 Whewell 1858a, p. 91, as cited in Snyder 2019.
43 See Snyder 2019.
44 See Cannon 1976. But cf. Ruse 1975 for a more nuanced account.
45 Whewell 1860, p. 373. See again Snyder 2019. It is worth noting that Whewell's concept of colligation has encountered considerable success precisely among philosophers of history. The latter saw in this concept a powerful means to grasp the kind of synthesis of the data that is proper to historical explanation. This use originated with Walsh 1942. For a more recent, insightful account, see Kuukkanen 2015, Ch. 6.

the facts from a new viewpoint, of "superinducing" a mental element to them; and not in the mere juxtaposition of punctual observations, as the empiricists would maintain.[46]

Whewell's metaphysics influenced Peirce no less than his epistemology. As the latter would state more clearly a few years later, when his own path toward realism had much progressed, the British polymath represented to him the model of a scientist who did not yield to the nominalist and materialist impulses of modern times. But equally important to Peirce was Whewell's attempt to reconcile his realist metaphysics with a historicized understanding of human intellectual faculties. Their divine nature notwithstanding, a priori conceptions cannot be derived once and for all. They have to emerge gradually in the process of scientific development. Both science and metaphysics unfold over time; they are processes. Moreover, the two processes are bound eventually to converge. As Peirce did not fail to notice, this entails a strong thesis about the virtual coincidence between the inductive results of science and the a priori or universal truths of philosophy: "[T]hough as clear conceptions they arise only after long study of nature and much colligation of facts, yet [...] they are, in reality, derived from within."[47]

Indeed, one of the aspects of Whewell's thought that most attracted Peirce was his emphasis on a historicized understanding of scientific development. The "appropriate ideas" and conceptions through which we are able to carry on our acts of colligation emerge in the course of history. This means that not all inductive inferences are possible at all times, but only those that are made possible by the ideas that have developed at a particular moment.[48] Moreover, Whewell placed great emphasis on the importance for philosophers of science to look at the history of science as a basis of their theories. He conceived of history as a repository of information, on the basis of which philosophers carry out their inductions about the dynamics of scientific processes.

Peirce dwelt at length on precisely this point in yet another series of lectures, delivered in 1869 (again at Harvard) on the history of British logicians from the Middle Ages on.[49] He devoted one of his lectures entirely to Whewell, insisting in particular on the latter's ability to seize upon the history of science as an inductive basis for his philosophy.[50] Contrary to Mill, Whewell "was not the man to write upon the Logic of Science solely on the basis of general qualifications.

---

46 Whewell 1858, p. 71, cited by Peirce in W1, p. 206.
47 W1, p. 207.
48 See Girel 2017, p. 38–40.
49 W2, p. 309–345.
50 W2, p. 337–345.

He prepared himself for his task by an exhaustive study of the history of all Natural Sciences." His historical books – which, Peirce added, "I do not think [...] can be rivalled by anything upon the same subjects in any language" – are a veritable and necessary basis for his theory. Whewell did not use his historical knowledge merely "to give a colour of verisimilitude" to a theory otherwise established; he did not "make use of facts of scientific history to support a theory which has really been derived [...] from a doctrine of a metaphysical origin." Instead, he "really derive[d] his theory from that." This is why he is also most "true [...] to all those characters of scientific investigation which leave their mark upon its history."[51]

The 1869 lecture also introduces another noteworthy facet of Peirce's reading of Whewell. I mean his emphasis on Whewell's conviction that the history of science should be studied, first and foremost, at the level of its public manifestations and, in particular, with an eye to the public controversies that unfold among scientists.[52] Whewell argued that scientific conceptions gain clarity not so much by means of definitions, as when they are deployed as a tool to articulate the public disagreements among researchers. Peirce paraphrased this thought as follows: "[S]cientific conceptions have always first become clear in debates."[53]

One is tempted to see in this insistence on the actual use of scientific conceptions an interesting analogy with what Peirce would say only a few years later on the pragmatist method for the clarification of ideas. Still, in his 1869 lecture, Peirce does not appear completely convinced by Whewell's emphasis on the epistemic primacy of controversies. In his opinion, this emphasis on the "public history of science" risks neglecting "the change and [...] the law of the change in the individual mind by which an obscure idea became clear."[54] This disagreement between the two men anticipates Peirce's belief – fully articulated only a few years later – that it is not so much the controversies among scientists, as, rather, the possibility of agreement among them, which should count as a paramount hallmark of scientific rationality (see Chapter 5). But it also anticipates a further methodological point, namely Peirce's emphasis on the importance of unintentional sources rather than on intentional or "public" ones in the study of history (see Chapter 7).

---

51 W2, p. 338–339.
52 See W2, p. 341–342. Cf. Girel 2017; Cowles 2016, p. 734.
53 W2, p. 342.
54 W2, p. 342. Cf. again Girel 2017.

1867–1869: Cartesianism versus Scholasticism

Between the two lectures on Whewell that I have just analyzed (the first in 1865, the second in 1869) lay the events of what has been called Peirce's "decisive year," the year 1867.[55] Around that year, Peirce's occupational status changed, and much for the better. His father Benjamin became superintendent of the Coast Survey and Charles was promoted to the rank of assistant. He thus took on more significant scientific responsibilities, such as the task of carrying out spectroscopic observations at the Harvard College Observatory. He also started reviewing books on science, mathematics and philosophy for the journal *The Nation:* an activity that he would continue almost until the end of his life (sometimes as his only source of income). Finally, he was elected fellow of the American Academy of Arts and Sciences. Within nine months, he delivered five papers on logic and philosophy at the Academy meetings, which contain an early exposition of some of his most important ideas in logic and semiotics.[56] In particular, the third essay of the series, "On a New List of Categories," contains the first systematic exposition of Peirce's theory of logical and metaphysical categories.[57] Here, the categories take on new names, namely Quality, Relation and Representation. These names make much more explicit the intimate connection between Peirce's metaphysics and his nascent theory of signs.

But Peirce could hardly conceive his work in logic and metaphysics as separate from his scientific and historical interests. It is thus no accident that the year 1867 was also the moment in which he started working more assiduously on the history of logic.[58] Among the topics he touched upon in his study, what stands out for breadth and importance is his interest in Scholastic philosophy. Initially wishing to provide deeper foundations to his own logical inquiries, Peirce found in the work of the Scholastics a crucial source to adjudicate anew the question of nominalism versus realism. What is more, he was struck by the theoretical rigor of the Scholastic authors, as well as by their quest for a scientific approach to philosophy.[59]

All these aspects become visible in the three texts Peirce published between 1868 and 1869 in the newly-born *Journal of Speculative Philosophy*. The papers were originally motivated by an exchange on Hegel's logic with the editor of

---

[55] Fisch 1984.
[56] W2, p. 11–97. Delivered in 1867, the papers were published in the *Proceedings* of the Academy the following year.
[57] W2, p. 49–59 (1867). For a commentary, see De Tienne 1989.
[58] See Fisch 1984, p. xxiv.
[59] On Peirce's reading of the Scholastics, and in particular of Scotus, see Boler 1963.

the journal, William T. Harris, who invited Peirce to explain his view of the validity of logical laws.[60] These are among the most famous of Peirce's essays, traditionally called "anti-Cartesian" because they put forward an anti-intuitionist view of cognition that is explicitly aimed at subverting "the spirit of Cartesianism."[61] In the first of these papers, "Questions Concerning Certain Faculties Claimed for Man," Peirce goes as far as to adopt the dialogic structure of a medieval *quaestio*, in a sort of rhetorical rejoinder to Descartes' model of philosophical inquiry.[62] Moreover, it was precisely in the course of writing these papers that Peirce made his transition from what he calls a nominalist to a realist position.[63] This is also a transition from the philosophy of Ockham to that of Duns Scotus, a philosopher whom Peirce had gotten to know during his study of Scholasticism, and whom he had quickly elected as one of his masters.[64]

In Chapter 3, I will return to the theories of mind and cognition expounded in the anti-Cartesian papers. For now, let me just remark that Peirce therein articulates a semiotic and processual view of the mind that can be related to what he wrote in the same period about the historical examination of concepts and ideas. Peirce claims that human beings do not have any faculty of intuition and can, therefore, only think with the aid of "external signs." What is more, the mind is conceivable in processual terms, as a "train of thought," a continuous flux of signs. The continuous character of this process may cause a sort of optical illusion in us and deceive us into thinking that this or that concept rests on indubitable assumptions. But in truth, "each age pushes back the boundary of reasoning and shows that what had been taken to be premises were in reality conclusions."[65]

To facilitate this task, one might resort to different tools. One such tool is conceptual analysis. Another is a historical investigation of concepts. As Peirce writes in the last Academy paper of 1867, "[a] philosophical distinction emerges

---

[60] See W2, p. 131–159.
[61] "Questions Concerning Certain Faculties Claimed for Man," W2, p. 193–211 (1868); "Some Consequences of Four Incapacities," W2, p. 211–242 (1868); "Grounds of Validity of the Laws of Logic: Further Consequences of Four Incapacities," W2, p. 242–272 (1869). See also the preparatory drafts: W2, p. 162–191. On the "spirit of Cartesianism," see the *incipit* of the second paper: W2, p. 211.
[62] See Colapietro 2007.
[63] See Fisch 1986a, p. 184–200.
[64] See, in particular, W2, p. 240 (1868), where Peirce explicitly equates his position with "the realism of Scotus." Fisch 1986a, p. 184–188 also quotes a later remark, CP 4.1 (1898): "Everybody ought to be a nominalist at first, and to continue in that opinion until he is driven out of it by the *force majeure* of irreconcilable facts."
[65] W2, p. 166 (1868).

gradually into consciousness; there is no moment in history before which it is altogether unrecognized, and after which it is perfectly luminous." Consequently, historical work can help us show that some concepts "are not so modern as has been represented." In the same paper, Peirce carries on this kind of philosophically-minded history of concepts with respect to the logical concepts of "comprehension" and "extension" (which he brings back to Scholastic philosophy).[66] But we will see that the idea of a possible use of the history of concepts as an aid to the analysis of concepts would stay with him throughout his life.

In the period immediately following the anti-Cartesian papers, Peirce found himself deploying his historical sensitivity in particular when he wished to articulate his misgivings about positivism. In a review of James Mill, for instance, he laments the positivists' tendency not to take seriously other philosophical perspectives and to be overly engrossed in their own method. "A method in which one is simply immersed, without seeing how things can be otherwise rationally regarded, is a sheer restriction of the mental powers." Against this tendency, Peirce ends up playing a quasi-Hegelian move: "It is a familiar logical maxim that nothing can be comprehended without comparing it with other things; and this is so true in regard to philosophies that a great German metaphysician has said that whoever has reached a thorough comprehension of a philosophical system has outgrown it."[67]

The polemic against the positivists is then continued in the lectures on British logicians from 1869. I have already mentioned these lectures in connection to Whewell; but this is also the place where Peirce welded together his interest in Whewell and his interest in the Scholastics. He framed these lectures as a contribution to the "history of logical thought," starting with an examination of the medieval dispute on the universals and running up to Whewell himself. But he also took the occasion to reflect on what he was learning from these thinkers with regard to the scientific nature of philosophy and its relation to historical knowledge.

The lectures open with an explicit plea for the historical perspective Peirce intended to adopt: "[T]he chief value of the study of historical philosophy is that it disciplines the mind to regard philosophy in a cold and scientific eye and not with passion as though philosophers were contestants."[68] And again: "[T]o understand the historical position, you ought not to lean either way."[69] This, of

---

[66] See W2, p. 70–86 (1867) and, in particular, p. 71 (1867). Cf. Short 2007, p. 276.
[67] "The English Doctrine of Ideas," W2, p. 302–303 (1869).
[68] W2, p. 310.
[69] W2, p. 327.

course, does not mean that philosophy is reduced to a striving for impartiality. Equally important is the question whether the authors "were right or wrong," which is properly "a question of philosophy and not of history,"[70] Still, philosophers ought to take most seriously the practice of impartial judgment that is secured by history. The reason for this, formulated here for the first time, is a crucial element of Peirce's pragmatist epistemology. No belief or proposition in science or philosophy, Peirce maintains, can be said to be certain as long as "competent men disagree about it."[71] In this perspective, history plays a major role:

> [P]erhaps by calling the Controversy of Nominalism and Realism trivial it is meant that any reasonable being can decide it in a jiffy. If you think then that all men who disagree with you on this question are foolish, I can only remark that whichever way your opinion lies there are certainly many men quite as competent in mental power, training, and information, who think that *you* have not fully probed the question.
>
> However though it doesn't seem to me so, yet to others whom I must respect, it does seem easy to decide the question. Let it be so then and let us all come to a unanimous decision upon it, only let our decision rest on a *historical basis, the only sound basis for any human institution* – philosophy, natural science, government, church, or system of education.[72]

"Metaphysical History": The Review of Berkeley

The threads we have pursued so far come together into a new configuration in another text of the same period: the lengthy review of Alexander Fraser's edition of Berkeley, which appeared in the *North American Review* in 1871.[73] This is one of Peirce's most significant pieces of philosophy. It develops some decisive ideas on metaphysics and epistemology and gives expression to Peirce's second and more decided turn toward Scholastic realism. While reading it, one should keep in mind that Berkeley played an important role in the development of Peirce's pragmatism. However, the Berkeley review itself gives very little indication of this circumstance.[74] Rather, Peirce here focuses on inscribing Berkeley within the history of the debate between nominalists and realists. This historical

---

70 W2, p. 310.
71 W2, p. 187 (1868).
72 W2, p. 336 (1869). The last emphasis is mine.
73 W2, p. 462–487. The work reviewed is Berkeley 1871.
74 But see the hint on W2, p. 483. Much more explicit is Peirce's later review of the second edition of Fraser's work, CN3, p. 36–39 (1901). See also RL 231 (1911), as cited in Moore 1984.

contextualization is the best strategy, Peirce suggests, to explain why Berkeley is still worth studying, notwithstanding the objections we might level against his philosophy:

> As a matter of history [...] philosophy must always be interesting. It is the best representative of the mental development of each age. It is so even of ours, if we think what really is our philosophy. Metaphysical history is one of the chief branches of history, and ought to be expounded side by side with the history of society, of government, and of war; for in its relations with these we trace the significance of events for the human mind.[75]

This passage contains two significant claims. First, considering philosophers historically is a useful way to shed light on the real purport of their doctrines. Second, "metaphysical history" – that is, the history of metaphysical ideas – should not be carried out in isolation. Rather, it ought to be put in relation to other branches of history, such as social, political, military history. The Berkeley review is a contribution to both tasks.

Let us first consider the first task: the analysis of philosophical figures – here, Berkeley – as a chapter of metaphysical history. Peirce goes about this task in two different ways: he looks both at the historical origins of Berkeley's thought and at his subsequent impact on subsequent philosophy. In other words, he seeks to show both what is the original context of Berkeley's philosophy, and "how large a part of the metaphysical ideas of to-day have come to us by inheritance from very early times."[76] Following up on his 1869 lectures on British logicians, he insists in particular on the role of medieval metaphysics. He claims that the latter "has so close a historic connection with modern English philosophy, and so much bearing upon the truth of Berkeley's doctrine," that it cannot be overlooked.[77]

Peirce goes on to provide an interpretation of the difference between nominalists and realists as ultimately depending on a more encompassing metaphysical disagreement over the nature of reality. Nominalists, he argues, conceive reality as what is external to the mind and not created by it. On this view, reality is the "fountain of the current of human thought," independent from thought itself, and directly influencing it, precisely on account of its being outside of the mind. Realists, on the contrary, see the real as the "unmoving form" which will be reached in an indefinitely distant future by means of converging trajectories that gradually do away with the partialities of individual viewpoints.

---

75 W2, p. 463.
76 W2, p. 485.
77 W2, p. 464.

Far from being external to the mind, reality is hence independent "not [...] of thought in general, but of all that is arbitrary and individual in thought," and presupposes the idea of a community of inquirers gradually approaching consensual truth. "[T]here is a general *drift* in the history of human thought which will lead it to one general agreement, one catholic consent."[78]

As is easy to perceive, Peirce's interpretation of the dispute aims at reading its logical "technicalities" as ultimately bearing on a much more general bundle of issues: something that pertains to our encompassing worldview, and that, for this very reason, every man, "if he is not less than man," has to confront. Nominalism is related to the morally "debasing," materialist and individualist drives that dominates the scientific outlook of the time. Realism, on the contrary, is only upheld by "the most conservative minds" – among which, as is apparent from the tone of the whole text, Peirce also counted himself. Yet, it remains possible to conceive of a scientific methodology that does not commit itself to materialism. As he writes, "science as it exists is certainly much less nominalistic than the nominalists think it should be. Whewell represents it quite as well as Mill."[79]

Let us now turn to the second task sketched in the passage I have quoted above. Metaphysical history deserves attention not only in its own right, but because of its relation with other branches of human history. To substantiate this idea, Peirce focuses on one specific phenomenon, which has to do, once again, with his fascination with Scholasticism: namely the "revolution of thought" that took place in Europe during the twelfth century. He tracks the consequences of this phenomenon in fields as diverse as commerce, law, ecclesial history, and most importantly, art and philosophy.

With respect to the latter two disciplines, Peirce opens a rather unexpected, architectural digression. "[I]f any one wishes to know what a scholastic commentary is like, and what the tone of thought in it is, he has only to contemplate a Gothic cathedral."[80] He offers four different rationales for this analogy. To begin with, both cultural phenomena show a "heroic" and "complete absence of self-conceit on the part of the artist or the philosopher." They both are, in this sense, "catholic" oeuvres. That is, they were meant to "embody" not the author's ideas, but "the universal truth." This is also due to the celebrated intellectual scrupulousness of the Scholastics. Their perusing abstract theological questions as though they were quite real no longer appears gratuitous if one takes seriously

---

78 W2, p. 469–471.
79 W2, p. 485–487. On Peirce's social and political conservatism, see Ch. 6.
80 W2, p. 465.

their unswerving faith in biblical revelation. A second shared trait is "a detestation of antithesis or the studied balancing of one thing against another [...], – a hatred of posing which is as much a moral trait as the others." The third is the "increasing sense of immensity" emanating from both. Finally, the two phenomena are comparable in the way they eventually faded, losing touch in the same period with their original religious impulse and sinking "first into extreme formalism and fancifulness, and then into the merited contempt of all men."[81]

Given what Peirce says about the relations between "metaphysical history" and other branches of human history, we may safely interpret his analogy between Scholastic commentaries and Gothic churches as a way to emphasize the "significance [...] for the human mind" of those cultural formations by reflecting on the common intellectual attitude displayed by both. But we should also note that the analogy was hardly chosen at random. In the course of the nineteenth century, the comparison between Gothic architecture and Scholasticism was a customary point of reference for scholars who wanted to pose the more general problem of the parallels between different cultural phenomena of the same period.

Probably initiated by Kant, the parallel was dealt with by many other scholars, such as Jules Michelet, Gottfried Semper and Heinrich Wölfflin, as a sort of *pars pro toto* of the general problem.[82] We do not know whether Peirce was aware of at least part of this literature. But the coincidence helps us see his reflections on "metaphysical history" as part of a broader nineteenth-century line of thought on the value of historical inquiries into the parallel cultural phenomena of a given period. We will see, moreover, that Peirce would return to the same parallel on many other occasions in his life, always with an eye to unearthing the intellectual or logical purport of architects' figurative choices. (Today, we are likely to look at Peirce's analogy through the lens of Erwin Panofsky's very influential study from 1951, *Gothic Architecture and Scholasticism*. Later in this book, I will show that there is, in point of fact, a historical relation, although a rather indirect one, between Peirce and the iconological studies carried forth by Panofsky.)[83]

---

81 W2, p. 465–467.
82 See Kant [1764] 2007, p. 61–62; Wölfflin [1888] 1964; Frankl 1960; Gombrich 1969; Dynes 1973. Particularly revealing of the paradigmatic status of the question are Wölfflin's words (Wölfflin [1888] 1964, p. 77). Once the need for a bridge between art and the "content" of an age ("Inhalt der Zeit") is assumed on a general level, he claims, "we still have to find the path that leads from the cell of the scholar to the mason's yard."
83 See Panofsky 1951. I return to this issue in Ch. 6 and Ch. 7.

At the same time, Peirce's theoretical concern with the relation between art and philosophy was also fueled by a genuine aesthetic appreciation of Gothic art. Peirce's trips to Europe were probably instrumental in the development of his taste. His first journey especially – from which he had returned just a few weeks before writing his review of Berkeley – was an occasion to see European art. Peirce's correspondence and private notes from that period give us a vivid image of his reactions, while also revealing a certain familiarity with the technical and art-historical vocabulary.[84] Then, in the second trip, which took place in 1875 (that is, after the Berkeley review), Peirce revived this interest, going as far as describing himself an "enthusiastic admirer of the Gothic."[85]

Finally, mentioning Peirce's European trips leads us to yet another reason why we should pay attention to what he has to say on Gothic architecture: namely, its being further evidence of the influence of William Whewell on his thought. In a note from Peirce's private diary dated January 30th, 1870, jotted down while he was in Strasbourg, we read: "Saw only cathedral. [...] In evening Z[ina] [i.e., Peirce's wife] read Whewell's Notes on German Churches. Very pleasant."[86] The reference is to Whewell's *Architectural Notes on German Churches*, the third edition of which came out in 1842. In that book, as in the chapters on the Middle Ages of the much more important *History of the Inductive Sciences*, Whewell betrays a pronounced tendency to put forth parallels between architecture, science and philosophy.[87] Although he does not advance a straightforward analogy between Gothic architecture and Scholastic philosophy, he gives enough hints in

---

84 The letters, addressed to Peirce's close relatives, are contained in RL 129; RL 333; RL 336; RL 337; RL 339; RL 341. In addition to these, I am taking into account R 1614 (a personal diary) and R 1560a (a list of suggestions for a friend's subsequent visit to Europe). This material is accessible online, together with a commentary and other related documents. See (Grupo de Estudios Peirceanos 2008-2019). Among the numerous churches Peirce visited, one may mention Netley Abbey (R 1560a), Salisbury Cathedral (RL 341) and Milan cathedral (R 1614), as well as many other buildings in Switzerland and Germany. While in Canterbury, he also purchased Robert Willis' *Architectural History of Canterbury Cathedral* (Willis 1845). See Nubiola 2009.
85 RL 341.
86 R 1614.
87 Peirce is likely to have known of Robert Willis precisely through this book, for the edition that Peirce consulted was issued under the influence of Willis's objections (see the preface). Compare a later passage in EP2, p. 46 (1898): "Whewell was a most admirable reasoner, who is underestimated simply because he stands detached both from the main current of philosophy and from that of science. It is worth the journey to the Rheingau, simply for the lesson in reasoning that one learns by reading upon the spot that remarkable work modestly thrown into the form of *Notes on German Churches*." On the relation between Whewell's history of science, his history of architecture, and his influence on nineteenth century biology, see Quinn 2016.

that direction to imagine Peirce having his pages in mind when giving shape to his ideas. This supposition is strengthened by a later text, in which, discussing the vexed topic of the historical origins of the Gothic, Peirce dismisses as "ridiculous" the hypothesis that it has come from the Arabs. "No" – he writes – "Whewell was right. [The Gothic] was simply forced upon the architects by their desire to open large spaces, and [...] to use compartments that were oblong not square."[88]

Clear and Cloudy Nights

The Berkeley review was published at the beginning of the most successful phase in Peirce's career. Between 1870 and 1883, he travelled five times to Europe, in charge of scientific missions. In 1872, his father appointed him to "take charge of the Pendulum experiments" of the Coast Survey, thereby inaugurating his long activity as a professional geodesist.[89] In all likelihood, 1872 was also the year when the Metaphysical Club at Harvard started meeting. The Club was a group of young intellectuals discussing philosophical issues, among which Peirce first developed the ideas that would later flow into his pragmatism. The most notable members of the group were Oliver W. Holmes, William James, Chauncey Wright, Francis E. Abbot and Nicholas St. John Green. Finally, in 1879 Peirce was appointed a professor of logic at the newly founded Johns Hopkins University in Baltimore, where he remained until 1884.[90]

Peirce's work from the early 1870s until his move to Baltimore progresses along two main axes. The first axis is Peirce's empirical research in the fields of geodesy and astronomy. The second is his theoretical work on philosophical and logical issues. The outcome of this second, more theoretical axis is a series of manuscripts (dated from 1872 to 1873) which were initially planned to become a book on logic, and then a more systematic series of papers on the logic of science (dated from 1877 to 1878), which are traditionally considered to mark the birth of pragmatist philosophy.[91] But Peirce was positive that his study of logic and philosophy went hand in hand with his empirical inquiries. In other words, the second axis of his work proceeded in parallel with the first. In a letter to his mother from April 1872, we read a statement that sounds like a motto in

---

[88] HP, p. 350 (undated).
[89] See (Fisch 1986b, p. xxiv).
[90] For biographical information on this period, see Houser 1989; Brent [1993] 1998. On the Metaphysical Club see Fisch 1986a, p. 137–170; Wiener 1949, Ch. 2; Menand 2001; Parravicini 2012.
[91] W3, p. 13–108 (1872–73); 241–374 (1878–79).

this respect: "On clear nights I observe with the photometer; on cloudy nights I write my book on logic[.]"[92]

What is especially interesting for us is that these two axes of Peirce's work entailed two quite different uses of history. Let us look first at the "clear nights," that is, Peirce's empirical work. Its most relevant result was *Photometric Researches* (1878), a book-length report that encompassed the observations carried forth at the Harvard Observatory from 1872 to 1875.[93] This book presents us with a genuine example of historical and philological work brought to bear on scientific inquiry. Peirce integrates his own direct observations with the records of much older star catalogues, which he analyses philologically, with an eye to increasing the accuracy of the data themselves. In particular, the book contains a critical edition of a manuscript of Ptolemy's catalogue of stars, which Peirce had found in Paris during his second European journey and which, as he wrote to the Survey Superintendent Carlile P. Patterson in 1877, "had never been properly transcribed."[94] The work Peirce conducted on this manuscript reveals better than anything else his idea that the data gathered by scientists of the past have to be interlaced with today's scientific inquiry as well as with the result of direct observation. The dialogue among scholars must go beyond the present and turn into a conversation with the past. Philology here becomes the *ancilla* of astronomy.

What about the cloudy nights? As I have already indicated, the logical studies carried out in the 1870s prelude in many ways the 1877 to 1878 series on pragmatism. What I would like to consider more specifically here is the renowned introductory essay of that series, "The Fixation of Belief" (1877).[95] For this is not only one of Peirce's best-known and most significant texts: it also displays a very peculiar use of historical arguments.[96] However, the use that Peirce makes of history in this essay could not be more different from the minute textual analyses that characterize the almost contemporaneous *Photometric Researches*. It is not fact-based and philological. Rather, it seems influenced by the project of a sweeping "philosophical archeology" of Kantian derivation.[97]

If one considers, furthermore, the introductory role that the essay plays for the whole series "Illustrations of the Logic of Science," one is tempted to recog-

---

[92] Quoted in Fisch 1986b, p. xxii.
[93] Peirce 1878, published in part in W3, p. 382–493. This is the only single-authored book Peirce published in his lifetime.
[94] HP, p. 645 (1877).
[95] W3, p. 242–257.
[96] See Topa 2016 for a very good analysis of this aspect of the text.
[97] See Kant [1793–1804] 2002, p. 417. Cf. Ferrarin 2015, p. 77.

nize the influence of yet another philosophical model, namely Hegel's *Phenomenology*. As in Hegel, we are confronted with a very *sui generis* historical reconstruction, which aims at introducing the reader to the realm of objective knowledge while assuming as little as possible from the start.

At the beginning of the essay, we read the following remark: "We come to the full possession of our power of drawing inferences the last of all our faculties, for it is not so much a natural gift as a long and difficult art. The history of its practice would make a grand subject for a book."[98] And as if signaling the route for this yet-to-be written history, Peirce goes on to trace a quasi-historical development of four different methods of fixing beliefs, a development that eventuates in the last and final method: the scientific one. Peirce thereby wished to provide a philosophical foundation for the scientific method by developing a reconstruction of the path of human reason. His argument, however, moves on a delicate balance between genetic narrative and systematic exposition. For although it takes actual historical events as a loose blueprint, and although a diachronic succession of the four methods is suggested, this succession cannot be intended as a strictly chronological one. Peirce's general strategy is to present the four methods one by one, in order gradually to show the insufficiency of the first three, thereby paving the way for the last stage.

The first method is the method of tenacity. This is the most immediate method of fixing beliefs, and consists in the arbitrary eradication of doubt, exerted by "learning to turn with contempt [...] from anything which might disturb it[.]" There are, indeed, a large number of people who adopt this method. Yet, there is something extremely powerful against it. This is "the social impulse," which forces us to suspect "that another man's thought or sentiment may be equivalent to one's own." "The man who adopts [this method] will find that other men think differently from him, and it will be apt to occur to him, in some saner moment, that their opinions are quite as good as his own, and this will shake his confidence in his belief."[99] In the attempt to abide by the social impulse, people find themselves forced to enlarge the scope of their method of fixing beliefs. For they cannot but feel "dissatisfaction at two repugnant propositions": the proposition that they themselves hold, and the proposition held by other people whom they feel obliged to take seriously.

They thus go on to adopt a method that is no longer based on the individual but on the community. This is the method of authority, in which a centralized institution like the state governs the opinions of individuals. Peirce is here think-

---

98 W3, p. 242.
99 W3, p. 248–250.

ing of concrete historical institutions that have been devoted to the defense of "correct theological and political doctrines" and to "preserving their universal and catholic character." In Rome, for instance, this method "has been practiced from the days of Numa Pompilius to those of Pius Nonus."[100]

Peirce is adamant that the method of authority cannot be separated from the "cruelties," the "moral terrorism," the "atrocities of the most horrible kind" which are perpetrated in its name.[101] But he considers them not only unavoidable, but also, quite ironically, the "natural" outcome of the social impulse. For "the officer of a society does not feel justified in surrendering the interests of that society for the sake of mercy, as he might his own private interests. It is natural, therefore, that sympathy and fellowship should thus produce a most ruthless power."[102] The method of authority has, moreover, enormous advantage over individual tenacity in terms of the "majestic results" in the arts and the sciences that it brings about (and an implicit reference is made, once again, to Gothic architecture).[103] Still, there is something profoundly flawed in it. To begin with, it cannot fix beliefs "upon every subject." But more importantly, it will soon appear imperfect to subjects who "possess a wider sort of social feeling," so as to be able to see "that men in other countries and in other ages have held to very different doctrines. [...] And their candor cannot resist the reflection that there is no reason to rate their own views at a higher value than those of other nations and other centuries; and this gives rise to doubts in their minds."[104]

"Men in other countries and in other ages"; "views [...] of other nations and other centuries." What Peirce is claiming here is that the very experience of a variety of opinions both across time and across countries pushes forward our search for a better method of fixing beliefs. In this sense, "The Fixation of Belief" is not only a quasi-historical account of the birth of the scientific method. It also locates in history itself – or more precisely, in historical and geographical diversity – the source of our dissatisfaction with the first two methods of fixing beliefs.

---

100 W3, p. 251. Pius IX was the pope when Peirce wrote these lines.
101 W3, p. 250–251, 255.
102 W3, p. 250–251. Peirce's argument turns upside down the eighteenth-century adage about private vices and public benefits (Mandeville [1714] 1924). See also immediately afterwards: "For the mass of mankind [...] there is perhaps no better method than this. If it is their highest impulse to be intellectual slaves, then slaves they ought to remain." On Peirce's conservative social philosophy, see Ch. 5.
103 W3, p. 251.
104 W3, p. 251–252.

The attention we pay to the opinions of people distant in time and space eventually forces us to abandon the method of authority in favor of a method "which shall not only produce an impulse to believe, but shall also decide what proposition it is which is to be believed." This is the a priori method: a method that hinges on "conversation" among human beings, on their tendency toward "regarding matters in different lights."[105] But this method, too, proves limited. And it proves limited for a new and powerful reason. Namely, it does not sufficiently take into account the coercive force of external reality. It thus ends up resting on nothing other than the relative agreeableness of a given system of beliefs. Peirce is here expressing his more general skepticism toward traditional philosophy. All major systems of metaphysics ultimately rest on an application of the a priori method, as do the major artistic "conceptions" that have followed one another in history.[106] But this method "makes inquiry something similar to the development of taste," which is as fleeting and unstable as fashion and thus cannot bring people to "any fixed agreement."[107] So, once again, it is the very fact of disagreement that constitutes the most intolerable outcome of a method of fixing beliefs. But this time Peirce makes clear that, in order to overcome this shortcoming, the social impulse is not sufficient. We need to base our cognitive endeavors on the recognition of the influence that external realities exert on us.

The last, finally objective, method of fixing belief is precisely the result of this conversion to realism. It rests on the basic idea that beliefs ought to be "determined by nothing human, but by some external permanency – by something upon which our thinking has no effect," and which "affects, or might affect, every man." Only this external permanency may guarantee "that the ultimate conclusion of every man shall be the same."[108] This basic profession of realism is the only method that will not give rise to doubt when it is put to the test of practice. The closing lines of the essay are devoted to an ardent plea for its adoption.

> Yes, the other methods do have their merits: a clear logical conscience does cost something – just as any virtue, just as all that we cherish, costs us dear. But we should not desire it to be otherwise. [...] The genius of a man's logical method should be loved and reverenced as his bride, whom he has chosen from all the world. He need not contemn the others; on the

---

105 W3, p. 252.
106 See W3, p. 252. This is yet another reference to the parallel between the history of art and the history of philosophy, as in the Berkeley review.
107 W3, p. 253.
108 W3, p. 254.

contrary, he may honor them deeply, and in doing so he only honours her the more. But she is the one that he has chosen, and he knows that he was right in making that choice.[109]

Transition to a New Phase

In 1879, a year after the publication of the *Photometric Researches*, Peirce accepted the job in Baltimore, where he taught courses on logic and its history. This was, in a sense, a slight diversion from the scientific career he intended to pursue. But it fitted very well with his growing conviction that the study of scientific methods has a fundamental importance for science. Peirce believed that the nineteenth century was the "age of methods" par excellence: an age in which the progresses of the sciences – chief among them, Darwinian biology – were made possible by progress in methodology and by the interbreeding of different techniques of inquiry.[110] The influence of Whewell's ideas about the complementary relation between factual discovery and theoretical work comes once again to the fore.[111]

This five-year period, never to be repeated, seemed perfectly to embody the Peircean ideal of science as the activity of a community of inquirers. Peirce set up a new Metaphysical Club, on the model of the older one in Cambridge. Moreover, he cultivated a circle of gifted students who left a deep mark on his thought, and with whom he started a number of cooperative research projects. The most remarkable among these projects is the collective book titled *Studies in Logic*, edited by Peirce himself in 1883.[112] But equally important is a series of experimental inquiries on unconscious perception carried out with his student Joseph Jastrow, later to become a well-known psychologist.[113] Overall, the group of students Peirce managed to build up during his Baltimore years was composed of truly exceptional scholars, who would go on to pursue many different paths in the intellectual history of the United States.[114] Besides Jastrow, we find well-known names such as John Dewey and Thorstein Veblen; but also less re-

---

109 W3, p. 257.
110 See HP, p. 940–944 (1882).
111 See Cowles 2016.
112 Peirce 1883, partly published in W4, p. 405–466.
113 See, in particular, "On Small Differences of Sensation," W5, p. 122–135 (1885). On Jastrow, see Pillsbury 1944. Jastrow himself wrote about his relation to Peirce. See, in particular, Jastrow 1914; Jastrow 1916.
114 In CP 7.265 (c. 1900), Peirce speaks of "one of those matchless classes, – the very salt of heart – which it was my privilege to enjoy in Baltimore."

nowned scholars, who nonetheless had a tangible impact on Peirce's philosophy. These include the logicians Christine Ladd-Franklin and Oscar H. Mitchell; or the eclectic figure of Allan Marquand, a logician and historian of logic, who influenced Peirce's understanding of topics as different as Greek philosophy and the mathematics of computing machines, and would later become an art historian and founder of the Princeton Department of Art History.[115]

During the Johns Hopkins years, Peirce started some new historical projects. These projects prefigure the work on the history of science that he would carry out in the 1890s, and are rather different from the writings we have been considering so far. Until the Baltimore period, Peirce was mainly interested in the philosophy of history – as in the 1863 text on "The Place of Our Age in the History of Civilization" – or in the history of philosophical ideas. Even when he widened his gaze to cover the whole spectrum of culture and society, as in the Berkeley review, "metaphysical history" remained the center of focus. In contrast, from the 1880s on, and for almost two decades, Peirce's historical interest would veer much more decidedly toward the history of science.

Three projects in particular need to be mentioned here, although they will be returned to in the following chapters. The first is archival and philological research. As we have seen, this strand of Peirce's activity had already manifested itself clearly during the composition of *Photometric Researches*. But during his fifth and last trip to Europe, in 1883, Peirce took it up more decidedly. He made a thorough study of a manuscript he found in Paris, at the Bibliothèque Nationale, containing the *Epistula de magnete*, a treatise on the physical properties of the lodestone written by thirteenth-century French scholar Petrus Peregrinus de Maricourt. We will have to come back to this text, because Peirce kept working on it well into the 1890s. He gradually came to consider it to be one of the greatest and oldest pieces of scientific thinking in history. In the early 1890s, with his professional perspectives growing more dire, he would place many hopes in the project of an edition, translation and historical commentary of that work (see Capter 6).

The second project is a systematic statistical study of the biographies of "Great Men," with an eye to extrapolating data about the causes of "human greatness" in art, politics and science. Again, I will come back to this facet of Peirce's work at much more length in Chapter 6, when I deal with the later phase of Peirce's thinking. Here, it will suffice to recall that Peirce began dealing with this topic around 1883, the year in which he gave a course on "great men" in Baltimore. Between 1883 and 1884, he covered dozens of pages with question-

---

[115] See Ketner/Stewart 1984; O'Donnell 2016.

naires, charts and biographical sketches about outstanding personalities of history from the ancient times to the nineteenth century.

Finally, the third project is an arrestingly large work in the field of lexicography. In 1882, a group of scholars led by the American philologist, linguist and Indologist William Dwight Whitney started the project of a new encyclopedic dictionary of the English language: *The Century Dictionary and Cyclopedia*.[116] First published between 1889 and 1891, the *Century Dictionary* still remains one of the most remarkable lexicographic projects on the English language. Its definitions have often been included in the actual editions of the *Oxford English Dictionary*. As the title betrays, one of its hallmarks is the encyclopedic character: the historical information gathered for every term is often much more exhaustive than those of other dictionaries. Peirce was asked to work on the entries pertaining to the fields of "Logic, Metaphysics, Mathematics, Mechanics, Astronomy, Weights and Measures, Color Terms, and many common words of philosophical import."[117] He worked hard on the project, especially while at Johns Hopkins, but also a few years after his dismissal, and ended up authoring, either totally or partially, more than five thousand entries.

This gigantic effort exerted a lasting impact on Peirce's thinking. First of all, he had to deal with methodological issues related to the field of historical semantics. It is possible to see some repercussions of his reflection on these issues in his later remarks on the "ethics of terminology," which we shall consider later on (see Chapter 5). Second, authoring the entries meant plunging into the history of science and philosophy to a hitherto unprecedented degree. It has been argued, for instance, that precisely his work for the *Dictionary* prompted Peirce to delve much deeper than he had done before into the history of Greek philosophy.[118] Overall, it is not an exaggeration to state that Peirce's work as a lexicographer was a turning point in his scientific and philosophical career, the real import of which still awaits a full assessment. For the specific perspective followed here, its chief significance lies in its having greatly heightened Peirce's interest in the history of scientific terminology (an interest which we have already spotted in his earlier writings) and, more generally, in the role of historical considerations for a sound understanding of the words we use.

---

116 Whitney 1889–1891. (I shall refer to Peirce's entries with the abbreviation CD). See Steger 1913, Ch. 6 for general information about the project.
117 I am quoting from the editors' note in W5, p. 526. The lists of all the entries Peirce worked on covers 39 three-column pages (Ketner 1986, p. 44–83). A critical edition of all these entries is planned to appear as the seventh volume of the *Writings*.
118 See Houser 1993, p. xl.

2 Not a Mere Wonder Book

Philosophy and History from 1884 on

In the previous chapter, I went through the first decades of Peirce's intellectual career, in an attempt to reconstruct diachronically his involvement in historical research. I have identified different aspects of that involvement. The grand philosophy of history captured in the 1863 talk on "The Place of Our Age in the History of Civilization" proceeded in parallel with a willingness to plunge into meticulous philological inquiries (as in his work on Shakespearean pronunciation). The archeology of scientific reason encapsulated in "The Fixation of Belief" was accompanied by the data-based approach of the *Photometric Researches*. Finally, during his years in Baltimore, Peirce started a number of new historical projects, such as his research on the biography of "great men."

Those happily busy years, however, were not destined to last long.[1] The death of Peirce's father, in 1880, ushered in a gradual deterioration of his position within the Coast Survey. In the same period, his relationship with Johns Hopkins worsened, until he was finally obliged to leave his post. From that moment on, Peirce would retire into an increasingly secluded life, marked by serious financial difficulties. This had a substantial impact on his intellectual production. The communal research atmosphere he could enjoy during his years at Harvard and Johns Hopkins was gone for good, and his thought took a more idiosyncratic turn. But Peirce's intellectual creativity was not jeopardized by that. In fact, the later period of Peirce's life is marked by an arresting sparkle of philosophical productivity. While in the 1870s and early 1880s Peirce had mainly focused on logic and natural science, after 1884 he gradually resumed his metaphysical inquiries. His first important work in this respect is the series of manuscripts known as "A Guess at the Riddle" (1887–88), which inaugurates many of the philosophical preoccupations of the following decades.[2]

It has become customary to see in this transition the beginning of a final phase of Peirce's philosophy. Although his later production can, in turn, be subdivided internally, commentators have agreed to regard the events of the mid-

---

[1] Beside the biographical sources I mentioned in Ch. 2, see Houser 1993.
[2] W6, 166–210. See in particular "Design and Chance," W4, p. 544–554 (1884), the paper that most explicitly inaugurates Peirce's metaphysical turn. But equally worth noting is the earlier essay on "The Order of Nature," W3, p. 306–322 (1878).

1880s as the most significant watershed in Peirce's intellectual life.³ From the perspective I am following here – namely Peirce's interest in history – this periodization needs to be blurred a bit, because the Johns Hopkins years had already substantially anticipated some of the most relevant historical projects that Peirce would carry out in his later years. Still, it remains true, also with regard to history, that Peirce's production post-1884 is qualitatively different from the earlier one. Just to mention the most obvious difference: Peirce's work becomes more centered on the history of science. Also, if compared with the earlier years, it is much more systematic.

In particular, the fifteen years between 1890 and 1905 embrace the kernel of Peirce's work as a historian.⁴ I suggest analyzing this period as consisting of three loosely demarcated phases.

The first phase circles around the years 1890 to 1893, just a few years after his dismissal from Johns Hopkins. In this period, Peirce experienced for the first time the strength of the financial difficulties that would vex him for the rest of his life. Indeed, his readiness to try out different intellectual paths should in part be related to his hope of finding possible new sources of income. He substantially intensified the amount of reviews he authored for *The Nation*, which led him to study a great number of texts in the history of science.⁵ He also resumed the work he had done ten years before, on Petrus Peregrinus's *Epistula de magnete*, which he now hoped to publish,⁶ and the statistical work on the biographies of "great men."⁷ Then, in 1892, he agreed to work on the English translation of Ernst Mach's *Mechanik*. This prompted him to reflect once again on the scope and implications of genetic accounts in the natural sciences.⁸ Further-

---

3 See Murphey [1961] 1993, p. 291–295; Fisch 1986a, p. 227; Apel [1967–1970] 1981, p. 40; Houser 1993, p. xix.
4 This period approximately coincides with what Max H. Fisch has called the "Monist period" of Peirce's mature philosophy, because the journal *The Monist* was the major outlet for Peirce's published works. See Fisch 1986a, p. 192–197. In any case, this does not mean that there are no significant texts from later years. See, e.g., a letter to sociologist Franklin H. Giddins, in HP, p. 996–1004 (1910).
5 The texts for *The Nation* are collected in CN.
6 HP, p. 58–65 (c. 1893).
7 "The Great Men of History," W8, p. 258–266 (1892).
8 The translation with Peirce's corrections was published as Mach [1883] 1893. On p. vii of that book, we read that "[i]t has had the sanction of the author and the advantage of revision by Mr. C. S. Peirce, well known for his studies both of analytical mechanics and of the history and logic of physics." In a subsequent review of that book, Peirce discusses critically Mach's genetic approach. He grants that while this approach is often relevant (especially when we need to teach "all those subjects in which the conceptions are really difficult"), it can "easily be carried too far, and it probably has been carried to far in this very treatise." HP, p. 545–550 (1893).

more, he planned some logical essays for the journal *The Open Court*, which involved some historical detours.[9] Most importantly, between 1892 and 1893, he delivered a series of lectures "On the History of Science" at the Lowell Institute, which was to become one of his most important historical works overall.[10]

If looked at from the viewpoint of the relation between Peirce's historical inquiries and his philosophy, one of the most remarkable aspects of this cycle of lectures is its being almost perfectly contemporaneous with another major piece of Peirce's intellectual production, namely the first series of essays that he published in *The Monist* between 1891 and 1893.[11] In these essays (which it has become customary to call the '*Monist* metaphysical series,' because of their subject matter), Peirce brought to completion some of the arguments he had started to formulate in "A Guess at the Riddle." He dealt in particular with the philosophical status of evolutionary theories in both the natural and the intellectual realm. In the next chapter, I will argue that this series of essays can indeed be read as a sort of speculative counterpart to the Lowell Lectures on the history of science. What holds these two works together is a concern about the laws of growth, evolution, or development of human ideas.

The second phase of Peirce's mature historical production covers the second half of the 1890s. In 1894, when he was busy with his project on Peregrinus, Peirce received an offer to work as a research consultant for the study of scientific manuscripts on behalf of publisher and philanthropist George A. Plimpton. He accepted the job, which led him to work on a good number of texts in the history of mathematics.[12] Two years later, he was invited to contribute review essays on the history of science to the newly founded *American Historical Review*. (In his invitation to Peirce, the editor of the journal wrote: "I know that you feel a great interest in the history of science.")[13] In the same period, he also authored short historical pieces for other journals. Particularly noteworthy is an 1898 article for *Science*, which tries to uncover the true historical identity of the early modern

---

9 See De Tienne forthcoming.
10 HP, p. 139–295. These lectures will be published in the forthcoming ninth volume of the *Writings* (W9). The *Writings* edition contains some important novelties when compared with HP. Throughout the book, I will give the page numbers of both editions. I thank the director of the Peirce Edition Project, André De Tienne, for having given me the opportunity to consult the *Writings* edition of the lectures before their publication.
11 W8, p. 83–205. Miller 1971 makes a similar remark about the relation between the Lowell Lectures and the *Monist* metaphysical series.
12 HP, p. 945–1010; see Eisele 1985a.
13 HP, p. 474.

alchemyst Basilius Valentinus.[14] Finally, in 1896 the publisher Putnam's Sons appointed him to work on a volume on the history of science. Peirce never finished writing up this work, but the material he left – which I shall henceforth refer to as 'the Putnam History' – is nonetheless remarkable. Dating from 1898, it develops in somewhat new directions the ideas of the Lowell Lectures.[15] Moreover, while in the case of the Lowell Lectures it is possible to establish a parallel with the *Monist* metaphysical series of 1891 to 1893, in the case of the Putnam History the closest philosophical counterpart is the series of lectures that Peirce delivered at Cambridge in 1898.[16]

Finally, the third phase I want to consider immediately follows the work on the Putnam History. This time, however, the main focus is not so much on the history of science as on a methodological problem: how are we supposed to go about reconstructing the facts of the past? This methodological issue is already visible in the Putnam History and other works from the mid-1890s. But it takes center stage in 1901, the year in which Peirce penned the lengthy treatise "On the Logic of Drawing History from Ancient Sources, Especially from Testimonies." This text sums up with unprecedented comprehensiveness Peirce's logical and epistemological theories as applied to the logic of historical inquiry and to the problem of historical testimony.

The task of the present chapter is not to put forth an in-depth analysis of Peirce's historical investigations, but to discuss his ideas about the scientific and philosophical relevance of those historical investigations. I will do so in two ways. First, I will consider the rationales by which Peirce justified his interest in the history of science. I will also explore some of the most relevant theoretical issues that are called upon by these rationales. Second, I will focus on the so-called "classification of the sciences," that is, that part of Peirce's work which is devoted to discussing the relations between different scientific disciplines. As we will see, both history and philosophy are part of the classification. Therefore, the classification can be read as Peirce's most explicit and comprehensive attempt to articulate the history-philosophy relation. However, I will close the chapter by claiming that the classification, while necessary, is not sufficient. To gain a complete picture of what roles history plays in Peirce's thought, we need to cross-reference the classification with an analysis of Peirce's actual work as a historian (Chapters 6–7) and with a comprehensive reconstruction

---

14 HP, p. 570–579. On Basilius Valentinus, probably a pseudonym used by one or more German authors around 1600, see Principe 2013, Ch. 6.
15 HP, p. 297–412. But see also CP 1.43–125, dated c. 1896 in the CP but more probably a part of the 1898 work. See, e.g., Atkins 2016, p. 20n5.
16 The lectures have been published under the title *Reasoning and the Logic of Things* (RLT).

of the most relevant arguments that sustain philosophy's relation to history (Chapters 3–5).

The Rationales for a History of Science

In a review of "Four Histories of Philosophy" published in 1894, Peirce wrote that "[i]f history is to be conceived neither as mere narration nor as the study of obsolete politics, but as an account of man's development, then the history of the mind is surely the main thing, and that of thought must stand at its head."[17] A couple of years later, in his first text for the *American Historical Review*, he declared that he was "no scholar of history except that of science, including philosophy"[18] These statements can be read in parallel with Carolyn Eisele's thesis that, by 1890, Peirce had come to see the history of science as a necessary support for his logical inquiries, on a par only with mathematics.[19] But what exactly does this mean? How can the history of "science," "thought," and "the mind" contribute to philosophical and logical work?

In one of the manuscripts for the first Lowell Lecture we find an initial answer to this question. This passage starts by presenting two rationales for studying the history of science.

> There are many ways in which the history of science is interesting. There is a personal interest in hearing how the truths we are familiar with got found out. Again, the history of science may be studied for the lessons it affords in regard to the investigation of new questions.[20]

---

17 The "Four Histories of Philosophy" are Windelband, Falckenberg, Bascom, Burt. See CN2, p. 73 (1894). In the same text, p. 75, Peirce makes another interesting remark. "That a history of philosophy ought to be written in the country where it is to be used, is a maxim that gains in weight the more one reflects upon it. [...] We need an American history of philosophy, upon an encyclopedic scale. It does not matter much whether we have good summaries of Aristotle, Descartes, Kant, nor even of the second grade of philosophers, but it is for information about writers whom few can find time to read, Samuel Parker, Toland, Arthur Collier, Jean Senebier, Tetens, Rosmini, and hundreds of other third-rate philosophers, that such a work is greatly needed."
18 Review to A. Dickson White's *A History of the Warfare of Science with Theology in Christendom*, HP, p. 474 (1896).
19 Eisele 1985a, p. 6.
20 W9, p. 97 / HP, p. 143.

The first rationale in this passage is the idea that "[t]here is a personal interest in hearing how the truths we are familiar with got found out." Although the adjective "personal" may seem to belittle the importance of this remark, by making it merely subjective, I think we should link it to a much broader issue that we started investigating in Chapter 1. Peirce often resorted to historical observations about philosophical or scientific ideas in order to suggest that they are less dubitable than one might think; or to contextualize their meaning, so as to be able to assess more objectively their effective force.

In the Lowell Lectures, for instance, Peirce places emphasis on the relatively short period that goes "from Copernicus to Newton," and explains: "[t]hat which specially interests me in this era is that it was then that was developed the modern idea of the absolute regularity of causation."[21] Now, we know that Peirce was a firm opponent of metaphysical determinism (see Chapter 3). So, he called upon history not only to better understand this idea but also to show that it is by no means so obvious and ineluctable as its "firmly established"[22] status would suggest. In this sense, history comes close to a genealogy in the loosely Nietzschean sense of the word: it is a tool to cast doubt on our established beliefs.[23] But genealogy can also have a more vindicatory or affirmative role: the history of concepts can be used not only to cast doubt on the validity of those concepts, but also to re-affirm that validity.[24]

More generally, history can help us understand the thoughts of other people, so as to better assess their influence on us; and it can help us understand ourselves, so as to nourish the ongoing process of self-consciousness. In a text that is chronologically close to the Lowell Lectures, Peirce claims that history can "cut the rope that ties us to the here and now."[25] Many years later he would claim that "one of the main purposes of studying history ought to be to free

---

21 HP, p. 149.
22 HP, p. 149.
23 In the same vein, in CP 7.54 (undated) Peirce launches upon a meticulous *Begriffsgeschichte* of the concept of "science," precisely in order to cast doubt on the idea that science should be understood as systematized knowledge. (On Peirce's definition of science, see Ch. 5).
24 See, e.g., the 1893 "Advertisement of the Principles of Philosophy," HP, p. 1113: "A definite affinity is traced between all these ideas and is shown to lie in the principle of continuity. The idea of continuity traced through the history of the Human mind, and shown to be the great idea which has been working itself out." On "affirmative genealogy" in a pragmatist sense, see Joas [2011] 2013, Ch. 4. For an interpretation of Nietzsche that emphasizes the affirmative and pragmatic nature of some of his genealogies, see Queloz 2019.
25 W8, p. 349 (1892).

us from the tyranny of our preconceived notions."[26] Also, cultivating a historical awareness is a gesture of intellectual fair play. "It is incumbent upon every philosopher in order to make himself understood to explain in what way he came up with his ideas. For we must all submit to be classified and ultimately to be pigeon-holed."[27]

The second rationale in the passage quoted above is the following: "[T]he history of science may be studied for the lessons it affords in regard to the investigation of new questions." In this sense, history is a practical instrument: one that helps us devise the best methods of scientific inquiry. In a text written in parallel with the Lowell Lectures, Peirce refers to his intention to write essays "relating to points in the history of human reason, treated mostly with special reference to the *practical lessons* they suggest."[28] But the same idea comes even more clearly to the fore in the Putnam History, where Peirce goes as far as to compile a detailed list of the "lessons" that working scientists may draw from the history of their discipline.[29] I will come back to this rationale in the next section.

Finally, the passage of the Lowell Lectures continues by pointing out "another point of view in which [history] is more interesting still."[30] Logic, Peirce claims, can be defined as "the analysis of reasoning. The anatomy of reasons." But the traditional syllogistic logic only captures a very small portion of this science. It is "so trivial, that a machine can be constructed to work it; and only a few conclusions, often only one, are to be drawn from a given premise."[31] By contrast, when we allow logic to encompass a much more "comprehensive view of reasoning" (as in the case of Peirce's logic of relatives), then the history of reasoning itself becomes relevant: "When so comprehensive a view of reasoning as this is attained, it becomes of the deepest interest to trace out the history of reasoning, with a view of ascertaining the general law of its evolution."[32]

In this sense, the history of science is the study of how logical reasoning has been deployed over time. Another statement contained in the Lowell Lectures puts the matter in similar terms: "It is not so much the history of science as

---

26 "On the Logic of Drawing History from Ancient Documents, Especially from Testimonies," HP, p. 761 (1901). For an analysis of this text, see Ch. 7.
27 R 1336, cited in Ambrosio 2016.
28 HP, p. 557 (1892). My emphasis.
29 HP, p. 406–411.
30 W9, p. 97 / HP, p. 143.
31 W9, p. 98.
32 W9, p. 98.

the history of sound scientific thinking that I am considering."³³ Just as logic is the theory of sound reasoning, the history of science investigates the unfolding of sound reasoning over time.³⁴

Even more generally, history may serve as a sort of empirical testbed for Peirce's general theory of evolution, with regard to both natural and intellectual phenomena. In order to express this idea, Peirce uses the metaphor I have adopted as the title of this chapter. History, he says, is not to be seen "as a mere Wonder Book, but as an instance, a specimen, of how the laws of growth apply to the human mind."³⁵ In other words, the history of science provides us with a partial answer to the paramount question of nineteenth-century science and philosophy, namely "*[h]ow things grow.*"

> [B]y far the most interesting aspect of the history of science, is that it shows how an important department of human thought has been developed from generation to generation, with a view of comparing this growth with the historical development of art, of religion, of politics, and of institutions generally, and not only with historical development, but also with the growth of the individual mind, and not only of mind, but of organisms both in their geological succession and in their individual development, and with the formation of worlds, and even with the gradual coming into being and crystallization of the fundamental laws of matter and mind, – from all of which facts taken together we are to expect in the future a grand cosmogony or philosophy of creation.³⁶

---

33 W9, p. 207 / HP, p. 245. Cf. the following claim, quoted in Eisele 1985, p. 9–10: "For that which the author had in mind throughout his studies in the history of science was to gain an understanding of the whole logic of every pathway to the truth."

34 Other texts from approximately the same period make use of a similar metaphor in a slightly different sense: what should be placed on the "dissection table" of the historian-anatomist are both sound and unsound reasonings. See Peirce's analysis of the controversy over spiritualism, W6, p. 380–381 (1890): "[H]e who looks upon speculative opinions as so many objects of natural history, calculated to excite lively interest by curious relationships and affinities, more so perhaps by being false than being true, but who lays them upon his dissection-table as things not calling for sympathy, as vivisection-subjects whose vehement logic-squirmings need excite no concern whatever, [...] this man may be aided in picking to pieces, disentangling, studying the intellectual component impulses urgent to the opinion in hand, in appreciating them, in considering their just limits of action, not so much himself to form definitive judgment *pro or con* (which mostly is not safe while controversy rages), as to assign it its schematic place in the natural history of opinion." Finally, see W8, p. 21 (1890): "The philosopher must regard opinions as so many vivisection-subjects, to be studied for their natural history affinities. He must even take this attitude to his own opinion. Opinion has a regular growth, though it may get stunted or deformed. To take the next step in philosophy vigorously and promptly, we must study our own historical position."

35 W9, p. 141 / HP, p. 202 (1892).

36 W9, p. 141 / HP, p. 202.

The "Mutual Aid" between History and Philosophy

For the moment, we should set aside the methodological implications of this impressive passage concerning the importance of developing parallels between the history of science and other branches of cultural, political and social history. Instead, we should focus on the kind of relation between history and philosophy that emerges out of it. The history of science, Peirce says, contributes to the emergence of a "grand [...] philosophy."

I have already said that in the period in which Peirce penned these lines he was laying out precisely such a grand philosophy, namely the *Monist* metaphysical project of 1891 to 1893. In that series of papers, Peirce says explicitly that there is a relation of "mutual aid" between his philosophical arguments about evolution and his historical studies of science. He adds: "The reader will, I trust, be too well grounded in logic to mistake such mutual support for a vicious circle in reasoning."[37] And the Putnam History is even clearer:

> The evolutionary theory in general throws great light upon history and especially upon the history of science – both its public history and the account of its development in an individual intellect. As great a light is thrown upon the theory of evolution in general by the evolution of history, especially that of science – whether public or private.[38]

Once again, I have to postpone the discussion of methodological issues – such as the interesting distinction between "private" and "public" history (see Chapter 7). What bears noting now is Peirce's claim that history throws light on the theory of evolution as much as the theory of evolution throws light on history.[39] To be sure, this claim cannot be generalized. Peirce is not saying that there is a relation of mutual aid between history and philosophy on a general level. He is more modestly saying that such a relation obtains when we confine ourselves to the relevance of the history of science to the development of a philosophical

---

[37] "Evolutionary Love," W8, p. 203 (1892): "I here take it for granted that such continuity of thought has been sufficiently proved by the arguments used in my paper on the 'Law of Mind' [...]. Even if those arguments are not quite convincing themselves, yet if they are reënforced by an apparent agapasm in the history of thought, the two propositions will lend one another mutual aid. The reader will, I trust, be too well grounded in logic to mistake such mutual support for a vicious circle in reasoning."
[38] CP 1.103 (c. 1896).
[39] Of course, whether or not this programmatic intention is actually fulfilled is a different question. As we have seen in the Introduction, for instance, Philip Wiener questioned precisely this point. I will return to this problem later.

theory of evolution. But we shall see throughout the book that there are many other senses in which the empirical observations of history may have a bearing on theoretical or philosophical generalizations.

If we go back to the Lowell Lectures, we note that one major justification of Peirce's conviction about history's relevance to philosophy is once again provided by William Whewell.

> The celebrated scientific philosopher, William Whewell, published, two years before I was born, a truly great book, the *History of the Inductive Sciences*, followed by another three years later called the *Philosophy of the inductive Sciences* founded upon their history. [...] A new book in the general spirit of Whewell is called for.[40]

What exactly is the "spirit" of Whewell that Peirce is referring to? The main answer to this question lies in what Peirce often called the "Law of Whewell": new scientific discoveries can only be made when suitable ideas are born that will enable those discoveries. Or, to put the same point in slightly different terms, "progress in science depends upon the observation of the right facts by minds *furnished with appropriate ideas*."[41] However, Peirce bent this "Law of Whewell" in a more decidedly evolutionist direction, thus strengthening the philosophical and scientific relevance of a historical investigation of ideas.

> [T]he nature of the mind is something itself due to an evolutionary process; and we want to know just how these ideas came to be implanted in the nature of the mind. Besides, these ideas have most of them grown up during the course of scientific history, and we want to know just how they have grown up and under what general agency.[42]

In this sense, scientific theories are historical in a double sense. First, they are historical because they are subject to evolution, to historical growth; they are a product of history. Second, since only appropriate ideas can engender scientific discoveries, the latter too are historical, in the sense that they are not possible at every time, but only at those historical moments in which the corresponding ideas have already been born.[43]

---

40 HP, p. 143–144 (1892). In an 1898 letter to G. Putnam, Peirce strikes a similar note, claiming that times are ripe for a "good History of Science to replace Whewell, and of the same instructive and intellectual kind." HP, p. 301–302.
41 "Reply to the Necessitarians," CP 6.604 (1893). I discuss this text more at length in Ch. 4.
42 HP, p. 144.
43 See the particularly explicit passage in HP, p. 469 (1899): "All our studies of scientific methods during the last half century have gone to confirm Whewell's sagacious induction of 1837, that scientific discoveries cannot be made until appropriate ideas have first grown up. [...] Very few

Finally, Whewell can also teach us a methodological lesson. He is "the only man of philosophical power conjoined with scientific training who had made a comprehensive survey of the whole course of science."[44] His writing a philosophy of the inductive sciences only after the history of the inductive sciences bears witness to this fact. Unlike Mill, who "bump[s] up against the facts of history at every turn like an awkward and overconfident walzer," Whewell's work is "distinguished for its truth to history."[45] Whewell uses the observation of historical facts as a genuine basis for a scientific induction on the laws that preside over human cognition. New ideas should always be put forth on the basis of the "observation" and "colligation" of facts; and the history of science fulfills precisely this function with respect to the philosophy of science.

A Pragmatist's History, Pragmatic History, Practical Lessons

Before concluding the first part of this chapter and going on to discuss Peirce's classification of the sciences, I would like to delve a bit deeper into the second aforementioned rationale for the history of science, namely history providing the philosopher with "practical lessons" about scientific reasoning. As I anticipated, the Putnam History goes so far as to list twenty-nine lessons on scientific method that we are allowed to draw from the history of science.[46] But more generally, Peirce often wrote on the assumption that all major turning points in the history of science contain a logical lesson. Here are a few examples of what Peirce meant. History shows the critical importance of experimentation, and confirms that the "great landmarks" in science "are to be placed at the points where new instruments, or other means of observations, are introduced."[47] It "proves" that there is something like a "natural light of reason" which guides our scien-

---

have been the exact general propositions drawn from history, perhaps none before Whewell's date, so eminently instructive as this; for it shows us that science is not unmixed receptivity, but essentially involves a conceptual element that has to go through a period of growth and a process of ripening." See also HP, p. 444 (1894).
44 CP 6.604.
45 HP, p. 144 (1892).
46 HP, p. 407–411. But cf. "The Chief Lessons of the History of Science," HP, p. 1117–1119. See also Miller 1971. Following this lead, the editors of the CP have titled the historical sections of that work "Lessons from the History of Philosophy" (1.15–1.42) and "Lessons from the History of Science (1.43–1.125).
47 CP 1.102. Cf. HP, p. 410: "Means of observation create science."

tific abductions.⁴⁸ It "shows that men cannot doubt at pleasure, or merely because they find they have no positive reason for the belief they already hold."⁴⁹ And so forth.

As I have already argued, to talk about the lessons of history is not the same as talking about history's ability to substantiate a general philosophical theory. Talking about "lessons" has a practical and normative sense. It amounts to saying that, as far as science is concerned, historical inquiry plays a crucial role in shaping our scientific methodology. What Peirce wanted to achieve with his history of science was not only a specimen of the general laws of growth. He wanted to carry out a diachronic assessment of our best intellectual practices with an eye to improving them. This is one of the reasons Peirce was so inclined to inveigh against "beautifully illustrated and excessively popularized books" of history.⁵⁰ History is not a mere wonder book: it is a necessary implement in every scientist's toolkit.

We could easily link this idea to a more general pragmatist motif (one articulated, for instance, by John Dewey). Since our practices are evolutionary in nature, we need history to assess their success over time, and to keep steering them in the best direction. But I would like to offer a slightly different contextualization here. I think it might be worthwhile to read Peirce's insistence on the practical lessons of history through the age-old conception of "practical" or "pragmatic history," or through the equally old topos of *historia magistra vitae*, history as life's teacher. These traditional notions suggest that history may teach us lessons about how we are supposed to deal with the most diverse circumstances of our own life.⁵¹

First formulated in antiquity, the idea that history may fulfill a "pragmatic" function and teach us something about life was the object of relatively steady fortune across the centuries. Through the end of the eighteenth century, however, it experienced both a successful re-articulation and a crisis.

---

48 CP 2.25 (1902): "The reasonings of the present treatise will, I expect, make it appear that the history of science, as well as other facts, prove that there is a natural light of reason; that is, that man's guesses at the course of nature are more often correct than could be otherwise accounted for." Cf. CP 5.604 (1896), which is particularly interesting because Peirce says explicitly that "the early history of modern science [...] *completes the proof*" about the existence of a light of reason "by showing how few were the guesses that men of surpassing genius had to make before they rightly guessed the laws of nature." (My emphasis.)
49 W5, p. 230 (1885).
50 HP, p. 201 (1892).
51 See Bouton 2018, p. 2; Hahn 1974.

The re-articulation was due largely to Kant, who used the adjective "pragmatic" with regard to two human sciences: anthropology and history. In his *Anthropology from a Pragmatic Point of View* (1798), he looked at human beings not as the mere object of the natural sciences, but as free acting agents.[52] And elsewhere, he defined "pragmatic history" as a history that makes us *klug* ("prudent," "wise") and is therefore able to teach us something.[53] During approximately the same years, Fichte defined his *Wissenschaftslehre*, his "science of knowledge," as a "pragmatic history of human mind." The science of knowledge in Fichte's sense is both a philosophy of history and an instructive history of the mind.[54]

As for the crisis, the case is best made by referring to an influential thesis put forth by Reinhart Koselleck.[55] The new historical sensitivity acquired during the Enlightenment, argues the German historian, made it impossible to stick to the idea of *historia magistra*. Nineteenth-century historians wanted to be more factual and less evaluative. But philosophers like Hegel also concurred with the criticism of the old topos. The only lesson we can draw from history, Hegel quipped in his *Lectures on the Philosophy of World History*, is that "nations and governments have never learned anything from history or acted upon any lessons they might have drawn from it."[56] However, Koselleck's thesis should probably be qualified. The notion of *historia magistra* does not really disappear after the Enlightenment period. Rather, it becomes more nuanced and survives in specific corners of the nineteenth century's historical consciousness.[57]

We might suggest that Peirce's insistence on the practical lessons of history is precisely a way to seize on the conception of a pragmatic history, although in a limited and qualified way. Peirce talks of practical lessons to be drawn from history because he is an heir to the Kantian concept of a pragmatic form of knowledge. However, the pragmatic kind of history that he talks about is confined to what Fichte would have called "the history of human mind," which in his terminology is the history of science, philosophy, and "human thought." In this sense,

---

[52] See Kant [1798] 2007.
[53] Kant [1785] 1996, p. 69n: "A *history* is composed pragmatically when it makes us *prudent*, that is, instructs the world how it can look after its advantage better than, or at least as well as, the world of earlier times."
[54] Fichte [1794] 1982, p. 198–199. See Topa 2016. Hahn 1974, p. 402, comments: "Damit ist die Wissenschaftslehre als Geschichtsphilosophie lehrhaften Charakters angesprochen: aus der Geschichte des menschlichen Geistes werden allein *die* Tatsachen erinnert, die in Beziehung stehen zum Werden der Freiheit [...]."
[55] Koselleck [1967] 2004.
[56] Hegel [1820] 1975, p. 21, quoted in Koselleck [1967] 2004, p. 37–38 and Bouton 2019, p. 3.
[57] I am relying on Bouton 2018.

the historically oriented, pragmatist epistemology put forth by Peirce might be read as one of the ways in which the motifs of pragmatic history and *historia magistra* survive the Enlightenment crisis and enter the nineteenth century.[58]

A crucial element that supports my interpretation is the strong historical link between pragmatist philosophy and the Kantian conception of "pragmatic" judgment or "pragmatic" science. It is Peirce himself who emphasized this link. In an attempt to recall the circumstances that led to the coinage of the word "pragmatism," he said that "some [...] friends" wished to call the doctrine "practicism or practicalism." However,

> for one who had learned philosophy out of Kant, [...] and who still thought in Kantian terms most readily, *praktisch* and *pragmatisch* were as far apart as the two poles, the former belonging in a region of thought where no mind of the experimentalist type can ever make sure of solid ground under his feet, the latter expressing relation to some definite human purpose.[59]

At this point, the interpretation I am suggesting may seem to stumble on an obvious difficulty: in his historical investigations, Peirce does not talk about pragmatic lessons, but about practical ones. Which is all the more significant as it is Peirce himself who stresses so emphatically the difference between the words "practical" and "pragmatic" when discussing the Kantian legacy on pragmatism. But while I recognize the difficulty, it seems to me that precisely the quote I have just brought up makes clear that when Peirce talks about practical lessons, he cannot be using the word "practical" in the Kantian sense. For in that sense, the word refers to something "where no mind of the experimentalist type" can operate. Now, Peirce's notion of the practical lessons of history goes precisely in the opposite direction. It refers to the lessons that experimentalist philosophers can draw from the history of scientific thinking whenever they have a specific purpose in mind, namely, the purpose of making progress in the pursuit of truth by dint of valid inference.

Does this mean that we can understand Peirce's historical work exclusively as the work of a pragmatic historian in the genuinely Kantian sense? I do not think so. It should have become clear by now that I am reading Peirce's recourse to history as an eclectic or pluralistic one. Indeed, the very fact that

---

58 Wiener 1949, p. 23, 253n explicitly notes that the teachings of history can be considered a pragmatic judgment in Kant's sense. While Topa 2016 has more recently suggested that the peculiar kind of historical approach that Peirce chose in his "Fixation of Belief" (see Ch. 1) can be related precisely to the Kantian and Fichtean understanding of a pragmatic history of the human mind.
59 EP2, p. 332–333.

he talks about "interspersing" his history of science with practical lessons suggests that his history of science is the product of a plurality of different conceptions of the role and the status of history. History oscillates between being a reservoir of practical lessons; a repository of empirical data for a "grand philosophy" of evolution; a tool to better understand the scope and purport of philosophical ideas; and so forth.

The Classification of the Sciences

Until now, we have examined Peirce's explicit arguments and rationales about the philosophical relevance of his history of science. Now, we have to turn to a second portion of Peirce's oeuvre that touches directly upon the history-philosophy relation, namely the "classification of the sciences": a comprehensive account of the scientific disciplines and of their position within the general system of the sciences.

For a late nineteenth-century scientist and philosopher, the drafting of a classification of the sciences was a rather conventional move. Over the course of that century, there were numerous attempts to order the different scientific disciplines within an encompassing classificatory system. Some of Peirce's most significant interlocutors, such as William Whewell, embarked on such an enterprise.[60] Convinced as he was of the importance of carefully studying other people's opinions, Peirce examined as many such systems as possible before producing his own. In doing so, he also let himself be guided by a more specifically philosophical source, namely Kant. In what Peirce himself called the "splendid [...] chapter" of the first *Critique* that deals with the "architectonic" of pure reason, Kant had maintained that there must be an architectonic principle that confers order on the whole system of philosophical and scientific activities.[61] Peirce's attempt to produce a system of the sciences is related to this Kantian idea.

The most conspicuous reason for my interest in the classification is that the two disciplines of history and philosophy are part of the classification itself. In articulating a comprehensive system of the sciences, Peirce needed to examine the relation that philosophy holds with many other disciplines, among which there is history. The relation between these two disciplines is therefore a pre-

---

[60] See Ambrosio 2016 for an in-depth historical contextualization of Peirce's classification.
[61] See "The Architectonic Character of Philosophy," CP 1.176–179 (c. 1896). Cf. Kant [1781–1787] 1998, p. 691–701, B860–879; Gava 2014, Ch. 1. I further discuss the architectonic in Ch. 5.

eminent object of study of the classification. In this sense, one might be led to think that the whole research question of this book is 'answered' by Peirce's classification. We shall see, however, that there are many reasons why this is not true. Although the classification is a necessary and very significant piece of our inquiry, it is not sufficient. As Joseph L. Esposito wrote, "it is not a good idea to try to understand Peirce's view of history from what he says about it only in the classification."[62]

There is also another, less obvious, reason why the classification is relevant. Peirce's explicit attempts to classify the sciences began precisely at the time of the momentous transition period of Baltimore and was, from the very beginning, closely tied to his activity as a historian. He made a first attempt while drafting the "science" entry of the *Century Dictionary*.[63] After that, three more phases of Peirce's interest in the classification can be identified, and these three phases roughly correspond to the three waves of Peirce's interest in historical inquiry that I pointed out at the beginning of this chapter. We may therefore conclude that the classification of the sciences is not only the place where Peirce explicitly discussed the relation between philosophy and history as disciplines. It is, more specifically, the conceptual tool that he deployed in order to reflect on the relation between his historical work-in-progress and other parts of the system, as well as on the historicity of the sciences. Indeed, I would suggest that Peirce's work as a historian was one of the major factors that spurred his urge to embark on the classification project.

Let us look more closely at the three phases I have just mentioned. The first dates from 1892. This is shortly after the publication of the *Century Dictionary* volume that contains the entry "science." We are in exactly the same year of the Lowell Lectures on the history of science. In fact, Chiara Ambrosio has pointed out that one of the manuscripts for the first Lowell lecture begins precisely with a diagram of the classification, as though Peirce wanted to use that diagram as a preface to his whole course.[64] As we know, moreover, the Lowell Lectures proceeded almost hand-in-hand with the *Monist* metaphysical series. In the same year, one essay of that series was published, "Evolutionary Love," which presents the most sophisticated version of Peirce's speculative theory of evolution, making the year 1892 really the *annus mirabilis* of Peirce's

---

[62] Esposito 1983, p. 161–162.
[63] CD, p. 5397.
[64] See the beginning of the manuscript R 1274a (1892), cited in Ambrosio 2016: "Gentlemen & Ladies: It will be convenient for the purpose of these lectures to use the classification of the sciences shown in Diagram I." On this issue, see also De Tienne forthcoming.

philosophy of history. But the *Monist* series had opened one year before, with "The Architecture of Theories," in which Peirce, for the first time, discussed in a comprehensive manner his architectonic conception of philosophy.[65]

A second phase of Peirce's interest in the classification is around 1898. Here again, a close relation with his historical inquiries can be detected. For although the main bulk of the classification is now discussed in a philosophical work, namely the Cambridge lectures on "Reasoning and the Logic of Things," there are constant references to historical data.[66] Moreover, it suffices to have a look at the manuscripts with the introductory plans for the Putnam History to see that they, too, like the 1892–93 Lowell Lectures, rely heavily on the classification as a guiding thread for the historical narrative.[67]

Finally, Peirce went back to the classification in a much more thorough and comprehensive fashion around the years 1902–03. One of the most significant texts in this respect is the 1902 "Minute Logic"; another is the 1903 "Syllabus of Certain Topics of Logic."[68] This later version of the classification is the one that commentators have most focused on, because it is the one Peirce himself ended up trusting most, and because it is the most comprehensive, encompassing not only what Peirce calls the "sciences of discovery" but also the arts, the practical sciences, and the so-called "sciences of review."[69] This time, the relation to his history of science is much more feeble. Still, in 1902 to 1903, Peirce had just finished his long treatise on the "Logic of Writing History from Ancient Documents" and he had recently taken up his work on "great men" and historical biography.

In order to discuss Peirce's classification in more detail, let me begin by presenting two diagrams, based, respectively, on the 1892 and the 1903 versions of Peirce's scheme (Schemes 1 and 2).[70] Even a quick glance at this scheme will show that the many differences coexist with robust structural similarities. I shall then set out from these diagrams to make two general remarks about the structure of Peirce's classification. These remarks will help us better under-

---

[65] W8, p. 98–110 (1891).
[66] EP2, p. 35–37, also in RLT, p. 114–117.
[67] HP, p. 307–309, 396.
[68] "Minute Logic," CP 1.203–283, also published in part as EP2, p. 115–132; "A Syllabus of Certain Topics of Logic," CP 1.180–202, also in EP2, p. 258–262.
[69] On the sciences of review, see Topa 2019. On the relations between Peirce's late classification and his metaphysics, see Atkins 2006.
[70] The first table is adapted from W8, p. 275. The second comes from CP 1.180–202. In both cases, I have omitted some details and sub-classifications, some of which will be discussed in later chapters. On the different versions of Peirce's Classification, see also Kent 1987.

stand in what sense Peirce's classification articulates the relation between history and philosophy, and conversely, what aspects of this relation it falls short of grasping.

- Mathematics
    - Pure
    - Applied
- Philosophy
    - Logic
    - Metaphysics
- Nomology
    - Psychology
    - General Physics
- Chemistry
- Physics of the ether
- Biology
- Sociology
    - Conduct
        - Ethics; Theology; Politics; Law; Etiquette
    - Communication
        - Art; Language
- Accounts of particular objects
    - Cosmology
        - Astronomy; Geognosy
        - Human History

Scheme 1

Sciences of Discovery
1. Mathematics
2. Philosophy or "cenoscopy"
    I. Phenomenology
    II. Normative Sciences
        i. Esthetics
        ii. Ethics
        iii. Logic
            a) Speculative Grammar
            b) Critic
            c) Methodeutic (or Speculative Rhetoric)
    III. Metaphysics
3. "Idioscopy" or special sciences
    I. Physical Sciences
        i. Nomological Physics
        ii. Classificatory Physics (Crystallography, Chemistry, Biology)
        iii. Descriptive Physics (Geognosy, Astronomy)
    II. Psychical or Human Sciences
        i. Nomological Psychics (Psychology)
        ii. Classificatory Psychics (Special Psychology; Linguistics; Ethnology)
        iii. Descriptive Psychics or History (History Proper; Biography; Criticism)

Scheme 2

The first remark I would like to make about these two diagrams has to do with the classification criteria. Peirce conceived of his classification as a ladder that goes from the most concrete to the most abstract sciences. In doing this, he was following one of his major sources of inspiration: Auguste Comte. ("My own classification" – he stated in 1892 – "is a direct reformation of that of Comte.")[71] For us, it is particularly rewarding to observe the position of philosophy and history within this ladder. In all versions of the classification, Peirce puts philosophy almost at the top, immediately after mathematics. Its characteristic hallmark is generality. (The *Century Dictionary*, for instance, says that philosophy is "the examination and logical analysis of the general body of fact."[72]) History, on the other hand, dwells at the very bottom of the ladder. In

---

[71] R 1336 (c. 1892), cited in Ambrosio 2016.
[72] CD, p. 5397.

all versions of the scheme, it is characterized as a descriptive science that deals with singular facts. Moreover, its object belongs to the "psychic" or human realm, as opposed to the facts of "cosmology" (1892) or "descriptive physics" (1903). In this sense, history and philosophy are not simply two disciplines among many; they occupy the extremes of the ladder. Thinking about their relation means thinking about how to bring into contact two seemingly opposite scientific methodologies.

The later version of the classification expresses a similar idea by means of a terminology borrowed from Jeremy Bentham. Philosophy is called "cenoscopy" (from Greek *koinos*, "common," "shared," "general," and *skopeô*, "to observe"). It is the study of "observations such as come within the range of every man's normal experience, and for the most part in every waking hour of his life."[73] In contrast, history is grouped together with other psychical and physical sciences under the label "idioscopy" (from *idios*, "peculiar," "separate"): the science of special observations.

Quite in keeping with the Comtian inspiration of his classification, Peirce maintains that the relation between the different sciences is the product of a twofold mechanism. Epistemologically, the relation goes in principle in one direction only, namely from the top to the bottom of the ladder. Lower, more concrete, sciences depend on higher and more abstract sciences. They borrow principles and general propositions from the latter. Higher sciences, on the contrary, remain relatively independent from lower ones. "Men may and do begin to study the different kinds of animals and plants before they know anything of the general laws of physiology. But they cannot attain any true understanding of taxonomic biology until they can be guided by the discovery of the physiologists."[74] But historically, the relation is reversed. Sciences go through a historical development that runs from the bottom toward the top of the ladder. That is, sciences display a "well-marked tendency to be first descriptive, later classificatory, and lastly to embrace all classes in one law."[75] In the 1898 version of the classification, a similar idea is expressed through a very explicit reference to the history-philosophy relation.

> As a general proposition, the history of science shows every science growing into a more abstract science, one higher in our scale. [...] The proverb that history is philosophy teach-

---

73 CP 1.241 (1902). Cf. Bentham [1816] 1843, p. 83–84.
74 CP 1.226. Compare 1.180: "[The classification] borrows its idea from Comte's classification; namely, the idea that one science depends upon another for fundamental principles, but does not furnish such principles to that other."
75 CP 1.226.

ing by examples, is another way of saying that the descriptive science of history tends to grow into a classificatory science of kinds of events of which the events of history are specimens.[76]

So, a descriptive and idioscopic science, like history, draws its principle from more general sciences and ultimately from philosophy. However, the only way it can, in turn, influence those general sciences is by producing its own generalizations and thus growing into a more general, classificatory science. But is this account of the relation between general and special sciences, or between cenoscopy and idioscopy, compatible with what we said before about the "mutual aid" that philosophy and history lend one another? Although in both cases Peirce is envisaging a reciprocal relation between philosophical and empirical sciences, we may still recognize a tension between the two models. The Comtian model that Peirce adopted in his classification led him to conceive of this relation as less symmetrical than was the case in the texts examined above.

The second remark I would like to make about the classificatory diagrams does not concern the relation between history and philosophy *within* the classification. Rather, it concerns the historicity of the classification itself as a theoretical object. While observing the diagrams above, we might ask: are the disciplinary relations captured by the classification historically contingent, or are they "rational," that is, non-historical? And does the classification follow a genetic method of reconstruction or a conceptual or morphological one? Finally, are the sciences themselves purely historical objects or rather ideal, non-historical entities?[77]

We can start answering these questions if we go back to the interesting circumstances noted before, namely, that the 1892–93 Lowell Lectures on the history of science begin with a diagram of the classification.[78] This can, once again, be related to the influence of Whewell and, more precisely, to the latter's conviction that the different sciences are governed by different "ideas," which develop

---

[76] EP2, p. 38–39 or RLT, p. 119. The "proverb" Peirce is talking about is attributed to Thucydides. See the editors' commentary on EP2, p. 506 n33.

[77] As early as in the *Century Dictionary*, we read that philosophy is a science "which *both in reason and in history* precedes successful dealing with special elements of the universe." CD, p. 537. My emphasis.

[78] See again Ambrosio 2016. Let me also note here that the classification placed at the beginning of the Lowell Lectures presents an odd detail. The two descriptive sciences at the bottom of the ladder are not "cosmology" and "history," as in W8, p. 275, but rather "cosmology" and "humanity." I am unable to say whether this is merely a slip of the pen, whether Peirce meant "humanities" (the *Oxford English Dictionary* attests the singular form as of the 1890s), or still something else.

in the course of history.⁷⁹ In fact, Peirce radicalized Whewell's thesis. Not only did he describe the sciences as the product of ideas that "have grown up during the course of scientific history," but he understood those ideas as the gradual development, or refinement, of primitive instincts. He remarked, for instance, that "the most fundamental division of the sciences" into physical and psychical sciences is the outcome of the distinction between the instinct of nutrition and the instinct of reproduction.⁸⁰ In virtue of its being placed at the beginning of the Lectures, the classification diagram serves as a guiding thread to follow the historical narrative about how the different human instincts have brought about the different domains of scientific knowledge.

An immediate consequence of this move is that the classification itself cannot pretend to be an eternal object, mirroring an atemporal structure. Rather, it is relative to the degree of development that scientific ideas display at the moment in which the classification itself is formulated. Depending on the stage of scientific development that we have reached, our classification will look different.⁸¹ This reading is consistent with a number of comments made by Peirce himself. In a hand-written annotation to Peirce's own copy of the *Century Dictionary*, we read: "I am convinced that we can only form a natural classification of science in its present state, looking forward just a little."⁸² In later versions of the classification, Peirce came back to the same problem. He emphasized that classifications are historical objects, likely to grow outdated over time:

> [I]f classifications are to be restricted to sciences actually existing at the time the classifications are made, the classifications certainly ought to differ from age to age. If Plato's classification was satisfactory in his day, it cannot be good today, and if it be good now, the inference will be that it was bad when he proposed it.⁸³

Also, Peirce claimed that his own classification is only concerned "with sciences in their present condition, as so many businesses of groups of living men."⁸⁴ The same idea can be found in a later letter to Victoria Welby, where Peirce says that

---

79 See Ambrosio 2016.
80 I am quoting from De Tienne forthcoming. I will come back to this point in Ch. 6.
81 Ambrosio 2016 expresses a similar idea by saying that Peirce bestows a certain "historicity" on the classification. But she also takes a step forward and claims that by prefacing his history of science with his classificatory scheme, Peirce is also implicitly recognizing that history can only be written from a specific historical angle, i.e., the stage of scientific development at which historians find themselves.
82 R 1597, quoted in Ambrosio 2016.
83 CP 1.203.
84 CP 1.180.

semiotics itself is, "for the present," a single science, although it might, in principle, be divided into three different branches. "But I have learned that the only natural lines of demarcation between nearly related sciences are the divisions between the social groups of devotees of those sciences."[85] This quote also makes clear that Peirce's classification of the sciences is closely intertwined with his definition of science, not as a specific corpus of knowledge, but rather as a mode of activity, a mode of life (see Chapter 5). Indeed, Peirce was positive that his pragmatic definition of science as a mode of activity made his classification necessarily relative to a given historical time.[86]

Natural Classes, Genealogy, Natural History

It should, however, be emphasized that the argument just given about the historicity of Peirce's classification is not aimed at advocating outright historical relativity. Peirce's remarks about the historical variability of the classification do not entail that the structure of the classification can be utterly revolutionized over history – say, by making logic or mathematics depend on the descriptive sciences. But how can we reconcile this fact with what Peirce himself says about the historical contingency of the classification? I think that we can start solving the conundrum if we posit a general structural trait of the classification, which transcends historical variability but can coexist with local changes. In the passage I have just quoted, Peirce talks about the "natural lines of demarcation *between nearly related sciences*," not about the classificatory structure in its entirety. The overall hierarchy is virtually immune to change but the specific lines of demarcation between the sciences are constantly redrawn.

Also, to better understand how exactly this combination of a historical and an ahistorical aspect in the classification is achieved, we should pay attention to the adjective "natural" in that passage. Especially in his later versions, Peirce was adamant that the classification of the sciences should be a "natural classi-

---

[85] CP 8.342 (1908). Cf. CP 1.190: "Phenomenology is, *at present*, a single study." (My emphasis.)
[86] CP 7.55–56 (c. 1902): "By *a* specific science will be meant a group of connected inquiries of sufficient scope and affinity fitly to occupy a number of independent inquirers for life, but not capable of being broken up into smaller coexclusive groups of this description. [...]"
"It seems plain that, with these definitions, the classification cannot be concerned with all possible sciences, but must be confined to actually realized sciences. If, however, this limitation is to be maintained, the question will arise, to what date or stage of scientific development is the classification to relate?"

fication,"[87] a concept borrowed from nineteenth-century biology. As such, this is not a particularly original move. If we look, for instance, at the *Kosmos* of Alexander von Humboldt, a book that Peirce explicitly mentioned as one of his sources, we note that natural history is developed in parallel with a number of observations about the history of the sciences.[88] In the same vein, Kant's architectonic is replete with biological metaphors.[89] But even more to the point, the claim that the classification of the sciences should be a "natural" one was virtually ubiquitous in the nineteenth century. Indeed, it has been claimed that the nineteenth-century classifications of the sciences differed from one another precisely in their taking different systems of biological taxonomy as their model.[90]

One of the many reasons behind this biological analogy was the intention to advance a claim to objectivity. By calling the classification "natural," it was implied that the classification itself did not follow arbitrary or artificial criteria but was faithful to the nature of its object. For instance, Whewell maintained that the sciences should not be classified according to the faculties of the human mind or to the nature of their objects, but according to a "more natural and fundamental criterion," namely the "fundamental ideas or conceptions" involved by each science. Geometry involves the idea of space; statics involves the idea of matter; chemistry involves the idea of substance or atom; and so forth.[91]

Like so many other scholars, Peirce was also taking inspiration from a specific model of biological taxonomy in order to advance his natural classification. In his case, the paradigmatic model was from a figure we have already encountered in Chapter 1: his teacher, Louis Agassiz. But Peirce intentionally mixed this biological model with another, very different source, namely archeology. Archeology, too, is a descriptive science: it is concerned with describing and classifying classes of objects, although these objects are not living organisms but artifacts. In particular, Peirce used the example of the ancient Egyptian balance-weights exhumed by English archeologist Flinders Petrie.[92]

---

87 See, in particular, the "Minute Logic," CP 1.203–237 (1902).
88 See Werner 2004, p. 45–56, for an overview of Humboldt's work. Cf. CP 1.182, and W1, p. 114, already cited in Ch. 1.
89 Ferrarin 2015, p. 34–42.
90 Csiszar 2010, p. 383, quoted in Ambrosio 2016.
91 See Whewell 1840, vol. 2, p. 277–282. I am once again relying on Ambrosio 2016 and De Tienne forthcoming. The latter emphasizes the complementary role of Comte and Whewell in Peirce's 1892 classification.
92 CP 1.209–210. I go back to Peirce's interest in archeology in Chs. 6 and 7.

Peirce's use of the concept of natural classification raises a crucial question: how should we go about identifying and defining the "natural classes" that his theory is supposed to organize and classify? Peirce makes three crucial remarks in this respect. First, he claims that the soundest way to define natural classes is to make them depend on those general ideas that have the power to generate the single items of a class. Second, this process of generation of the single items of a class from a general idea does not follow the dynamic of efficient causation but that of final causation. In this sense, the relevance of the archeological model becomes apparent. We can talk of a certain group of artifacts forming a real, natural class when they are produced according to a general goal that is common to all of them. But Agassiz had advocated a similarly teleological view of generation in the realm of zoology. Third, the classes thus formed do not have sharp boundaries. "[I]t may be quite impossible to draw a sharp line of demarcation between two classes, although they are real and natural classes in strictest truth."[93]

These remarks led Peirce to elaborate a specific method for investigating the natural classes: a method that is extremely significant for us because it is aimed precisely at striking a middle course between a historical and an ahistorical approach. The "Minute Logic" (1902) is particularly explicit in this respect. Since a natural class is "a family whose members are the sole offspring and vehicles of one idea," the best way to identify them is not by "abstract definitions," but rather by "trac[ing] the *genesis* of a class and ascertain[ing] how several have been derived by different lines of descent from one less specialized form."[94] This means that "*genealogical classification* [...] is the classification we can most certainly rely upon as being natural."[95] But the kind of genesis that is at stake here has a strong ideal dimension, one that directly derives from its relation to final causes.

If we apply this methodological argument about natural classes to the specific case of the classification of the sciences, we reach precisely the result I anticipated above: the classification of the sciences is a partly historical but partly non-historical enterprise. On the one hand, "[t]he natural classification of science must be based on the study of the history of science."[96] But on the other hand, the history of science is itself guided by an ideal and teleological dimension:

---

[93] See, in particular, CP 1.205–210. But cf. the much earlier "Deduction, Induction, and Hypothesis," W3, p. 332 (1878): "Classifications in all cases perfectly satisfactory hardly exist."
[94] CP 1.222. My emphasis.
[95] CP 1.225. My emphasis.
[96] CP 1.268.

> All natural classification is then essentially, we may almost say, an attempt to find out the true genesis of the objects classified. But by genesis must be understood, not the efficient action which produces the whole by producing the parts, but the final action which produces the parts because they are needed to make the whole. Genesis is production from ideas. [...] A science is defined by its problem; and its problem is clearly formulated on the basis of abstracter science.[97]

Peirce's classification is thus based on a specific kind of history, namely genealogy, which is aimed precisely at reconciling a sensitivity to historical change with an investigation of ideal elements. The latter are, in turn, defined as final causes. This concept of genealogy (which is also related to the concept of "natural history"[98]) is indeed among Peirce's most significant uses of history, not only in connection to his classification of the sciences, but on a more general scale. We shall see in the next chapter that both the specific kind of teleology that it brings with it and its relation to naturalistic metaphors are crucial elements of Peirce's conception of historicity at large. For now, let me just repeat that the idea of the classification of the sciences as a genealogical study entails at the same time a genuinely historical reference to the past and the ability to look to the future. While the past provides us with irreplaceable information about how the sciences have been developing over time, only a reference to their future developments can do justice to their ideal and teleological character. In this sense, the Peircean concept of genealogy meets a quintessentially pragmatist requirement: although its subject matter lies partly in the past, it cannot be carried out without reference to the future. This idea finds expression in a passage that deserves to be cited at length:

> According to the general spirit of this book, which values everything in its relation to Life, knowledge which is altogether inapplicable to the future is nugatory. Consequently, our classification ought to have reference to the science of the future. [...] Meantime, let it not be understood that the classification is to ignore the scientific discoveries of the past. For the memoirs of that work are not so poor as not to merit being read critically, precisely as we shall read the memoirs of tomorrow. Such reading is, therefore, of the nature of scientific inquiry. True, it is not original research; but there is original research still to be done in the same specific science. For none of the sciences of the past is finished. If it be one of the positive sciences that is in question, there is not a single conclusion belonging to it which has in the past been made sufficiently precise or sufficiently indubitable. If it be a branch of mathematics, its propositions require to be further generalized, as well as to be

---

97 CP 1.227.
98 See, e.g., CP 1.568–572 (1910).

more accurately limited. For these reasons all the old science that still stands is to be retained in the classification, but in its most modern forms.[99]

We can reach quite similar results from a slightly different angle if we focus not on the method of the classification but on its object. As we have seen, Peirce maintains that natural classes have vague boundaries.[100] This means that, when we go about classifying the sciences, we cannot hope to draw clear-cut lines of demarcation between them from a purely a priori standpoint. The only way to trace those lines of demarcation is by relying on historical and sociological observations, such as whether a definite science has reached the point at which it has become the exclusive subject matter of a group of experts. Since these observations necessarily vary with time, the lines of demarcation constantly move. As I already said, however, there are some general traits of the classification that do not vary with time. This applies in particular to the general hierarchical ladder that Peirce derives from Comte: whether, say, mathematics is higher or lower than descriptive physics is not a matter that can be settled by historical observation. So, Peirce was willing to allow for historical variation *within* the sciences, as well as across the lines of demarcation between neighboring sciences, while insisting on invariance at the level of the general hierarchy. This means that not only is the method of the classification half historical and half ideal; the very subject matter of the classification is so. The sciences conceived as natural classes preserve a history-transcendent structure while continually changing over time.

This argument captures quite successfully the process of historical differentiation and the increasing division of labor that have affected the scientific disciplines over time,[101] while dismissing the possibility of drastic revolutions in the general organizing scheme. In this sense, I am tempted to compare Peirce's natural classification of the sciences to yet another traditional biological metaphor of human knowledge, namely the *arbor scientiae*.[102] In Peirce's "tree of science," new branchings can pop up at certain historical times; old branches can disappear; and most importantly, a single branch can divide into two or more sub-

---

99 CP 7.56–57 (c. 1902).
100 I return to this point in Ch. 3.
101 Let me bring up yet another example. Using, once again, a biological metaphor, Peirce describes the philosophical discipline of phenomenology as "still in the condition of a science-egg, hardly any details of it being as yet distinguishable." See Atkins 2019, p. 228.
102 The metaphor dates back to Llull [1295] 2000.

branches. But the general structure of the tree – the general pattern according to which it reproduces itself – is bound to endure.[103]

An Alternative Approach

The foregoing discussion has alerted us to a fact that might have escaped our notice at the outset. Peirce's classification of the sciences is relevant to the history-philosophy relation in two different senses. The first sense is internal to the classification itself. It conceives of history and philosophy as two scientific disciplines and articulates their relation according to the twofold mechanism I have already described. As a descriptive science, history may borrow its principles from philosophy. Vice versa, it tends to "grow" into a more general science by producing increasingly general observations. The second sense is related to the issues discussed in the last section: does a "natural" classification of the sciences mirror historical facts (i.e., the historically contingent relations between scientific disciplines at a given time in history) or non-historical, ideal facts (i.e., some sort of eternal structure of human knowledge)? While laying out our classification do we need to adopt a more historical or a more philosophical – conceptual, systematic, "rational" – methodology? In this second sense, the relation between history and philosophy becomes a methodological or meta-theoretical issue, which Peirce himself had to confront when critically reflecting on his own work.

But here we stumble on a problem. The concept of "history" that Peirce placed at the bottom of his classificatory ladder does not appear adequate to grasp this new sense of history that we have seen emerging at the level of the classificatory method. What Peirce dealt with in his classification is history conceived as a self-enclosed discipline. It is not a specific method or a specific approach to problems which may possibly concern other disciplines as well. In order to grasp this latter aspect, we will have to go beyond Peirce's classificatory scheme.

---

103 Peirce studied trees as a mathematical object, in particular with regard to their ability to picture recursivity and complexity across a wide spectrum of phenomena, from biology to logic. He took inspiration from the work of his colleague at Johns Hopkins, mathematician Arthur Cayley. See, e.g., W8, p. 173 (1892). Cf. Houser 2010, p. xlviii-xlix, and the editors' comments on W8, p. 225, 407, 424, 613. I found inspiring remarks on trees as a model that reconcile historical variability with structural invariance, although applied to a different historical epoch, in Kemp, 2004, p. 135–141.

By the same token, Peirce's classification does not seem adequately equipped to grasp the idea that there may be different strategies, more or less rival, for broaching a single scientific topic; and that, moreover, one of the issues on which this rivalry hinges is precisely the way these different strategies resort to historical explanations. In line with his understanding of science as a community-driven pursuit of truth, Peirce produced quite an ecumenical classification: one in which all big conflicts over methods, objectives and theoretical paradigms have been set aside for the sake of inquiry. In this model, scientific disciplines can only split up as a result of the growing complexity of their object of inquiry or as a result of an increasing community of practitioners. But they do not split because of methodological and theoretical conflicts that arise within the discipline itself. The complexity of Peirce's classificatory system is the complexity of organic growth. It is not the complexity of conflict.

In the subsequent chapters (in particular, Chapter 5), I will return to this problem and argue that it is related to a more general difficulty of Peirce's conception of disagreement in science and philosophy. For all his appreciation of Whewell's emphasis on controversies as an engine of scientific progress, Peirce thought about science as primarily oriented toward agreement and consensus. This position, however, risks downplaying the essential role of controversies in the actual unfolding of science.

What would happen to our problem, the problem of the history-philosophy relation, if we shifted our focus from consensus toward conflict? One major consequence, I think, would be to give much more emphasis than Peirce did to the idea that the apparently simple dichotomy of history and philosophy is, in fact, decomposable into a plurality of issues. In other words, we would need to stop considering history and philosophy as self-enclosed or monolithic disciplines and, instead, admit that the boundaries between them are complex, multi-faceted and always open to re-negotiations that are, in turn, spurred by methodological or disciplinary controversies.[104]

---

[104] The pragmatist-oriented sociology of disciplines put forth by Chicago sociologist Andrew Abbott (Abbott 2001) may be taken as an example of what I mean here. Abbott presents a very peculiar *arbor scientiae*; one in which what remains stable over time is not the hierarchy among the sciences but rather the possibility of engaging in conflict over fundamental issues of method. Abbott speaks in this sense of a "fractal" structure, precisely because the same lines of division tend to appear at any point of the scientific controversy. See p. xvi: "[I]f we take any group of sociologists and lock them in a room, they will argue and at once differentiate themselves into positivists and interpretivists. But if we separate those two groups and lock *them* in separate rooms, *those* two groups will each in turn divide over exactly the same issue."

In closing the chapter, I would like to point to one possible way to analyze the history-philosophy dichotomy, which will in turn help me structure the chapters that follow. Peirce, it will be recalled, had organized the argument of "The Fixation of Belief" around a specific claim. It is by observing the opinion of "men *in other countries* and *in other ages*" that we come to realize the inadequacy of pre-scientific ways of fixing beliefs. I have already suggested linking this remark to the positive role of history in shattering our inveterate beliefs. History exerts an influence on us that can be broken down into two domains: space and time; "other countries" and "other ages"; what is past and what is alien to us.[105] But now we can take a step further. That is, we can turn these two domains into a heuristic device that helps us isolate two different axes along which history's bearing on philosophy can be understood. The first is the axis of temporality, or of the relation between past and present. The second axis, by contrast, understands history as the knowledge of what is foreign and other.

The first axis centers around the question whether, and in what measure, the past is relevant to the philosophical understanding of the present. Should we take into account the past in order to understand the present? What is the use of our knowledge of the past? Following the German philosophical tradition, we may call this question the question of *historicity* (*Geschichtlichkeit*). I have already sporadically used the concept when dealing with the classification of the sciences. But in the following chapter I aim to discuss it more closely. I will deal precisely with the philosophical issue of the relation between past and present and suggest that one of the ways in which we should hope to make headway on Peirce's philosophy of history is to ask what conception of historicity is at play in his philosophy.

The second axis takes a different stand. Instead of asking what uses we can make of the past, or how the past is embedded in the present, it asks what role a confrontation with alterity should play in our use of rational faculties. Here, we face the question whether our faculty of judgment and our intellectual creativity can be exercised in *autonomy*, without recourse to the opinions of others (or to the lessons of experience). This second set of questions has a decidedly more epistemological flavor than the first one. But it also reflects a different under-

---

105 See Chapter 1. I am here borrowing my terminology from a passage in Nietzsche's second *Untimely Meditation:* "There were centuries in which the Greeks found themselves threatened by a danger similar to the one we face today, the danger, namely, of perishing in a flood of things alien and past [*Überschwemmung durch das Fremde und das Vergangne*], of perishing of 'history.'" (Nietzsche [1874] 1995, p. 166). The idea that time and space are structuring distinctions of historical research is as old as Herodotus. See Carbonell 1985.

standing of history, more centered on a conversational and dialogic attitude than on diachrony. It will be the object of Chapter 4.

Part II

3 Historicity as Process

An "Attraction for Living Facts"

We have seen that the place Peirce allotted to philosophy and history in the classification of the sciences cannot be considered his last word on the matter. Peirce's approach to history is complex and multi-faceted; and it is occasionally based on a tighter, more reciprocal relation than the classification would have it. In the last part of the book, I will return to Peirce's actual historical work by isolating some themes of his history of science that have a bearing on his philosophical preoccupations. By contrast, in this and the following two chapters I aim to delve deeper into the theoretical underpinning of Peirce's recourse to history. I would like to ask whether, and in what ways, his philosophy allows history to play a significant role in philosophical inquiry. As I suggested at the end of the preceding chapter, this problem can, in turn, be broken down into two different questions, which I have dubbed the question of historicity and the question of autonomy. The first hinges on whether the past is a constitutive dimension of the present. The second asks whether we can articulate our individual philosophical ideas independently of external sources.

Here I start by considering the question of historicity. I wish to ask in which sense it is legitimate to say that Peirce's metaphysics allows the past to have a decisive influence on the present.[1] I shall look for the answer to this question in the processual ontology that is shared by signs, habits and laws of nature (in short, by all elements of reality that have to do with the metaphysical category of Thirdness).

As such, this is not a particularly original claim. The metaphysics of Peirce, and of the pragmatists in general, has long been discussed under the heading of processualism, along with related terms, such as evolutionism or "temporalism."[2] However, these discussions have also brought to the fore a predicament I will need to address. Because of their emphasis on the future consequences

---

[1] Von Renthe-Fink 1974 points out three different sense of the German word *Geschichtlichkeit*, with the second almost perfectly overlapping with my use of the word "historicity." A classic study of the Hegelian concept of historicity is Marcuse [1932] 1987. See also the introduction by Seyla Benhabib, in particular p. xxvi, xxiii. After Hegel, the concept of historicity was most prominently taken up by Dilthey, and, via Dilthey, by phenomenologically oriented thinkers such as Heidegger, Jaspers and Raymond Aron. See Aron 1950, p. 322. For a pragmatist use of the concept, see Koopman 2009; Margolis 2019.
[2] On evolutionism, see Wiener 1949; on temporalism, Lovejoy 1963; on processualism, Browning/Myers 1998.

of ideas and actions, Peirce and the other pragmatists have often been read as future-oriented rather than past-oriented philosophers.³

I aim to show that this opposition, at least in the case of Peirce, does not cut deep enough. It is true that Peirce's processualism acquires its distinctive profile from the role it bestows on the future. Still, it cannot be understood without taking into account its appreciation of the past. By defending this thesis, I also hope to lay the ground for a renewed understanding of the complex relation that Peircean philosophy holds with other historically oriented philosophies such as Hegelianism, historicism or hermeneutics.⁴

I will proceed in a loosely chronological fashion. Going through the main phases of Peirce's intellectual career, I will examine the development of his processualism and the main philosophical challenges it encounters. My starting point will be the analysis of thought-processes, but I will look at the way Peirce gradually widened his gaze to encompass habits, laws of nature, laws of history and symbols at large. In doing so, I aim to show that Peirce's processualism is one of the original insights of his philosophy, one that may even antedate his full-hearted espousal of evolutionism. Indeed, the basic structure of Peirce's processualist argument remains quite stable over time. The argument aims precisely at striking a balance between a past-oriented and a future-oriented attitude by inquiring into the different ways the past and the future influence the present, as well as into the possible existence of a teleology in nature which does not rule out chance and contingency.

While discussing these issues, I will note how Peirce finds himself going back again and again to a terminology that rests on organicist metaphors. All phenomena that have to do with the metaphysical category of Thirdness are described as "living" and "growing." This gives us a first, intuitive sense of the position Peirce wished to defend. When we say that something grows, we mean that it changes over time in a way that comes closer and closer to its *telos*, yet to a *telos* which is not necessarily predetermined. Moreover, living entities can be described as having a history – indeed, a "life-history"⁵ – and preserving their stability over and above the constant change. We will have to take this simile very

---

3 Lovejoy 1963 is a classic account. To say that pragmatists are future-oriented is not to deny that they are processualist philosophers, because a processualist position does not need to be past-oriented and historicist. It can, on the contrary, be radically presentist, if it looks at reality as a flux where only the present exists. See, e.g., Abbott 2016. Or it can be future-oriented if it takes the relation between present and future to be more significant than the relation between present and past.
4 For similar approaches, see Colapietro 2003a; Koopman 2009; Joas 2016.
5 CP 2.111 (1902).

seriously: in a sense, Peirce's ontology of historicity rests precisely on the attempt to see signs, habits, and laws as growing, living things. His pragmatism is "a sort of instinctive attraction for living facts."[6]

Early Semiotic Processualism

The first substantial contribution to the formulation of a processualist metaphysics can be found in Peirce's early writings on logic and semiotics, which investigate the nature of thought and signs. One way to sum up Peirce's argument is by looking at it as a series of consecutive steps.

The first step is the definition of the sign as being in a triadic relation. The sign refers to something for someone. It is related to both an object and an "interpretant," that is, the person or thing that interprets the sign.[7] However, the interpretant itself is a semiotic entity. More precisely, it is a sign that refers to the same object as the first sign and makes its meaning available to other interpretants. In this way, the sign ceases to be a static entity and becomes dynamic: it is part of a potentially infinite chain of interpretants that lets its own meaning develop. In the course of this development, a peculiar balance between change and stability is attained: while the interpretants follow each other, their object remains fixed.

A second argumentative step is articulated in the anti-intuitionist essays from 1868 to 1869.[8] Thought, Peirce maintains, must be understood semiotically, as a flux of signs. We cannot have a conception that is not itself a sign. But a sign is always embedded in a chain of interpretants; therefore, a conception is always embedded in a flux of other conceptions. Moreover, we cannot have a conception that is not preceded by other conceptions, as this would amount to a sign that is not itself the interpretant of another sign. This amounts to saying that we have no power of intuition.

One possible objection to this argument might be to claim that it gives rise to an infinite regress. If all thoughts are interpretants of previous thoughts, the objection might run, there cannot be a moment in time in which a thought process begins; but this seems plainly contradicted by facts. Thus, we must grant the ex-

---

6 EP2, p. 158 (1903). On the relation between historicity and the concept of life, see again Marcuse [1932] 1987. Cf. Gerhardt 2000, p. 25–26.
7 See W1, p. 464–467 (1866); W2, p. 54 (1867).
8 See W2, p. 193–211; 211–242 (1868).

istence of a first thought that is not preceded by anything else. Peirce, however, counters the objection with a third argumentative step. Thought, he claims, is not only a flux of signs but a continuous flux of signs. One property of continuity is precisely its infinite divisibility: between any two members of a series there is always an infinite number of other members.[9] Therefore, it is possible to claim both that the flux of thought has a temporal beginning and that every conception has an infinite number of antecedents. The only further assumption we need to make to reach this conclusion is that the point of origin of thought is not itself a conception, but rather, a non-cognitive fact that triggers a process of cognition.

Peirce helps us visualize his argument through a geometrical analogy. Take the diagram of a triangle "resting upon its apex" (fig. 1).[10] The triangle represents the flux of thought. The infinite number of cross-sectional segments that we can draw on it (like the one I have drawn in the figure) represent the different conceptions contained in the flux. The down apex, however, is not itself a segment but a point of zero length. Hence, it does not represent a conception but rather the non-cognitive point in time in which the thought-processes has its origin. Now, since we are dealing with continuous quantities, we can admit that between this point in time and any given segment there is an infinite number of other segments. This stands for the fact that the flux of thought can have a chro-

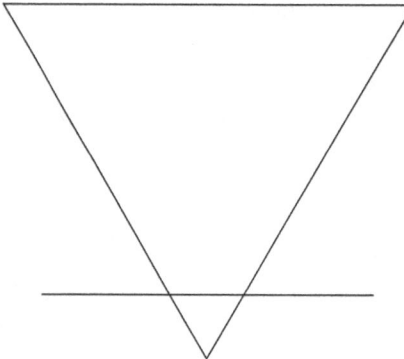

Fig. 1

---

9 W2, p. 256 (1868). Later in his career, Peirce would come to regard the property of infinite divisibility as necessary but not sufficient for the definition of continuity. See W8, p. 143–145 (1892).
10 W2, p. 178, 210. The diagram drawn by Peirce is slightly different from mine, and less clear.

nological beginning (the apex of the triangle) without there being any absolutely first conception (i.e., an absolutely first cross-sectional segment). Rather, whenever a conception presents itself as first, we can be confident that it has been preceded by an infinite number of other conceptions of which we have not been aware.

The fourth and last argumentative step is already implicit in the preceding one. It consists in modeling the continuity of thought processes after the continuity of time. That time is a continuous quantity entails that between any two instants there is an infinite number of other instants. But since thought takes place in time, it borrows its ontological structure from the latter.

Thus, a major outcome of Peirce's anti-Cartesian argument is indeed a historical-processual account of thought, which rests on "the familiar axiom that in intuition, i.e., in the immediate present, there is no thought, or that all which is reflected upon has past."[11] Peirce took up the same idea in his logical writings from the early 1870s: writings in which the relation between time and thought is indeed crucial. "[N]ot only does it take time for an idea to grow, but after that process is completed the idea cannot exist in an instant. During the time of its existence it will not be always the same but undergoes changes."[12] Or again: "Thought [...] is a stream, which as it goes on, is enlarged by new additions. And yet, all that we can distinctly trace is the flow; and we cannot put our finger on the points at which the new matter emerges."[13]

A corollary of this idea is that in the immediate or instantaneous present there is neither thought nor consciousness but, at most, a *feeling* of consciousness. In other words, there is a difference between immediate feelings, which

---

[11] W2, p. 207. The passage continues: "That, since any thought, there must have been a thought, has its analogue in the fact that, since any past time, there must have been an infinite series of times. To say, therefore, that thought cannot happen in an instant, but requires a time, is but another way of saying that every thought must be interpreted in another, or that all thought is in signs."

[12] W3, p. 104 (1873). This comes from a manuscript entitled "The Conception of Time essential in Logic." On the manuscript page, after the sentence "the idea cannot exist in an instant," Peirce added: "but is itself the nature of a process." He then barred the addition. See Kevelson 1983, p. 90.

[13] W3, p. 34 (1872). Peirce's definition of thought as a "stream" antedates William James's better-known conception of the "stream of thought" in James [1890] 1981, Ch. 9. See Girel 2003 for a comparison between the two conceptions on the basis of Peirce's later reading of *The Principles of Psychology*. See also W3, p. 35 (1872), which makes a similar point with regard to the process of inquiry. "All inquiry [...] presupposes a passage from a state of doubt to a state of belief; and therefore there must be a succession of time in the thoughts of any mind which is able to inquire."

can be instant-like, and genuine thoughts, which are mediated and temporally extended. This difference not only reflects the metaphysical distinction between the categories of Firstness and Thirdness, or immediacy and mediation. It also dovetails with a phenomenological remark about the temporal structure of consciousness. We cannot be immediately aware of our present ideas, if by "present" we mean the punctiform instant now occurring, as deprived of any duration. If, on the contrary, we take the present to mean a lapse of time (however short), then we can certainly say that we are aware of it, although mediately so. But at that point, nothing prevents us from expanding at our pleasure the lapse of time that we take to constitute the present. "The events of a day are less mediately present to the mind than the events of a year; the events of a second less mediately present than the events of a day."[14] So the distinction between memory of the past and consciousness of the present is only a matter of degree. Following this argumentative line, the very concept of memory gets re-defined as our ability to gain access to an infinite series of variously extended presents.[15]

The processualist results Peirce obtained through his early logical analyses are not confined to mental phenomena but apply to signs at large. After all, Peirce's aim was not to ground logic on psychology, but rather the other way around. The real object of his investigation was the general structure of signs as they contribute to logical processes. These signs may be both internal and external to the mind. In fact, there is a constant interplay between the internal and the external. In a typical example of the organicist metaphors that I mentioned at the beginning of the chapter, Peirce compared symbols to living beings, because of their ability to grow, learn, and generate.

> Does not electricity mean more now than it did in the days of Franklin? Man makes the word, and the word means nothing which the man has not made it mean, and that only to some man. But since man can think only by means of words or other external symbols, these might turn round and say: "You mean nothing which we have not taught you, and then only so far as you address some word as the interpretant of your thought." In fact, therefore, men and words reciprocally educate each other; each increase of a man's information involves and is involved by, a corresponding increase of a word's information.[16]

The passage should be understood against the background of Peirce's logical inquiries on the two basic components of a symbol's meaning, namely its "exten-

---

14 W3, p. 70 (1873).
15 See Brunson 2007, Brunson 2010 for a more comprehensive analysis of Peirce's concept of memory than I can provide here.
16 W2, p. 241 (1868). See also the lengthy comparison between words and human beings in the Lowell Lectures. W1, p. 494–500 (1866).

sion" and its intension or "comprehension." According to traditional logical theory, there is a relation of inverse proportionality between these two components of a concept's meaning. For example, the concept of "mammal" has a smaller comprehension than the concept of "lion," because its definition includes a lower number of qualities; but it has a larger extension, because it may be applied to more individuals.[17] Peirce amended this theory by observing that the relationship between extension and intension is not fixed. Instead, it changes in function of the amount of information that is attached to the concept itself. We can discover new things about mammals, thus enlarging the concept's intension without altering its extension. When this happens, the information has "increased," as we read in the passage above. Hence, the concept has grown.[18]

Habit and the Law of Mind

In the early 1870s, while reflecting on the relation between time and thought from a logical viewpoint, Peirce also started paying increasing attention to what would become a major concept of his philosophy: the concept of habit. In particular, he introduced a notion that he would articulate more fully a few years later, in "The Fixation of Belief" (1877): beliefs or general ideas are not only temporally extended but are "of the nature of a habit."[19] Therefore, the very concept of inquiry – that is, the process through which we formulate new beliefs – can be defined as a habit-taking process.

By taking this path, Peirce opened up the possibility of translating his processualist conception of thought and signs into the new language of habit. Habits, like signs, refer to the category of Thirdness. Both are general, mediating elements that preside over singular events. But as much as the two concepts of sign and habit may be equivalent on a metaphysical level, recasting Peirce's semiotic arguments in terms of habit does contribute substantially to the development of his processualist outlook. A focus on habits helps us understand the sense in which Peirce's arguments apply not only to thought and cognition but also to inquiry and human conduct. And it sheds light on some specific qualities of Peirce's processualism that would have remained hidden otherwise. Using

---

17 See, e.g., Kant [1800] 1992, p. 593.
18 See W1, p. 287 (1865), where the concept of information is defined as "the amount of comprehension a symbol has over and above what limits its extension." See also "Upon Logical Comprehension and Extension," W2, p. 70–86 (1867).
19 W3, p. 24 (1872); p. 248 (1877). Cf. p. 75–76 (1873).

Peirce's own terminology, we might therefore say that a reflection on habit lets his processualism grow, both in extension and in comprehension.

Let me focus on two points that are particularly significant for the aims of this book. First, habits graft a certain teleology onto human conduct. As Peirce recognized in 1879, they make sure that "the actions of an animal come to be directed toward an end: that end being the removal of irritation."[20] In other words, the gradual establishment of a habit as a rule to action is the establishment of a purposefulness in the action itself. (For instance, practicing my skills with a musical instrument is to let my action be directed toward the goal of making music.) But second, habits are the one component of human conduct that most clearly exhibits its historicity. Through habits, past actions come to affect present ones, as they are internalized and embedded into a general rule of action. (Again, my musical skills are the outcome of a long process of practice and learning, which I have internalized.)

The historicity of habits may in turn be explained in terms of a peculiar balance between generality and particularity. On the one hand, habits are general rules, which preside over particular actions but cannot be reduced to them. On the other hand, the particular actions can always feed back into the rule and modify it. In other words, only by performing particular actions can we create, strengthen or correct a general rule of action. To put it yet another way, we cannot define a general habit as the mere sum of the finite collection of actions that it elicits; but neither can we assume that those actions have no power whatsoever to determine the rule.

Peirce's solution to this apparent predicament is to emphasize the rule's orientation toward the future. The purport of a general rule – be it a habit, a belief or a symbol – is not reducible to its particular instantiations, because it also takes into account those potential instantiations that may be brought about in the future. This idea is related to the pragmatic maxim, as formulated in 1878.[21] It is also related to Peirce's conviction, expressed later in his life, that "the rational meaning of every proposition lies in the future," and that knowl-

---

[20] W4, p. 39 (1879). At this point in his career, Peirce took this idea to be fully compatible with a Darwinian perspective. Indeed, he explicitly claimed that habit "plays somewhat the same part in the history of the individual that natural selection does in that of species," as in both cases a series of chance-like events engender purposefulness. (W4, p. 46, 1880). As we will see, he would later change his opinion on this point.

[21] "How to Make Our Ideas Clear," W3, p. 266 (1878): "Consider what effects, which might conceivably have practical bearings, we conceive the object of our conception to have. Then, our conception of these effects is the whole of our conception of the object."

edge is always future-oriented.²² However, this emphasis on the future goes hand in hand with an acknowledgment of the influence of the past, without which the very concept of habit would indeed be deprived of meaning.

The balance between generality and particularity lies at the center of Peirce's subsequent reflections on habit, which follow the publication of the 1877 to 1878 essays on pragmatism and culminate in one of the key texts of Peirce's midphase, the "Guess at the Riddle." In these writings, Peirce dwells on the possibility of drawing up a list of "principles" or "laws" of organic phenomena which may explain the insurgence of habits.²³ The most important of these laws, which Peirce calls the "universal law of habit," epitomizes his quest for a balance between the general and the particular. The law says that "all vital processes tend to become easier on repetition."²⁴ That is, vital processes can establish and strengthen a general rule by the simple repetition of singular actions.

But if we now turn to the series of speculative essays Peirce wrote for *The Monist* between 1891 and 1893, we can observe a slight change of approach. Peirce is now more explicit in seeking to subsume the whole physiology of habit-taking under a single law, called "The Law of Mind" (which is also the title of one of the essays).²⁵ The terminological shift is motivated by Peirce's claim that obedience to this law is a distinctive trait of all mental phenomena. However, an important qualification needs to be made here. Saying that the law concerns mental phenomena is not to say that it applies exclusively to human thought. In fact, in the years of the *Monist* essays, Peirce was particularly explicit about his espousal of a "Schelling-fashioned idealism" that postulates the continuity between matter and mind.²⁶

The law of mind is based on the attempt to describe the two main components of thought, namely "feelings" and "ideas" (or "general conceptions"), in a processualist manner. This is not something entirely new: we have seen that a processualist account of feelings and ideas was already entailed in Peirce's early logical writings. In this sense, Peirce's essay can be read as an attempt to articulate more fully his older insight that "thought [...] is a stream" – possibly with an eye to William James's almost contemporaneous publication of the *Principles of Psychology*, which contains a renowned articulation of that insight.²⁷

---

22 "What Pragmatism Is," EP2, p. 340 (1905).
23 W4, p. 39 (1879); W6, p. 191 (1886–1887).
24 W4, p. 39. Peirce is here citing from from the Irish philosopher Joseph J. Murphy (Murphy [1869] 1879, p. 87). Cf. W6, p. 448 (1887–1888).
25 W8, p. 135–157 (1892).
26 W8, p. 135.
27 See James [1890] 1981, Ch. 9, and Girel 2003.

However, there is a significant difference between "The Law of Mind" and Peirce's earlier logical writings. This difference makes "The Law of Mind" a new, pivotal contribution to Peirce's processual philosophy. The difference is this: feelings and ideas are no longer two qualitatively different entities. Instead, they are the two poles of a continuum. Ideas are generalized feelings. Moreover, the process of generalization through which feelings gradually turn into ideas is precisely the process of habit-taking. "Feelings, by being excited, become more easily excited, especially in the ways in which they have previously been excited. The consciousness of such a habit constitutes a general conception."[28] In addition, Peirce claims that this transformation of feelings into general conceptions or ideas takes place by means of two complementary tendencies: a decrease in intensity of the feeling-idea and an increase in their generality.

Using Peirce's categories, we may remark that the distinction between feelings and ideas mirrors the distinction between the inarticulate immediacy of Firstness and the generality of Thirdness. But this distinction is now conceived more dynamically than in the earlier logical writings. Habit-taking now stands for a dynamic process through which Firstness may evolve into Thirdness. This idea is consistent with the overall metaphysics of potentiality on which the idea of Firstness rests. Firstness is an entity *in potentia*, which awaits to be actualized by its embodiment in effectual reality. It is also consistent with Peirce's insistence on the continuous character of the stream of thought. Indeed, Peirce went as far as to coin a new technical concept, the concept of *synechism*, to denote his claim that "continuity governs the whole domain of experience in every element of it."[29]

As we know from Peirce's earlier semiotic writings, this insistence on continuity runs in parallel with his appreciation of the temporal structure of the stream of thought. It comes, therefore, as no surprise that the *Monist* series takes up Peirce's analysis of time and supplies some new details.[30] First of all, Peirce maintains that the process described by "The Law of Mind" dovetails with the flow of time as is perceived and experienced. "One of the most marked features about the law of mind is that it makes time to have a definite direction of flow from past to future." What does it mean? It means that "[t]he present is affectible by the past but not by the future;" and that, in turn, "[t]he future is suggested by, or rather is influenced by the suggestions of, the past."[31] Here we

---

[28] W8, p. 104 (1891).
[29] "Immortality in the Light of Synechism," EP2, p. 1 (1893). See also "The Law of Mind," W8, p. 136, 156.
[30] W8, p. 146–150.
[31] W8, p. 150.

reach the kernel of what I have been calling the historicity of Peirce's philosophy: his processualism is a way to articulate the insight that the present is necessarily affected by the past, without forgoing his emphasis on the future.

Second, Peirce goes back to his idea that consciousness "essentially occupies time." To say that we are conscious of the present is to grant that the present has a duration. By contrast, of the perfectly instantaneous present we cannot even be conscious. "[W]hat is present to the mind at any ordinary instant, is what is present during a moment in which that instant occurs." This, in turn, means that the present of which we are conscious is but the point of convergence between the past and the future: "the present is half past and half to come."[32]

In other texts, Peirce expressed a similar thought by making recourse to a metaphor that he found in Emerson's poem, "The Sphinx." We cannot be fully conscious of those feelings, ideas or habits that are immediately present to us, because they are like the beams of our own eyes: they cannot be seen by the eyes themselves. They are similar to the blind spot that is always present in our visual field.

> [W]hatever we say of ideas as they are in consciousness is said of something unknowable in its immediacy. The only thought that is really present to us is a thought we can neither think about nor talk about. "Of thine eye I am eyebeam," says the Sphinx. We have no reason to deny the dicta of introspection; but we have to remember that they are all results of association, are all theoretical, bits of instinctive psychology.[33]

We shall have to return to the epistemological implications of this metaphor in the following chapters. For now, let me go back to "The Law of Mind," so as to enunciate yet another reason why it should be considered a milestone in Peirce's processual thinking. By reflecting on the law, Peirce answered an additional, important question about the nature of processes – the question about determin-

---

32 These quotations are taken from a short section of the paper entitled "Analysis of Time," W8, p. 146–147.
33 CP 7.425 (c. 1893). See already W1, p. 498 (1866), one of the early texts in which Peirce developed a comparison between symbols and human beings. "Each man has an identity which far transcends the mere animal; – an essence, a *meaning* subtile as it may be. He cannot know his own essential significance; of his eye it is eyebeam." Cf. Emerson [1841] 1888, p. 12–13: "'Dull Sphinx, Jove keep thy five wits; / Thy sight is growing blear; / Rue, myrrh and cummin for the Sphinx, / Her muddy eyes to clear!' / The old Sphinx bit her thick lip, / Said, 'Who taught thee me to name? / I am thy spirit, yoke-fellow; / Of thine eye I am eyebeam.' // 'Thou art the unanswered question; / Couldst see thy proper eye, / Always it asketh, asketh; / And each answer is a lie.[']" On Peirce's reading of Emerson, see Houser 1993, p. xlii. Later in his life, Peirce would return to this issue. See CP 1.310 (1907): "[T]he feeling [is] completely veiled from introspection, for the very reason that it is our immediate consciousness."

ism. Do processes develop in a deterministic fashion, or are they open to contingency? Peirce's answer was clear-cut. He coined yet another brand-new term, namely "tychism" (from Greek *tychê*, "chance" or "fate"), to denote his belief that absolute chance plays an irreducible role in "nature and mind."[34] But what is chance? It is an objective indeterminacy of natural events. It is, also, a creative agency: a principle of "spontaneity" by means of which new phenomena may come about. "[D]iversification is the vestige of chance-spontaneity; and wherever diversity is increasing, there chance must be operative."[35] Thus, Peirce read chance as a principle of life and as tantamount to feeling. "Wherever chance-spontaneity is found, there in the same proportion feeling exists. In fact, chance is but the outward aspect of that which within itself is feeling."[36]

The parallel between chance-spontaneity and feeling brings us back once again to the metaphysical categories. Both chance and feeling are an expression of Firstness, as habit is an expression of Thirdness. So, the relation between chance and general regularities in nature is the same as the relation between feelings and habits. That is, it is an inverse relationship: while habits grow, chance-spontaneity and feeling decrease. If a habit suddenly breaks up, an "intensification of feeling" and of "renewed fortuitous spontaneity" takes place.[37] Being creative, spontaneity has the power to trigger a process of habit-taking. But in the course of the process, it is gradually reduced by the establishment of habit-like regularities. This reduction, however, never reaches its end. Indeed, if this happened – that is, if spontaneity were to be completely replaced by habits – habits themselves would deteriorate into dead matter.[38]

We also know, however, that habits are related to teleology; that is, to our actions' being "directed toward an end." Thus, the interplay between spontaneity and habit-taking which we have just analyzed reflects a more general interplay between chance and final causes. Habits gradually replace spontaneity,

---

[34] W8, p. 135: "[T]ychism must give birth to an evolutionary cosmology, in which all the regularities of nature and mind are regarded as products of growth." To fully understand Peirce's application of tychism to both "nature and mind," recall what I have said about his quasi-spiritualist metaphysics: nature and mind are not separate realms.
[35] "Man's Glassy Essence," W8, p. 181 (1892).
[36] W8, p. 181. For similar remarks, see the "Guess at the Riddle," W6, p. 181 (1887–1888): "Indeterminacy is really a character of the first. But not the indeterminacy of homogeneity. The first is full of life and variety."
[37] W8, p. 180.
[38] See the "Guess at the Riddle," W6, p. 191 (1887–1888): "Were the tendency to take habits replaced by an absolute requirement that the cell should discharge itself always in the same way [...] all possibility of habit developing into intelligence would be cut off at the outset; the virtue of thirdness would be absent. It is essential that there should be an element of chance[.]"

but they could not exist if spontaneity itself ceased to exist. By the same token, final causes could not exist if they left no place for chance-like variation. In fact, one of the central problems of Peirce's processualism is precisely to find a balance between three complementary forces: objective chance, efficient causation, and teleology. Since all three forces are always at play, Peirce's insistence on final causation can never be read as a form of teleological determinism. Processes remain always open to unforeseen developments.

Evolution, Love, and Teleology

Another key text of the *Monist* speculative series, namely "Evolutionary Love" (1892),[39] is devoted to spelling out this conception of an anti-deterministic teleology. But in addition, this essay marks the point at which Peirce's processualist outlook on signs, thought and habits starts to be systematically applied to the macro-phenomena of nature and history. This means translating Peirce's general processualism into a fully-fledged evolutionary perspective – evolutionary, but not Darwinian.

I said that Peirce's evolutionary scheme can be applied to both natural evolution and human history. With regard to the latter, we should recall that Peirce wrote "Evolutionary Love" almost in parallel with his 1892–93 Lowell Lectures in the history of science, which support his account of intellectual evolution from a more empirical angle. With regard to the former, we can simply remark that laws of nature, being general regularities that govern individual events, partake of the same metaphysical structure as habits. As a consequence, natural laws, too, can be described in an evolutionist and processual manner. Here, Peirce's "Schelling-fashioned" belief about the continuity of matter and mind comes again to the fore. As the "Guess at the Riddle" had already made clear, laws have a "natural history" and evolve over time, passing from a state of indeterminacy to a state of greater regularity.[40] But the process of increasing regularity never goes as far as completely to erase chance and spontaneity. "[A]n element of pure spontaneity or lawless originality mingles, or at least must be supposed to mingle, with law everywhere."[41] Peirce's philosophy of nature is as anti-deterministic as his theory of human agency.

---

[39] W8, p. 184–205.
[40] W6, p. 166 (1887–88).
[41] W6, p. 207 (1887–88).

"Evolutionary Love" opens with a tirade against Darwin's exclusive focus on chance-like variation and the "struggle for existence" of individuals. It pinpoints the devastating consequences of this idea for social philosophy.[42] To overcome these consequences, Peirce suggests not substituting but, rather, expanding Darwinism. He outlines three different models of evolution, all three of which are directly inspired by different theories that were discussed at that time. The difference between the three models lies in their being based on, respectively, one of the three major forces that are at play in evolutionary processes: chance, deterministic causation, and teleology.[43]

The first model is called *tychasm:* a clear reference to *tychism*, since it is the model that emphasizes the role of chance. This is essentially the Darwinian model: evolution is propelled by the random fact of variation, conjoined with natural selection. The second model is *anancasm,* from Greek *ananchê,* "necessity," which conceives of evolution as a necessary and predetermined process. This model is inspired by those theorists who thought that the main engine of the historical succession of species was a geological "cataclysm" (the most notable example is Georges Cuvier).[44] Finally, the third model is *agapasm,* from *agapê,* the "love" or "charity" of the Biblical tradition. This model takes evolution to be propelled by "creative love." In this case, the crucial inspiration is Lamarck. The species do not evolve because of variation and natural selection but, rather, because of a teleological effort toward achieving a certain goal, the result of which is then transmitted by a habit-taking process.

How can we make sense of Peirce's recourse to the concept of love in conjunction with the Lamarckian model of evolution? The first thing to recall is the social-philosophical undertone of the whole essay. Peirce was trying to hit back at Darwinian individualism, and he wished to do so with the help of a social philosophy inspired by Christianity. Thus, he pitted the "Gospel of Christ" against the "Gospel of Greed" of laissez-faire liberalism.[45] But we can also give an answer more internal to Peirce's theory. Peirce used the concept of love precisely to support a defining trait of the Lamarckian model, namely its emphasis on individuals' effort to attain something they do not, as yet, possess and to pass it on to their offspring. Finally, the concept of love suggests a reconciliation between teleology and chance. Love is what exhibits a teleological orientation without thereby foregoing the possibility for unforeseen circumstances

---

42 W8, p. 189.
43 See W8, p. 190–195.
44 See Wiener 1949, p. 329.
45 W8, p. 184–189. Cf. further, Ch. 5.

to take place. As Peirce said with yet another recourse to organicist metaphors, it is "vital freedom which is the breath of the spirit of love."[46] To love our children, for instance, means to want them to flourish, yet without necessarily imposing a fixed goal on them. In this sense, Peirce explicitly remarked that love is "creative."[47] It is by the very force of love that we are able to create something new – new ideas, new living beings – in a way that is not completely predetermined.

Although Peirce thought that all three models play a role in evolution, it is *agapasm*, he claimed, that offers the soundest and most encompassing model, hence the most valid alternative to Darwin. Agapasm is also, quite explicitly, "the representative and derivative within the physiological domain of the law of mind."[48] This becomes even clearer if we turn to Peirce's application of his theory to the specific case of the evolution of *ideas*. According to him, intellectual history provides examples of all three models of evolution: chance-like phenomena (*tychasm*), purposeless and blind changes (*anancasm*), and teleological changes (*agapasm*). However, agapasm enjoys pride of place. Let me present the general traits of these three models as related to intellectual evolution. For a more specific examination of the concrete historical phenomena discussed by Peirce, we will have to wait until Chapter 6.

The tychastic model puts emphasis on the "slight departure from habitual ideas in different directions indifferently [...] these new departures being followed by unforeseen results which tend to fix some of them as habits more than others."[49] Also, tychasm is the model that most unambiguously embraces a form of methodological individualism. Ideas change by means of gradual, random variations in individuals. These variations have a greater or lesser chance of surviving and of being transmitted to other individuals. "[W]herever we find men's thought taking by imperceptible degrees a turn contrary to the purposes which animate them, in spite of their highest impulses, there, we may safely conclude, there has been a tychastic action."[50] As we shall better see in the following chapters, Peirce recognized that this model was very widespread in nineteenth-century science, but wanted to counter this tendency by relegating tychastic action to secondary, and mostly retrograde, intellectual phenomena.

Turning to anancasm, things become a bit more complex. In general, anancasm emphasizes determinism. It puts emphasis on the creation of "new ideas

---

46 W8, p. 195.
47 W8, p. 194. On creativity in pragmatist philosophy, see Joas [1992] 1996.
48 W8, p. 192.
49 W8, p. 196.
50 W8, p. 197.

without foreseeing whither they tend,"⁵¹ in a way that is perfectly predetermined. However, we have to differentiate between two forms of such determinism: an "external" and an "internal" one.

External anancasm focuses on the force of external circumstances, the brute force of facts, as a factor of intellectual change. Peirce did not wish to deny the importance of this model. Indeed, "in combination with other elements, nothing is commoner."⁵² Moreover, the very meaning of "external circumstances" is extremely broad. This concept can encompass the influence of non-intellectual historical events on the evolution of ideas, but it can also encompass the plain interaction with the external world that continually occurs within the process of intellectual development. The latter case is "on the border between the external and the internal forms" of anancasm.⁵³ In sum, "[d]evelopment under the pressure of external circumstances [...] has numberless degrees of intensity, from the brute force, the plain war, which has more than once turned the current of the world's thought, down to the hard fact of evidence [...] which has been known to convince men by hordes."⁵⁴ So, unlike with tychasm, the question here is largely "quantitative." Peirce did not deny that external circumstances have a crucial role in the development of ideas. Rather, he asked how much of intellectual history could be explained as a result of that. External anancasm, he suggested, is "the fluorine of intellectual elements":⁵⁵ it reacts extremely easily but has to be combined with other elements.

Internal anancasm, for its part, foregrounds another kind of brute force: not the force of facts, but the logical compulsion of arguments. Peirce had a clear model in mind here: the model of Hegel. This is extremely important for us, because it is a clear symptom that Peirce wished to differentiate very explicitly his own (indeterministic, agapastic) model of teleology from that of the German thinker. However, Peirce's words about Hegel are, as usual, avowedly ambivalent. They oscillate between admiration and critique.⁵⁶ Peirce claims that Hegel was "aiming" at developing an agapastic model of evolution, similar to his own, but ended up with a mere variant of anancasm, that is, of blind determinism. According to him, the only difference between Hegel's anancasm and other forms of determinism is that the Hegelian one is steered by a final cause rather than by an efficient one. But the outcome is analogous. "[T]he whole

---

51 W8, p. 196.
52 W8, p. 200.
53 W8, p. 200.
54 W8, p. 199.
55 W8, p. 200.
56 On Peirce's complex relation to Hegel's metaphysics, see (Stern 2009, Chs. 7–10).

idea of the theory is superb, almost sublime. Yet, after all, living freedom is practically omitted from its method. The whole movement is that of a vast engine, impelled by a *vis a tergo*, with a blind and mysterious fate of arriving at a lofty goal."[57] And again:

> Internal anancasm, or logical groping, which advances upon a predestined line without being able to foresee whither it is to be carried nor to steer its course, this is the rule of development of philosophy. Hegel first made the world understand this; and he seeks to make logic not merely the subjective guide and monitor of thought, which was all it had been ambitioning before, but to be the very mainspring of thinking, and not merely of individual thinking but of discussion, of the history of the development of thought, of all history, of all development. This involves a positive, clearly demonstrable error.[58]

What is this error? It is Hegel's conviction that logic is sufficient to itself, and that "from given premises only one conclusion can logically be drawn."[59] This amounts to saying that there is a crucial difference between Peirce's conception of teleology and the one that Peirce attributed to the German philosopher. The kind of final causation that Peirce was trying to articulate is not a deterministic *vis a tergo*. Rather, it is a final causation that can be reconciled with creativity and freedom.

This reconciliation between teleology and anti-determinism is carried out in Peirce's third and final model of intellectual evolution. Agapasm puts emphasis on "the adoption of certain mental tendencies, not altogether heedlessly, [...] nor quite blindly by the mere force of circumstances or logic," but rather, by means of two complementary forces. The first is the "immediate attraction for the idea itself, whose nature is divined before the mind possesses it, by the power of sympathy, that is, by virtue of the continuity of mind." The second force is the energy of habits, which gradually push this propulsive attraction "to take practical shapes, compatible with the structures they affect, and [...] gradually replac[e] the spontaneous energy that sustains them."[60] Taken together, these two forces delineate a model that is "distinguished by its purposive character, this purpose being the development of an idea."[61]

Whilst anancasm, an instance of Secondness, was internally divided into two kinds (internal and external), now the division is in three kinds, depending on the kind of "sympathetic" link that is established between individuals and ideas. In the first case, the idea affects individuals as members of "the collective

---

57 W8, p. 195.
58 W8, p. 200.
59 W8, p. 201.
60 W8, p. 192–193.
61 W8, p. 203.

people." In the second case, it affects a private person "by virtue of his sympathy with his neighbors, under the influence of a striking experience or development of thought. The conversion of St. Paul may be taken as an example of what is meant." In the third case, it affects the individual without any form of intermediation: the idea becomes attractive to a person "even before he has comprehended it." Peirce links this third modality to the "*divination* of genius" and interprets it as the sign that there may ultimately be a direct link between individuals and God.[62]

The third modality of agapasm, in particular, is well suited to grasping the gradual process by means of which ideas develop over time. This process starts out as a vague feeling of attraction toward a new, not yet fully articulated, idea and then goes on to produce a chain of interpretants that increasingly determine the purport and the scope of the idea itself.

The Growth of Symbols

During the mid-1890s and early 1900s, especially in his writings about logic, Peirce took up his earlier interest in the growth of symbols. But this time, his approach was enriched by the evolutionary perspective laid out in the *Monist* series. The outcome was a multi-faceted doctrine of symbolic growth. This doctrine represents yet another crucial stage of Peirce's processualist philosophy and is also the best starting point from which to reflect on the historicity of symbols from a Peircean angle.

Let me start by quoting a rather well-known passage from 1894, which presents in compressed form all the most difficult philosophical issues that are entailed by Peirce's doctrine.

> Symbols grow. They come into being by development out of other signs, particularly from likenesses or from mixed signs partaking of the nature of likenesses and symbols. We think only in signs. These mental signs are of mixed nature; the symbol-parts of them are called concepts. If a man makes a new symbol, it is by thoughts involving concepts. So it is only out of symbols that a new symbol can grow. *Omne symbolum de symbolo.* A symbol, once in being, spreads among the peoples. In use and in experience, its meaning grows. Such words as *force, law, wealth, marriage,* bear for us very different meanings from those they bore to our barbarous ancestors. The symbol may, with Emerson's sphinx, say to man,
>
> Of thine eye I am eyebeam.[63]

---

62 W8, p. 196.
63 EP2, p. 10 (1894).

Unlike the earlier writings considered at the beginning of this chapter, this passage lumps together at least three different senses in which symbols grow.[64] First, symbols "develop" out of something else. Second, they "spread among the peoples." Third, they grow in "meaning." In turn, the first sense can probably be interpreted in two slightly different ways. When we talk about the "development" of symbols, we may either be referring to the way a specific symbol comes to be used by individuals in their reasoning processes ("if a man makes a new symbol, it is by thought involving concepts…"); or we may be referring to the way a new symbol is created in the course of history (symbols "come into being by development out of other signs").[65]

The second interpretation, if taken seriously, makes fully visible the impact of Peirce's evolutionary perspective. Read in this way, the passage I am analyzing seems to suggest that the historical origin of symbols is in simpler signs, in particular "likenesses" or icons. And other texts from approximately the same period corroborate this reading. Peirce says, for instance, that the evolution of language may be conceptualized as a systematic progression from more iconic to more symbolic signs:

> In all primitive writing, such as the Egyptian hieroglyphics, there are icons of a non-logical kind, the ideographs. In the earliest forms of speech, there probably was an element of mimicry. But in all languages known, such representations have been replaced by conventional auditory signs. These, however, are such that they can only be explained by icons.[66]

To be sure, this quote cannot be taken to mean that symbols are *always* the product of former icons. For in a metaphysical sense, symbols are always already present in nature. They are not necessarily the result of a historical development, nor are they necessarily derived from icons. However, there are cases in which

---

64 I am following Short 2007, p. 285–286 and the whole of Ch. 10.
65 Bellucci 2017, p. 135 interprets it in a slightly different way. He reads the whole passage as being about what I am here calling the individual level. Thus, he understands Peirce's mention of "likenesses" as a reference to the interplay between symbols and diagrams in inferential reasoning.
66 CP 2.280 (c. 1895). What I am leaving aside here is the very interesting double role that icons have in this passage: on the one hand, there are "icons of a non-logical kind," which are more "primitive" than today's "conventional auditory signs." On the other hand, there are logical icons, which provide a logically perspicuous translation of those conventional signs even today. On the diachronic relation between icons and symbols, see also the later "Ethics of Terminology," EP2, p. 264 (1902): "Every symbol is, in its origin, either an image of the idea signified, or a reminiscence of some individual occurrence, person, or thing, connected with its meaning, or is a metaphor." I will return to this passage in Ch. 5.

symbolic systems do evolve over time. Natural languages are the most obvious example; and the passage just quoted is suggesting precisely that a gradual development from icons to symbols is at play in the evolution of language.[67]

A second question that deserves to be discussed is whether the development of symbols over time follows a general blueprint and whether this blueprint applies to both historical and individual processes. Here, Peirce's dialogue with Hegel comes once again to the fore. In a passage of his "Minute Logic," Peirce asks himself whether he ought to be working on an "objective logic" in the Hegelian sense. This sub-discipline of logic would be devoted to inquiring "whether there be a life in Signs, so that [...] they will go through a certain order of development."[68] While Peirce fails to provide an unambiguous answer to his question, he nevertheless subscribes to the Hegelian notion that symbols are living and growing entities. (Compare the "Syllabus," 1903: "[E]very symbol is a living thing, in a very strict sense that is no mere figure of speech. The body of the symbol changes slowly, but its meaning inevitably grows[.]"[69])

Another passage of the "Minute Logic" returns to Hegel from a slightly different viewpoint. The German philosopher – Peirce argues therein – believed in the possibility of establishing a parallel between the logical development of thought and its historical development. This amounts to admitting that history displays both reasonableness and directionality.

> It must be acknowledged that if [Hegel's] method of thought can be carried out, it is the best possible. It must represent the history of thought, too, as far as that history is not merely accidental. Now, considering the immense multitude of minds, and that it is the normal minds who are influential, the history of thought can hardly be very seriously accidental. It is true that there will be, in history, perturbations, due to the fact that all minds are not at exactly the same stage of development.[70]

Once again, Peirce appears sympathetic to Hegel's most basic insight: "It is of the nature of thought to grow," and we are therefore required to explore

---

[67] Not accidentally, Peirce's ideas about the way symbols "come into being" have been read in two quite different ways. On a more historicist or evolutionary interpretation, symbols are the result of a historical process of development that starts with simpler signs and gets more complex over time. Deacon 1998 has advocated a similar idea, as applied to the evolution of language. On a more structuralist interpretation, those simpler signs are the mere components of a primitive process of symbolization. Stjernfelt 2014 has recently championed this second interpretation, precisely as a rejoinder to Deacon.
[68] CP 2.111.
[69] EP2, p. 264. See further, Ch. 5.
[70] CP 2.32.

"some of the directions that growth will take." However, he suggests going about this task not by "adher[ing] strictly to Hegel's text [...], but guided rather by the history of thought."[71] In other words, the Hegelian insight about the rationality of history ought to be married to a more robust consideration of empirical data. We should read this empirical qualification of Hegel's philosophy in conjunction with the argument advanced in the *Monist* about the difference between anancasm and agapasm.

Finally, let me say something about the growth of symbols' meanings. In the 1894 passage cited at the beginning of this section, Peirce suggests linking the growth of meaning to "use and experience." This phrase can be related to Peirce's earlier logical writings, where the growth of a word's meaning was dependent on the increase of its "information." But it can also be related to the pragmatic maxim, according to which the meaning of a concept depends on the practical consequences of its acceptance. Following the pragmatic maxim, a concept grows in meaning when we learn new things about the practical consequences of its use.[72] However, Peirce also believed that the growth of a symbol's meaning could be reconciled with the preservation of a semantic core that remains more or less stable over time. Much like what happens with a living being, the growth of a symbol does not erase its self-identity over time. Growth is attained through a balance of change and stability.[73]

This problem is also related to Peirce's remarks on another major concept of his semiotics, namely the concept of vagueness.[74] Vagueness is, for Peirce, a specific kind of semiotic "indeterminacy." A sign is indeterminate if its interpretation is not absolutely fixed; and it is vague if it can only be further determined with the help of "some other possible sign or experience."[75] A vague sign suggests that there may be a better, more determined characterization of its object, but stops short of providing it. Only further information or further experience will enable that better characterization to emerge.

---

71 CP 2.32.
72 See Haack 2009; Short 2007, p. 285–288.
73 In this respect, Shapiro 1991, p. 92 quotes a very relevant passage from 1905: "[A symbol] may have a rudimentary life, so that it can have a history, and gradually undergo a great change of meaning, while preserving a certain self-identity."
74 See, in particular, the essays "Issues of Pragmaticism," EP2, 346–359 (1905); "Consequences of Critical Common-Sensism," 5.502–537 (1905). I am relying substantially on Short 2007, p. 274–276; Short 1980. But see also Brock 1981; Tiercelin 1992.
75 CP 5.505.

Peirce held vagueness to be a ubiquitous phenomenon in semiotics, because no sign can ever be so precisely defined as to foreclose any further determination (or growth) through some other sign or experience.[76] But he saw a particularly strong link between vagueness and common sense. In fact, some of his most sophisticated analyses of vagueness take place while discussing the relation between science and common sense. The feeling of indubitability that goes hand in hand with common-sense beliefs, Peirce argued, is due precisely to their vagueness. "It is easy to speak with precision upon a general theme. Only, one must commonly surrender all ambition to be certain. It is equally easy to be certain. One has only to be sufficiently vague."[77] Science, for its part, has the task of reducing that vagueness, gradually substituting the certitudes of common sense with beliefs that are both more accurate and more questionable.

However, we ought to make an important qualification here. Although gradually reduced by science, vagueness can never be completely eliminated and is, in fact, absolutely vital to the correct functioning of science itself. Following T. L. Short, we can say that a scientific theory "is vague in Peirce's sense if and only if it implies that there is *some* more detailed (precise, informative, specific) account of exactly the same things but does not imply what this account would be."[78] This is an ideal situation for scientific research: we have a relatively clear object of inquiry, but one about which we still know too little. The vagueness of a theory or of a concept is precisely what drives us to carry on our inquiry. This is what lets our concepts and theories grow.[79]

Embodiment, Final Causation, and Genealogy

The process of symbolic growth that I have just described may be reminiscent of what I said about habit-taking and the law of mind: it does not proceed blindly but conforms to a teleological pattern. It is oriented toward the attainment of a meaning that is already prefigured at the outset, although in a way that is not yet sufficiently definite. Peirce expressed this idea by saying, for instance, that the symbol is "essentially a purpose, that is to say, a representation that seeks to

---

[76] CP 5.512: "[V]agueness [...] is no more to be done away with in the world of logic than friction in mechanics." On this point, see Tiercelin 1992.
[77] CP 4.237 (1902).
[78] Short 1980, p. 321.
[79] See Brock 1981, p. 138: "[I]ndeterminacy of meaning is a necessary condition for certain kinds of conceptual growth, change, development. Vagueness is a mother of invention."

make itself definite, or seeks to produce an interpretant more definite than itself."⁸⁰

Symbols are thus teleologically oriented toward making their own meaning increasingly explicit, accurate and perspicuous. In the terminology of Peirce's later semiotics, this is tantamount to saying that they tend to approach more and more a diagrammatic form. However, the purely diagrammatic form, the perfectly perspicuous representation, is unattainable: a minimal amount of indeterminacy must be there in order for the symbol to exist at all. "The meaning of a representation [...] is nothing but the representation itself conceived as stripped of irrelevant clothing. But this clothing never can be completely stripped off; it is only changed for something more diaphanous. So there is an infinite regression here."⁸¹

We may compare the latter sentence to another passage, in which Peirce resorts to an apparently bizarre metaphor. "To try to peel off signs and get down to the real thing is like trying to peel an onion and get down to the onion itself."⁸² This simile evokes quite effectively Peirce's effort to hold together two apparently conflicting ideas. On the one hand, we can peel off signs of their inessential layers, coming closer and closer to a perspicuous or diagrammatic representation. But on the other hand, a perfectly perspicuous representation is actually a contradiction in terms. If we strip the onion of all its layers, we are left with nothing.

One way out of this apparent dilemma is, once again, to insist on the future-oriented character of semiosis. The heart of the symbol is a final cause that orients the processes of semiotic determination toward a goal that is increasingly approached, without ever being completely attained. Furthermore, the final cause is not perfectly determined at the outset, but becomes such in the course of the process.

To make this point even clearer, Peirce deployed another concept which brings us back to his frequent use of organicist metaphors: the concept of embodiment. To say that signs are embodied is to say that they must find expression, they must govern individual instances. If this process of embodiment does not take place, Peirce says with a Shakespearean phrase, the meaning of a sign evaporates into "airy nothingness."⁸³ That is, it turns into something pri-

---

80 EP2, p. 323 (1904). See Short 2007, p. 287; and Shapiro 1991, who applies Peircean semiotics to the study of linguistic change. Gava 2014 spells out the teleology of semiotic processes with an eye to Kant. See in particular p. 83–87 for a discussion of Peirce's concept of final interpretant.
81 CP 1.339.
82 From a letter to F. C. Russell (1905), quoted in Brent [1993] 1998, p. 357.
83 "Minute Logic," CP 4.241. See also "A Neglected Argument for the Reality of God," EP2, p. 435 (1908). The phrase comes from *A Midsummer Night's Dream* (5.1.14–17): "And as imagination

vate and ineffable: a purely qualitative experience (a pure Firstness). This idea can be traced back to the delicate balance between particularity and generality that I have already dealt with when speaking of habits. Since no finite collection of individual events exhausts the purport of a Thirdness, we can only define the latter as a general rule that constantly produces the very individual events in which it is embodied:

> The very being of the General, of Reason, *consists* in its governing individual events. So, then, the essence of Reason is such that its being never can have been completely perfected. It always must be in a state of incipiency, of growth. It is like the character of a man which consists in the ideas that he will conceive and in the efforts that he will make, and which only develops as the occasions actually arise. Yet in all his life long no son of Adam has every fully manifested what there was in him. So, then, the development of Reason requires as a part of it the occurrence of more individual events than ever can occur. [...] This development of Reason consists, you will observe, in embodiment, that is, in manifestation.[84]

Peirce's comparison of "the General, [...] Reason" (in other words: Thirdness) with the "character of a man" suggests once again that he was thinking of a model of growth that is teleological but not deterministic. The final cause grows more determinate as the chain of individual events that it governs unfolds. Similarly, the character of a person is not predetermined at the outset but grows more determinate in the course of a person's life.

In other passages, Peirce says that not only are historical processes unpredictable, but this unpredictability is an essential character of growth. "[T]o say that the variety of Nature grows is to say that events do not exactly conform to any law."[85] Thus, to conceive of history under the heading of growth is to admit that history bristles with unforeseen events and unintended consequences of action. As Peirce wrote to Victoria Welby in 1904, "we never can foresee all the consequences of a great change."[86]

Peirce sought to better explain the non-deterministic character of final causation by clearly demarcating the latter from efficient causation. An efficient cause is a "compulsion acting to make [a] situation begin to change in a perfectly determinate way."[87] It is the determination of an individual fact by another indi-

---

bodies forth / the forms of things unknown, the poet's pen / turns them to shapes and gives to airy nothing / a local habitation and a name."
84 EP2, p. 255 (1903).
85 From a late manuscript, quoted in Wiener 1949, p. 86.
86 S&S, p. 19 (1904).
87 EP2, p. 120 (1902). See Short 2007, p. 136–139.

vidual fact, with no space for indeterminacy in between. A final cause is precisely the opposite. It is not the compulsion of an individual fact upon another, but the attraction that a general, ideal element, such as a symbol or a habit, exerts on individual events. Peirce, therefore, did not reduce all final causes to conscious purposes or intentions.[88] Nor did he conceive of final causation as mere 'backward' efficient causation – that is, as a causation that flows from the future to the present rather than from the past to the present. Rather, a final cause is just a "general result," which does not rule out chance-like variations. "The general result may be brought about at one time in one way, and at another time in another way. Final causation does not determine in what particular way it is to be brought about, but only that the result shall have a certain general character."[89]

We are not far from the agapastic model of "Evolutionary Love": "the idea [...] confers upon [individual events] the power of working out results in this world, [...] it confers upon them, that is to say, organic existence, or, in one word, life."[90] In this sense, final causes are not only reconcilable with chance, but they are complementary to efficient causes. Final causes provide the general direction of change, but only efficient causes have the power to actually implement the change. Incidentally, this is also the reason why symbols grow not only in development and in meaning but also – as we know from the preceding section – by spreading "among the people." *Qua* final causes, symbols "have a power of finding or creating their vehicles, and having found them, of conferring them the ability to transform the face of the earth."[91]

Peirce was not always completely successful in demarcating his variety of teleology from a more deterministic, "anancastic" one. He sometimes talked of historical processes as ineluctably destined to bring about a certain state of affairs – for instance, the emergence of scientific thinking.[92] But putting aside this difficulty, what is most relevant to us is that there is a strong connection between his peculiar understanding of teleology and his reliance on historical in-

---

88 Thus, in the sentence I quoted in the preceding section, Peirce was slightly inaccurate. Strictly speaking, a symbol is not "essentially a purpose," but "essentially a final cause."
89 EP2, p. 120.
90 EP2, p. 124.
91 EP2, p. 123.
92 See, for instance, CP 7.50 (undated, but probably after 1900): "Given the oxygen, hydrogen, carbon, nitrogen, sulphur, phosphorus, etc., in sufficient quantities and under proper radiations, and living protoplasm will be produced, will develop, will gain power of self-control, and the scientific passion is sure to be generated. Such is my guess. Science was preordained, perhaps, on the Sunday of the Fiat lux."

quiry. For it is precisely the indeterminate nature of final causes that makes it necessary to study their historical development. In other words, history is a way to reconstruct how a final cause has grown, or has determined itself over time, by bringing about certain individual facts. One of the defining traits of Peirce's take on historicity and processualism is thus confirmed: his overall orientation toward the future does not amount to a depreciation of the past. Rather, the opposite is true.

The best way to understand this point is to go back to the issues of genealogy and natural classification that I considered in Chapter 2. We will recall that Peirce defined the concept of natural class teleologically, as a class "the existence of whose members is due to a common and peculiar final cause."[93] However, it is precisely this reference to teleology which demands that the historical development of natural classes be taken into account. For the many final causes that are operative in nature cannot be distinguished from one another through a merely analytical, ahistorical gaze. Given their indeterminacy, only a historical or genetic examination can accurately pinpoint them and tell us whether a certain individual is a member of one class or of another. In other words, the members of a natural class can only be discriminated from the members of another class if we factor in the historical path by which they have evolved and the "active causality" that the defining idea has exerted on them. Peirce's example is quite telling here: "no degree of resemblance between two men is proof positive that they are brothers." Only genealogical analysis can provide us with such a proof.[94] As we know from Chapter 2, "genealogy" was indeed the word Peirce used to denote that kind of historical inquiry which focuses on final rather than efficient causes.

A Pragmaticist's Analysis of Time

In the years around 1905, Peirce was very busy defending his logical, anti-nominalistic version of pragmatism, which he renamed "pragmaticism" so as to distinguish it from other variants, such as James's.[95] Peirce's pragmaticism is, first and foremost, a doctrine about the "intellectual purport" of symbols and concepts. Building on the pragmatic maxim, it asserts that understanding the meaning of a concept means being acquainted with the conceivable practical conse-

---

[93] EP2, p. 120.
[94] EP2, p. 126. See also p. 121: "The word *natura* evidently must originally have meant birth." There is perhaps no need to say that DNA tests have made Peirce's example slightly obsolete.
[95] The bulk of these texts is published in EP2, p. 331–433.

quences of that concept upon our conduct.⁹⁶ In "Issues of Pragmaticism," published in 1905, Peirce chose to exemplify his pragmaticist approach by analyzing a concept that has stood at the very center of my own analysis: the concept of time.⁹⁷ A brief examination of Peirce's ideas on time around this period will, therefore, help me close the chapter by recapitulating some of the most characteristic traits of Peirce's processualism.

First of all, Peirce's discussion of time is "pragmaticist" because it pivots on the concept's conceivable effects upon our conduct. Peirce did not focus on the concept of time as a neutral, mathematically ordered sequence but, rather, on time as a common-sense conception; on time as it is experienced and lived.⁹⁸ This, however, is not a new idea: it was already implicit in his earlier reflections on time as a property of the stream of thought.

Using slightly different terminology, we might say that Peirce's approach to time is phenomenological, because it hinges on the role of time for the constitution of a distinctively human experience. As a consequence, his description of the temporal flux is tensed: that is, the flux is endowed with a specific direction and its three dimensions – past, present and future – can be distinguished on the basis of their different experiential qualities. However, Peirce was not content with staying at a purely phenomenological level. He claimed that past, present and future have not only different experiential qualities, but also a different metaphysical status. Though all three temporal dimensions are real, their modes of existence are different and mirror the modes of existence of the three categories. While analyzing in detail these three different modes of existence, Peirce found himself forced to navigate through some very difficult philosophical puzzles.

Let me start with the present. The main puzzle here is the contradiction between the feeling that the present is all there is and the fact that the more we try to focus on it, the more it escapes us, dissolving into the other two dimensions, the past and the future. Peirce expressed this contradiction with a powerful met-

---

96 EP2, p. 346 (1905). "I will restate [the maxim of pragmaticism] in other words[.] […] The entire intellectual purport of any symbol consists in the total of all general modes of rational conduct which, conditionally upon all the possible different circumstances and desires, would ensue upon the acceptance of the symbol."
97 EP2, p. 357–359.
98 For a classic discussion of the distinction between the two conceptions of time, see McTaggart 1908. Cf. Markosian 2016, par. 4–5.

aphor, possibly borrowed from Shakespeare: the present is a "Living Death."[99] It is both what is most real and what is most unreal. But while this metaphor appears for the first time in Peirce's later writings, the basic insight behind it goes back to his much older attempt to distinguish two conceptions of the present in order to accommodate the contradiction I am discussing. The present conceived as a pure instant is almost a limit-concept: "nothing is more occult than the absolute present."[100] But the present conceived as the moment in which we are now thinking is not an instant: it is a lapse of time, which cannot be "utterly cut off from past and future."[101] Here, we have a paradigmatic application of Peirce's synechism: the past and the future impinge directly and seamlessly on the present. They do so, however, in different ways.

The past's mode of existence is analogous to Secondness: it represents what is most actual because it is unchangeable; it is what exerts power on us by brute force. "If you complain to the Past that it is wrong and unreasonable, it laughs. It does not care a snap of the finger for Reason."[102] Here again, however, we cannot avoid a sense of paradox. The past is, by definition, what is no more; but Peirce nonetheless equates it to Secondness, the category that stands for the most tangible mode of existence. (As we shall see later, some of the tensions and conundrums that affect Peirce's philosophy of history find a metaphysical counterpart in this paradox about the nature of the past.)

Peirce sought to alleviate the paradox by noting that everything we know or think already belongs to the past. "When we say that we know that some state of things exists, we mean that it used to exist, whether just long enough for the news to reach the brain and be retrasmitted to tongue or pen, or longer ago." So, "[t]he Past is the sole storehouse of our knowledge"; it definitely "acts upon us."[103] As with all instances of Secondness, it does so by means of efficient causation. Every individual event of the past is connected to another individual event by means of a causal chain. In the realm of mental phenomena, the same can be said of memory, which is the way past ideas have an influence on our present and future conduct.[104]

---

99 EP2, p. 358. See *Richard III*, 1.2.337: "[N]ow they kill me with a living death" (Richard referring to Lady Anne's eyes). In the history of poetry, the metaphor of the living death is traditionally associated with love.
100 EP2, p. 358 (1905)
101 CP 2.85 (1902).
102 CP 2.84.
103 EP2, p. 357–358.
104 Cf. CP 1.325: "Constraint is a Secondness. In the flow of time in the mind, the past appears to act directly upon the future, its effect being called memory."

The future is almost the perfect opposite of the past. "I remember the past, but I have absolutely no slightest approach to such knowledge of the future."[105] The future, too, is real and acts upon us; but it does so in a different sense. It is not related to Secondness but to Thirdness. Thus, it does not act by efficient causation but by final causation, "as a law acts."[106]

However, since Peirce's teleology must be reconciled with anti-determinism, the future must have a modal status that combines necessity and possibility, or teleology and contingency. On the one hand, chance and free will are always operative, hence the future must be indeterminate and open. On the other hand, nature is governed by laws and makes room for a certain degree of predictability. As Peirce adds in another text, "[t]his factor of reality is specially prominent in the reality of personality. It is what the man is destined to do, what of the future is wrapped up in him, that makes him what he is."[107] In other words, a man's or woman's personality can be understood as a final cause that unfolds over time.

Although Peirce framed his complex analysis of the future as a return to common-sense conceptions, we can better understand it as a way of taking up his lifelong attempt to reconcile teleology, determinism and contingency. On the one hand, nature is governed by laws. This makes future events predictable and necessary. But on the other hand, chance is always operative. The possibility that something turns out differently than predicted can never be ruled out. The consequences for human agency are momentous: thanks to this modal status of the future, we are free to try and shape the future in conformity with our wishes and ideals. This is another crucial difference from the past, which by definition cannot be modified. "I have considerable power over the future, [while] nobody except the Parisian mob imagines that he can change the past by much or by little."[108]

Let me sum up by saying that Peirce's pragmaticist analysis of time puts in a nutshell the most characteristic traits of his philosophy of process. The present is a "living death," it is our eye-beam: so immediately close to us that we cannot even think about it. The past is what constantly acts upon us. It is, really, everything we are: our "ego" and what we "go upon" whenever we think or act.[109] Finally, the future orients the present in a teleological, but not deterministic fashion. The specific kind of historicity that is at work in Peirce's process-oriented pragmatism results from the conjunction of these three ideas.

---

105 CP 6.70 (1898).
106 EP2, p. 358.
107 "Telepathy and Perception," CP 7.666 (1903).
108 CP 6.70. On Peirce's social and political ideas, see Ch. 5.
109 EP2, p. 357–359.

4 Autonomy and the Value of Experience

Wading into the Slough

The ideas presented in the previous chapter have shown us to what extent Peirce let considerations about the past play a role in his philosophical and scientific inquiries. It is now time to turn to the second axis of the history-philosophy relation, as I characterized it at the end of Chapter 2. I suggested that this axis revolves around the problems of autonomy and alterity in thinking. What does it mean for a philosopher or scientist to think for oneself? To what extent should we rely on external sources of knowledge, or on other people's opinions, when we carry out our inquiries? Is this reliance on external sources of knowledge a hindrance or an asset for autonomous thinking?

To tackle these questions, we will have to move our discussion on to a more distinctly epistemological level; but we will have to do so without abandoning the discussion of historicity spelt out in the previous chapter. For the very concept of intellectual autonomy that we are going to discuss in this chapter is not left unchanged by the processualist framework laid out in Chapter 3. If thought is a stream, autonomy in thinking is the ability to steer that stream in a way that accords to certain rules that one sets oneself.[1] Moreover, we know that Peirce held the past to be "the sole storehouse of all our knowledge."[2] So there is a sense in which asking about philosophers' relation to external sources of knowledge is to ask about their relation to the past. From this angle, the arguments of the two chapters are inextricably bound up with one another.

Let me try to narrow down the question I will be considering by pointing out Peirce's most significant interlocutors. First of all, a major foil of Peirce's reflections is, of course, Descartes, and his fight against all prejudices by the exercise of radical doubt. But my use of the concept of autonomy is a way to suggest the relevance of another crucial figure, namely Kant. Peirce followed the German thinker in conceiving of philosophy in terms of intellectual autonomy. He embraced the Enlightenment ideal of *Selbstdenken* as the fight against prejudice, epitomized by Kant's epoch-making call for the use of our intellect "without direction from another."[3] He did so, however, in a way that partly departs from Kant.

---

1 Hampe 2006, p. 62–69.
2 EP2, p. 358. See Ch. 3.
3 Kant [1784] 1996, p. 17.

To see in which sense this is so, it may be worthwhile to have a brief look at one specific aspect of Kant's conception of philosophy. In the chapter of the first *Critique* called "The architectonic of pure reason," Kant distinguishes, first, between "rational" and "historical" cognition, and then, internal to rational cognition, between a "cosmic" and a "scholastic" notion of philosophy.[4] Learning the contents of a given philosophy means to learn historically. It is an exercise neatly distinguished from the practice of philosophizing in its proper sense, which is rational learning. Kant thereby separates the study of historically given philosophies from a more properly productive judgment, which stems from the activity of pure reason. The history of philosophy is thus conceived as an auxiliary tool: a set of examples that at best prepare us for the exercise of philosophical thinking.

This conception of philosophical *Selbstdenken* finds a counter-model in Hegel.[5] No thinking, Hegel says, can be other than for oneself: "nobody can think for someone else."[6] There is no purely imitative thinking, as there is no learning that simply amounts to a merely passive absorption of content, "as if I did not myself produce these determinations in my own thought but rather tossed them in my head as pebbles."[7] Conversely, there is no thinking that is a purely formal and subjective act: thinking is only thinking through contents.[8] This means that learning a given philosophical content is already a philosophical activity. All thinking, and philosophy is no exception, has to go through learning and interpretation.

While holding on to the Kantian conception of philosophy as *Selbstdenken*, Peirce's reflections on the role of history come, at times, much closer to the Hegelian position. Or to express the same idea in slightly different terms: Peirce wanted to safeguard the ideal of *Selbstdenken* without thereby condemning historical work to a merely auxiliary function.

One of the most significant texts in this respect is Peirce's polemical piece against "necessitarian" philosophers, published in 1893 in *The Monist*.[9] In that

---

4 Kant [1781/1787] 1998, p. 693–605, B 864–868. I am following Ferrarin 2015, Ch. 1.
5 See Ferrarin 2015, p. 79–80; Dierse 1995.
6 Hegel [1830] 2010, p. 57: "One can often hear the expression 'to think for oneself' [*Selbstdenken*], as if something significant is thereby said. In fact, nobody can think for someone else, just as little as they can eat and drink for them. That expression is thus a pleonasm."
7 Hegel [1812] 1984, p. 280.
8 Hegel [1830] 2010, p. 57: "[T]hinking is true in terms of content only if it is immersed in the *basic matter* [*Sache*] at hand and in terms of form only if it is not a *particular* instance of being or doing of the subject[.]" Ferrarin 2015, p. 79 remarks that "when we learn the content of philosophy, we are not simply learning to philosophize, but are actually practising philosophy."
9 "Reply to the Necessitarians," CP 6.588–6.615. All the citations that follow are from CP 6.604.

essay, Peirce carries out a reflection on the relation between *Selbstdenken* and history hinging on the concept of "originality." On the one hand, he inveighs against "positivistic" methodology, precisely because it shies away from the very ideal of intellectual autonomy. "Eschew originality is its pious formula; do not think for yourself, nor countenance results obtained by original minds." This epistemic and methodological ideal, Peirce remarks, is completely delusional; for "to look an inch before one's eyes involves originality." But on the other hand, Peirce levels an equally sharp criticism against those thinkers that equate originality with a sort of solipsistic thinking, "untrammeled by historic facts."

In order to articulate his own alternative to these two methods, Peirce invokes two main sources. One is the Kantian concept of "architectonic"; the second is William Whewell.[10] In fact, he reads the first through the second source. Without giving too much weight to Kant's neat separation of rational and historical learning, Peirce argues that the "essence" of the architectonic method is precisely the conjunction between the two. "My method of attacking all problems has ever been to *begin with an historical and rational inquiry* into the special method adapted to the special problem. This is the essence of my architectonical proceeding […]."[11] The architectonic philosopher, Peirce continues, should shy away from "taking ideas at haphazard, or being satisfied with those that have been handed down from the good old times." For this reason, he describes his own way of building a system of philosophy by first making a systematic survey of "facts." Among them, there are also the facts "of the history of philosophy. I waded right into this fearful slough of 'originality,' in order to gather what seemed to throw a light upon the subject."

Peirce's emphasis about the "facts" that the architectonic philosopher ought to take into account is a good illustration of his departure from the strictly Kant-

---

10 "My own historical studies, which have been somewhat minutely critical, have, on the whole, confirmed the views of Whewell, the only man of philosophical power conjoined with scientific training who had made a comprehensive survey of the whole course of science, that progress in science depends upon the observation of the right facts by minds *furnished with appropriate ideas*." I have already referred to this passage in the Introduction and in Ch. 2.

11 My emphasis. Note that Peirce is, here, talking primarily about the work he conducted for the *Monist* metaphysical series of 1891 to 1893, which I have already related to his history of science. The "Reply to the Necessitarians" can indeed be read as a continuation of that series of papers, since it appeared in the same journal. On the conjunction between historical inquiry and creative philosophizing, see also Anderson 2008, p. 41: "Peirce was clear that his pragmatism […] and overall philosophical outlook were a creative development from his reading of the history of philosophy."

ian model of *Selbstdenken* toward a position that is closer to Hegel.[12] However, we should add another important point here: Peirce was a scientist, an empirically-oriented thinker. For him, individual thought must take into account not only the facts of history but also the facts unearthed by experience and scientific inquiry. To think for oneself means first and foremost to be willing to consider whether the propositions we inherit from tradition pass the test of our own experience. In this sense, Peirce found himself in agreement with yet another Enlightenment thinker, namely John Locke. Notwithstanding the irreducible philosophical differences between the two, Peirce recognized in the Englishman a truly "grand word": "Men must think for themselves, and genuine thought is an act of perception. Men must see out of their own eyes, and it will not do to smother individual thought [...] beneath the weight of general propositions."[13] Granted, Locke thought of such general propositions as "only traditional – oppressive and unwholesome heritages from a barbarous and stupid past," while Peirce held generality to be the real object of knowledge.[14] Nonetheless, he held on to the Lockean conviction that only a recourse to experience can provide intellectual autonomy with a solid foothold.

This understanding of intellectual autonomy – or critical thinking – in terms of a recourse to experience has in turn a significant implication: it means that our discussion will have to keep together two apparently distinct questions. The first is: what is the right attitude for the philosopher toward tradition and history? This is the question that my brief discussion of Kant and Hegel was meant to highlight. The second is: what is the right attitude for the philosopher toward empirical knowledge? This is the question I have just traced back to the influence of classical empiricism but which was, in fact, taking quite a new shape in the post-Hegelian scientific era to which Peirce belonged. As we shall see toward the end of the chapter, a crucial piece of that era was the debate about psychologism, which became a sort of paradigmatic conceptualization of the more general question of whether philosophers should be receptive to information coming from the nascent human and social sciences.[15] Also, it should be noted that the two questions are related to two slightly different conceptions of history. According to the first question, history is first and foremost the history

---

12 I will return to the architectonic in Ch. 5.
13 W8, p. 41 (1890).
14 W8, p. 41.
15 See Kusch 1995.

of past philosophical opinions. According to the second question, history is simply a specific – if peculiar – kind of empirical knowledge.[16]

The present chapter is organized in such a way as to mirror the double nature of the problem at hand. In the following section, I will begin by discussing Peirce's general stance toward tradition, prejudice and common sense. As we shall see, Peirce wished not only to reconcile tradition and critical thinking but also to indicate that historical knowledge has a vital role to play, precisely as a tool to think critically about tradition. Then, in the three central sections of the chapter, I will focus on empirical knowledge at large, and show in which sense the latter represents a crucial source of information for philosophy. Finally, the chapter's last two sections will consider history under the heading of empirical knowledge. They will ask accordingly about history's relation to philosophy and, more specifically, to logic.

Tradition, Prejudice, Common Sense

The pragmatist epistemology sketched in Peirce's early anti-Cartesian papers is a good starting point to investigate his attitude toward tradition. There Peirce argues that doubt cannot be elicited at will. Doubt is a state of privation, an unpleasant irritation that derives from the lack of a stable belief. Belief is, in turn, defined as a habit. The normal, unproblematic state of our behavior is the possession of a belief. When this belief is shattered, we find ourselves in a state of doubt. But we cannot decide to enter this state; and when we do enter it, we try leave it as soon as possible. In order to do so, we start a process of inquiry that eventually leads to the possession of a new belief. This dynamic has an important corollary: we cannot doubt everything that we have come to believe by tradition or by unconscious learning. In fact, our intellectual life teems with prejudices and traditional ideas that have not been subject to critical examination. To start from scratch, by wiping out at one single stroke all uncritical ideas, is an impossible feat. "We cannot begin with complete doubt. We must begin with all the prejudices which we actually have when we enter

---

[16] It can, of course, be argued that there is an important difference between history and empirical knowledge. The latter does not necessarily deal with temporal development, while the former does. So here again we see how we have to keep the arguments of Ch. 3 and Ch. 4 together if we want to provide a satisfying account of historical knowledge. Cf. Koopman 2010, p. 18.

upon the study of philosophy. These prejudices are not to be dispelled by a maxim, for they are things which it does not occur to us *can* be questioned."[17]

But Peirce's criticism of Descartes is not tantamount to a plea for a placid acceptation of tradition. In fact, Peirce grants that Descartes's legacy still lives on precisely because of its emphasis on the critical nature of philosophical understanding. Only in the course of time has philosophy learnt to strike the right balance between these two attitudes.

> Descartes marks the period when Philosophy put off childish things and began to be a conceited young man. By the time the young man has grown to be an old man, he will have learned that traditions are precious treasures, while iconoclastic inventions are always cheap and often nasty. He will learn that when one's opinion is besieged and one is pushed by questions from one reason to another behind it, there is nothing illogical in saying at last, "Well, this is what we have always thought; this has been assumed for thousands of years without inconvenience." The childishness only comes in when tradition, instead of being respected, is treated as something infallible before which the reason of man is to prostrate itself, and which it is shocking to deny.[18]

A similar attitude toward tradition dominates Peirce's later doctrine on common sense. This doctrine is labelled "critical common-sensism," precisely because it is aimed at finding a balance between critical thinking and the acceptance of unquestioned beliefs – or, as Peirce also puts it, between Scottish philosophy and Kantian criticism.[19] Traditional Scottish common-sensism is right, Peirce claims, in thinking that the rationalist ambition to apply criticism to all our beliefs is misguided. What distinguishes the totality of our stream of thought from the more specific phenomenon of logical reasoning is the fact that only the latter is self-controlled. Thus, it is not correct to apply rational criticism to those as-

---

[17] "Some Consequences of Four Incapacities," W2, p. 212 (1868). See also, much later, "What Pragmatism Is," EP2, 336 (1905): "[T]here is but one state of mind from which you can 'set out,' namely, the very state of mind in which you actually find yourself at the time you do 'set out,' – a state in which you are laden with an immense mass of cognition already formed, of which you cannot divest yourself if you would; and who knows whether, if you could, you would not have made all knowledge impossible to yourself?"

[18] "Grand Logic," CP 4.71 (1893). This ambivalent attitude toward Descartes might be compared to Peirce's take on Locke in the passage quoted above. Peirce explicitly places Locke "nearly upon a level with Descartes" in W8, p. 41 (1890).

[19] Peirce took these two philosophical traditions to be the two most significant "ways of answering Hume." See "Consequences of Critical Common-Sensism," CP 5.05 (1905). See also "Issues of Pragmaticism" EP2, p. 346–359 (1905) For a very good commentary, see Haack 1994. In a much earlier text, W2, p. 189 (1868), common sense is also called "common prejudice." This terminological overlap strengthens the link between Peirce's early reflections on prejudice and his late philosophy of common sense.

pects of our reasoning that have not (as yet) been submitted to rational thought. However, Kant, too, was right in demanding that "first principles be scientifically established," as against the common-sensist claim that it is unavoidable to "come to a halt somewhere" in the justification of our knowledge.[20]

But how can these two opposite intellectual tendencies be reconciled? Peirce believed that this could be done by suggesting a number of corrections to the classical common-sensist picture. First and foremost, the critical common-sensist needs to recognize that some of our beliefs, although not dubitable or actually doubted, may very well be false. Accordingly, we can imagine a future state of knowledge in which those beliefs are no longer uncritically accepted. In turn, this means admitting the existence of a complementary relation between the doubting attitude of critical thinking and the uncritical attitude of common sense. This complementary relation is similar to the relation of inverse proportionality between the (unquestioned) vagueness of common sense and the (fallibilist) definiteness of science that we discussed in the preceding chapter.[21] Science is, thus, a critical activity that gradually puts our uncritically accepted beliefs in doubt. However – and again similarly to what happens with vagueness – this does not mean that science can pretend to cast doubt at once on the totality of these uncritical beliefs; nor does it mean that scientific thinking is free of unquestioned assumptions. Rather, scientists are busy with exerting doubt, "provided only that it be the weighty and noble metal itself, and no counterfeit nor paper substitute."[22]

A corollary of this argument is that the set of our indubitable beliefs does not remain the same over history. There is historical development of common sense, to a degree that the traditional Scottish school had underestimated. This means bringing the concept of common sense implicitly closer to the concept of historical tradition. Granted, Peirce did admit that there is a domain of our life where the original beliefs remain almost perfectly stable over time, because they are hardly touched by scientific progress. This is the domain of "affairs that resemble those of a primitive mode of life" and mostly concern practical conduct. However, not even this distinction is absolute. Primitive beliefs do change: those

---

20 See CP 5.505.
21 Cf. CP 6.494 (c. 1906), where ordinary language is conceived in a similar fashion: "No words are so well understood as vernacular words, in one way; yet they are invariably vague; and of many of them it is true that, let the logician do his best to substitute precise equivalents in their places, still the vernacular words alone, for all their vagueness, answer the principal purposes."
22 EP2, p. 353.

changes are "slight from generation to generation, though not imperceptible even in that short period."[23]

Finally, one last difference between Peirce's common-sensism and the traditional Scottish school is the idea that reasoning rests not only on acritical beliefs but also on "acritical inferences." This point should be related to a remark I made in Chapter 3. The habits of thought that govern our reasoning here and now are the least obvious for consciousness. They are our eye-beams.

> It should surprise nobody that the most characteristic form of demonstrative reasoning of those ages is left unnoticed in their logical treatises. The best of such works, at all epochs, though they reflect in some measure contemporary modes of thought, have always been considerably behind their times. For the methods of thinking that are living activities in men are not objects of reflective consciousness. They baffle the student, because they are a part of himself.
>
> "Of thine eye I am eye-beam,"
>
> says Emerson's sphinx. The methods of thinking men consciously admire are different from, and often, in some respects, inferior to those they actually employ.[24]

In his later logical writings, Peirce sought to capture this distinction between conscious and unconscious methods of thinking by means of a Scholastic terminology. He distinguished between *logica docens* and *logica utens*. The first is the logic that we "teach": our explicit logic. But this is hardly sufficient to the exercise of sound reasoning, because reasoning is mostly done in a tacit or unconscious way: it is embodied in implicit logical rules, the logic that we "use."[25] As suggested by the final sentence of the passage just quoted, Peirce thought that the implicit methods of thinking are often worthier than the explicit ones. In fact, our inability to become fully conscious of the logic that we use dovetails with the need to exert originality and critical thinking. Let me recall a statement I have already referred to: "To look an inch before one's nose involves originality: *therefore*, it is wrong to have a conscious method."[26] However, Peirce also re-

---

23 EP2, p. 349. On the distinction between theory and practice, see further, Ch. 5.
24 "The Critic of Arguments," CP 3.404 (1892). The text continues (3.405) with a quip about the two senses of the word "beam" – a joist, or a ray of light – and a citation from the Gospels. "One has to confess that writers of logic-books have been, themselves, with rare exceptions, but shambling reasoners. How wilt thou say to thy brother, Let me pull out the mote out of thine eye; and behold, a beam is in thine own eye? I fear it has to be said of philosophers at large, both small and great, that their reasoning is so loose and fallacious, that the like in mathematics, in political economy, or in physical science, would be received in derision or simple scorn."
25 See, e. g., HP2, p. 892 (1901). On *logica docens* and *logica utens* see Pietarinen 2005.
26 CP 6.604. My emphasis.

marked that the gap between implicit and explicit logic should not be taken as an ahistorical constant. There have been times in which "the discrepancy was not very great," which is why some logical works do in fact "exhibit well the character of thought of [their] time."[27] Only history can determine how the relation between the two logics looks like at different epochs.

This complex web of connections between implicit logic, "originality," and history helps me articulate one last, crucial point: Peirce's writings about common sense and the *logica utens* are not simply meant to make us aware of the importance of tradition. There is a much deeper point to be taken: for the critical common-sensist, history itself may become a tool for rational, critical inquiry. Critical common-sensism invites a detailed study of the ways we entertain unquestioned beliefs, of how we think and act on their basis, of how we change them and submit them to criticism over time. And within this framework, historical knowledge contributes precisely to the critical assessment of beliefs, because it investigates the proper meaning of such beliefs as related to their historical context. With the help of history, for instance, we can better understand what the scientific and cultural conditions of a certain epoch would have allowed people to doubt and what not. Or even more specifically, we can discriminate the beliefs that should be ascribed to a truly primitive bedrock of human culture from those which are, instead, the result of contingent, historical factors. (One of Peirce's examples in this sense is our belief that suicide is morally wrong).[28]

To put the same point in slightly different terms, cultivating historical awareness is by no means the same as revering tradition for its own sake. Rather, historical awareness helps us understand tradition; it helps us assess it with a critical eye. In the book's first two chapters, we saw that Peirce nurtured a life-long interest in the history of philosophical and scientific ideas as a tool to look critically at the force that those ideas exert on us. The doctrine of critical common-sense elaborates on the same idea: history is a tool to assess the scope and purport of our philosophical or scientific beliefs. Moreover, this strategy can be adopted not only with regard to beliefs defended by other people, but also with regard to ours. In this sense, history acts as a reminder that what we consider most certain is not necessarily destined to remain so. The critical common-sensist "acknowledges that what has been indubitable one day has often been proved on the morrow to be false."[29] He or she recognizes that common sense

---

[27] CN1, p. 48 (1872).
[28] See EP2, p. 350.
[29] CP 5.514.

is subject to historical change and that, precisely because of this, history may turn into a powerful instrument of critique.

Experience: The Outward Clash and the Little Mouse

Let me now turn to the other strand of Peirce's reflections on *Selbstdenken*, namely the question of empirical knowledge. Peirce conferred on experience and empirical observations the power to place a check on the abstractions and generalizations of philosophy, as they represent a source of information without which the conceptual arguments of philosophy risk running astray. He did so by insisting on the relation between philosophy and science and on the strong realistic basis of both.

As we have seen while discussing "The Fixation of Belief," Peirce's conception of rationality is profoundly shaped by the model of science. As all other rational modes of inquiry, philosophy *is* a scientific enterprise, although a peculiar one. And science as a whole hinges on the willingness to learn something about reality by means of experience. The concept of learning is indeed crucial to understanding Peirce's view of philosophical and scientific rationality. "[M]en of science [...] want above all to learn – that is, to change their mind."[30] There is, at least in principle, no space for a "will to believe" in Peirce's epistemology, because scientific reasoning aims precisely at establishing beliefs that we cannot in any way anticipate. The only aim we are allowed to have when we carry out a scientific inquiry is the overthrow of ignorance. "The object of reasoning is to find out, from the consideration of what we already know, something else that we do not know."[31] One pivotal component of this conception of scientific and philosophical rationality is its emphasis on realism. Reality is something other than our beliefs; it is something external to us, which has the power to force our beliefs into a direction that was not foreseeable at the outset.

In 1885, Peirce articulated this insight in a particularly successful manner while reviewing a book by Josiah Royce, namely *The Religious Aspect of Philosophy* (1885).[32] He took the occasion of that review to level a general objection against the Hegelian kind of idealism that he saw at work in Royce's book. Hegel and Royce, Peirce argued, neglect the epistemic value of our immediate,

---

[30] HP, p. 477 (1896).
[31] W3, p. 244 (1877).
[32] "An American Plato," W5, p. 221–234 (1885). See Oppenheim 2005 for Peirce's broader influence on Royce, and Pfeifer 2017 for Royce's influence on Peirce. On the crucial role of the 1885 review of Royce in Peirce's intellectual development, see also Girel 2011.

non-conceptual relation with external reality as a constraint on our conceptual arguments. Peirce was, here, resuscitating the well-known Kantian dictum that being is not a predicate.[33] The existence of something cannot be derived from its concept but must be grounded on something other than conceptual reasoning. However, while Kant identified such a something other with intuition, for Peirce this solution was blocked, on account of his rebuttal of non-inferential cognition (see Chapter 3). He thus substituted Kantian intuition with the "sense of action and reaction, resistance, externality, otherness"[34] that belongs to the category of Secondness and is the necessary counterpart to the category of Thirdness.

With this argument, Peirce was merely taking up the second fundamental criterion of an objective belief as outlined in "The Fixation of Belief," namely the existence of "something upon which our thinking has no effect [...] and which affects, or might affect, every man."[35] But he gave it a twist. He decreased the importance of a definition of reality as something toward which our opinions will converge in the long run, and increased the role of Secondness here and now: the brute resistance that the external world exerts on our cognitive undertakings, completely irrespective of what we happen to think.[36] Peirce found a felicitous name for this notion: "The capital error of Hegel which permeates his whole system in every part of it is that he almost altogether ignores the *Outward Clash.*"[37]

The concept of the outward clash is also linked to another crucial point of Peirce's epistemology. Namely, it dovetails with a distrust for those sweeping generalizations that underplay the richness and variety of empirical reality. This is precisely the point where we can recognize the empiricist undertone to

---

[33] See Kant [1781/1787] 1998, p. 567, B598–599. Cf. a later review to Royce 1899–1901, CP 8.129 (1902): "Professor Royce is blind to a fact which all ordinary people will see plainly enough; that the essence of the realist's opinion is that it is one thing to *be* and another thing to *be represented*; and the cause of this cecity is that the Professor is completely immersed in his absolute idealism, which precisely consists in denying that distinction." On realism and idealism in Peirce see Lane 2018.
[34] W5, p. 225.
[35] W3, p. 253. See above, Ch. 1.
[36] This insight goes hand in hand with an insistence on the semiotic role of the index, which "like a pointing finger, exercises a real *force* over the attention [...] and directs it to a particular object of sense." W5, p. 224. Gava 2014, p. 100–101 places emphasis on precisely this shift from agreement in the long run toward indexicality and Secondness in Peirce's mid-phase. Cf. Girel 2011, p. 80.
[37] W5, p. 225. My emphasis. On the outward clash, see also Hookway 1985, Ch. 5. Stern 2009, Ch. 9 counters Peirce's criticism of Hegel on this point.

Peirce's reflections on *Selbstdenken:* general propositions must be brought to the test of experience by every single individual who aims to think autonomously.

Especially in the later phase of his career, Peirce was at pain to articulate precisely the delicate balance between the virtues and vices of generalizations in science and philosophy. The "Minute Logic," for instance, says: "Broad generalization is glorious when it is the inevitable outpressed juice of painfully matured little details of knowledge; but when it is not that, it is a crude spirit inciting only broils between a hundred little dogmas, each most justly condemning all the others. It is the usual fruit of sloth."[38] And again, in the 1903 "Harvard Lectures"*:* "My way of philosophizing [...] is nothing if not minute. I certainly endeavor to generalize as far as I can find support for generalization; but I depend on the sedulous care with which I scrutinize every point."[39]

We can recognize in these passages the same attempt to balance generality and particularity that I considered in Chapter 3 (only, from an epistemological rather than a metaphysical angle). No amount of theory will ever grasp the richness of the empirical world. Human reality bristles with unintended consequences of actions, with unforeseen turns of events. Therefore, history cannot be grasped as the mere realization of the grand laws of philosophy.

To use the terminology of the classification of the sciences, *idioscopic* observations are not merely there to fill in the *cenoscopic* scheme. Sometimes, they have the ability to orient that cenoscopic scheme in one direction or in another. In the "Minute Logic," for instance, Peirce remarks that there are "certain special yet obtrusive points" of metaphysics that cannot be settled without appealing "to the most specialized and refined observations, in order to ascertain what minute modifications of everyday experience they may introduce." This means that certain idioscopic observations may come to have a truly philosophical significance. One of the examples Peirce gives is a problem investigated by the "history of science and art": namely, whether there is progress in history or simply cyclical repetitions.[40] Factual history, in other words, is a necessary step to settle those problems that we normally subsume under the philosophy of history. At least in this

---

38 CP 2.14 (1902).
39 EP2, p. 526. See Turrisi 1997, p. 40.
40 CP 1.273 (1902). Let me quote the passage more in full: "Speculative minds have asked whether there may not be a complete cycle at the expiration of which all things will happen again as they did before. Such is said to have been the opinion of Pythagoras; and the stoics took it up as a necessary consequence of their philistine views. Yet in our day, certain experiences, especially the inspiring history of science and art during the nineteenth century, have inclined many to the theory that there is endless progress, a definite current of change on the whole of the whole universe."

particular case, the distinction between cenoscopy and idioscopy does not follow a rigid Comtian hierarchy.

More generally, idioscopic observations can enrich cenoscopic experience by making it more complex and nuanced. This may happen when idioscopic observations take the form of disturbances, exceptions, anomalies. Or, as an outstanding reader of Peirce, namely Robert K. Merton, would have put it, when they take the form of virtuous serendipities.[41] A little-known logical manuscript dating from 1906 gives poetic expression to this idea. It does so, moreover, by establishing a remarkably clear connection between the two issues I have dealt with in this section: on the one hand, the "outward clash" of reality; on the other, the power of minute details.

> [A]n approach to reality, something that is not in the slightest of the nature of a pretense is found wherever an object of thought is sufficiently obstinate to enable us to say, it has *not* these characters but it *does* have these. There is already a lesson in logic. Namely, that one may lay down the very best of definitions, going to the very heart of things; and yet there will be, as it were, a little living mouse of a quasi exception which will find or make a hole to get in when all seemed hermetically closed. This mouse will not be a mere pest to be got rid of and forgotten. It will be a fellow being to be remembered and to be appraised.[42]

Pragmatism, Analysis, and the A Priori

One further thought that is entailed by what we just said is that philosophy cannot be defined as a purely a priori activity. To better articulate this thought, we have to look in more detail at Peirce's attempts to redefine the classical distinctions between a priori and a posteriori cognition and between analytic and synthetic reasoning. Although Peirce did not wish to conflate the empirical with the non-empirical, he offered a number of arguments to show that philosophical methodology is neither completely a priori, nor is it exhausted by the practice of conceptual analysis. In turn, these arguments will help us introduce the last problem I would like to deal with in this chapter, namely the relation between logic, empirical knowledge and history.[43]

---

41 Merton/Barber 2004. On Peirce and serendipity, see Merton [1957] 1968, p. 158fn: "Charles Sanders Peirce had long before noticed the strategic role of the 'surprising fact' in his account of what he called 'abduction,' that is, the initiation and entertaining of a hypothesis as a step in inference."
42 R 498 (1906). The manuscript has been published by Pietarinen 2015.
43 The questioning of the distinctions between a priori and a posteriori, or analytic and synthetic reasoning, is a classical theme of pragmatism, which comes to play center stage in the linguis-

A first argument I would like to consider is laid out in the series of essays on pragmatism from 1877 to 1878. In particular, one essay of that series, "How to Make Our Ideas Clear,"[44] is on a par with "The Fixation of Belief" in formulating an explicit attempt to make philosophy a scientific activity, oriented toward finding out what we do not yet know. Peirce takes his cue from two classical concepts of early modern epistemology, namely the concepts of "clear" and "distinct" ideas. These concepts, Peirce argues, successfully define the first two "degrees of clarity" of an idea. "Clear" ideas (the first degree of clarity) are ideas that we feel familiar with, and which we can recognize in every circumstance. "Distinct" ideas (the second degree of clarity) are ideas for which "we can give a precise definition." When analyzed and broken up into its different components, a distinct idea remains as clear as it was before. "A distinct idea is defined as one which contains nothing which is not clear."[45]

Early modern philosophers, Peirce goes on to argue, took this second degree of clearness to be a sufficient criterion for the clarity of thinking. But this cannot be true. For the validity of this criterion is circumscribed to situations where we limit ourselves to "analyzing definitions" and forgo any possibility of learning anything new about our own ideas. "Nothing new can ever be learned by analyzing definitions."[46] Or, in other words, "the machinery of the mind can only transform knowledge, but never originate it, unless it be fed with facts of observation."[47]

Thus, we need a third degree of clarity, capable of satisfying the needs of modern science by allowing knowledge to actually advance. This "higher perspi-

---

tic pragmatism of Quine. See Quine [1951] 1953; White [1950] 2005. Maddalena 2015 offers an even more radical criticism of the analytic-synthetic distinction on a Peircean basis.
44 W3, p. 257–276 (1877).
45 W3, p. 258.
46 W3, p. 260.
47 W3, p. 259. We may locate a first step toward this argument in an 1869 criticism of James Mill and his followers, W2, p. 303: "The chief methodical characteristic of their thought is 'analysis.' [...] By mental analysis the English mean the separation of a compound idea or sensation into its constituent ideas or sensations. [...] The same thinkers reason in a manner entirely analogous when they are not dealing with the mind at all; and in general their method may be described as simplifying existing hypotheses and then endeavoring to show that known facts may be accounted for by these simplified hypotheses. In this way, a highly elegant and instructive system has been created; but it is not pre-eminently scientific. It might be scientific if these philosophers occupied themselves with subjecting their modified theories to the test of exact experience in every possible way [...]. But that is not their business; they are writers. Their energies are occupied in adjusting their theories to the facts, and not in ascertaining the certainty of their theories."

cuity of thought"⁴⁸ is the pragmatic one. It dictates that we look at the practical actions that are produced by the habits of conduct to which our ideas are linked. Peirce's well-known pragmatic maxim is introduced precisely as a means to define the third degree of clarity of ideas:

> It appears [...] that the rule for attaining the third grade of clearness of apprehension is as follows: Consider what effects, which might conceivably have practical bearings, we conceive the object of our conception to have. Then, our conception of these effects is the whole of our conception of the object.⁴⁹

Peirce's definition of the pragmatic clarity of concepts has two consequences that relate to what I have argued in Chapter 3. First of all, the emphasis on the conceivable effects of concepts is the cornerstone of Peirce's conviction that the real purport of knowledge lies in the future. Second, it is only by the third degree of clarity of ideas that we can take into account the growth of meaning. For the first and the second degrees of clarity are unable to grasp the way a symbol grows by absorbing new empirical information. The third degree of clarity, on the contrary, makes meaning depend more decidedly on experience. Thus, it helps understand what it means for a concept's meaning to change as a result of new experiences. T. L. Short remarks in this respect that Peirce's views about the growth of meaning "undercuts definitions of philosophy as 'conceptual analysis,' that is, as usefully employed in explicating received meanings. The point is not to understand our meanings but to change them."⁵⁰

A later version of this argument can be found in what the "Minute Logic" has to say about the limited validity of definitions in the context of that discussion of natural classes and final causation which I have already considered (see Chapters 2 and 3). Peirce compares definitions to the dissection of a living being. A definition "will not really work in the world as the object defined will. It will enable us to see how the thing works, in so far as it shows the efficient causation.

---

48 W3, p. 260.
49 W3, p. 266.
50 Short 2007, p. 264. Cf. Haack 2009, p. 17: "Peirce's three grades of clarity can be seen as located along a continuum of degrees of depth of understanding: from being able to use a word more or less correctly (the first grade of clarity), to being able to give a verbal definition (the second grade), to being able to work with the terms in the course of inquiry, to employ them deftly and adapt them as needed (the third grade). So the idea Hilary Putnam calls 'division of linguistic labor' has a significant place in the picture I am sketching. Perhaps unlike Putnam, however, I think of this division of labor gradualistically, because understanding comes in degrees; and dynamically, because both specialists' and lay people's understanding of specialized scientific (etc.) terminology changes over time."

The final causation, which is what characterizes the *definitum*, it leaves out of account."[51] We might compare the analytical definition of a concept to the second degree of clarity of ideas as presented in the 1877 essay: while helping us get a clear view of the structure of the *definitum*, it has no pragmatic efficacy. In turn, Peirce relates this fact to definitions' inability to grasp the final cause of their object and thus to identify natural classes. (If we keep in mind what we saw in previous chapters, it becomes clearer that Peirce is pitting the purely analytical method against what he calls "genealogy").

> I am not decrying definitions. I have a lively sense of their great value in science. I only say that it should not be by means of definitions that one should seek to find natural classes. When the classes have been found, then it is proper to try to define them; and one may even, with great caution and reserve, allow the definitions to lead us to turn back and see whether our classes ought not to have their boundaries differently drawn.[52]

The second argument I would like to highlight is articulated in Peirce's mid-phase work. Instead of addressing the pragmatic limitations of analytic reasoning, as the first argument does, it addresses the very distinctions of analytic and synthetic reasoning, and of a priori and a posteriori cognition. Its goal is to suggest that these distinctions need to be substituted by a more dynamic, processual model, one that insists on continuities rather than on sharp dichotomies.

As might be easily imagined, Peirce's polemical objective in this case is not so much early modern rationalism (as it was in the first case), but Kant. This in no way diminishes his "profound and almost unparalleled admiration for that [...] indispensable stepping-stone of philosophy" that is the *Critique of Pure Reason*.[53] But it does cast a shadow of doubt on the viability of Kant's terminology. Peirce criticizes both the distinction between a priori and a posteriori cognition and the distinction between analytic and synthetic – which he also calls "explicative" and "ampliative" – reasoning. These distinctions, he claims, are confusing, and they run the risk of mixing up questions of psychology and questions of logic.[54] He thus suggests substituting them with new distinctions.

---

51 CP 1.220 (1902).
52 CP 1.222.
53 "Grand Logic," CP 4.92 (1893).
54 See CP 4.85; CP 4.92. Cf. NEM4, p. 58 (1902), as well as EP2, p. 218 (1903): "Kant's conception of the nature of necessary reasoning is clearly shown by the logic of relations to be utterly mistaken, and his distinction between analytic and synthetic judgments, which he otherwise and better terms explicatory (*erläuternde*) and ampliative (*erweiternde*) judgments, which is based on that conception, is so utterly confused that it is difficult or impossible to do anything with it." Cf. a much earlier remark, W1, p. 111–112 (1863): "In one point of view indeed, pure *a priori*

First, we can legitimately distinguish between necessary reasoning, which proceeds only from hypotheses, and contingent reasoning, which proceeds from facts.[55] Second, we can distinguish between inner and outer experience. On that basis, mathematics can be defined as necessary reasoning; however, this does not mean that it is not based on experience. Mathematics is based on a certain kind of inner experience, namely the experimentation with, and manipulation of, *diagrams*. Mathematical reasoning is an experimental process, which laboriously extracts or "evolves" necessary consequences out of the premises.

> Everything is involved which can be evolved. But how does this evolution of necessary consequences take place? [...] It is not by a simple mental stare, or strain of mental vision. It is by manipulating on paper, or in the fancy, formulae or other diagrams – experimenting on them, *experiencing* the thing. Such experience alone *evolves* the reason hidden within us and as utterly hidden as gold ten feet below ground – and this experience only differs from what usually carries that name in that it brings out the reason hidden within and not the reason of Nature, as do the chemist's or physicist's experiments.[56]

The crucial point here is that Peirce wants to stretch the concept of experience to cover all forms of reasoning and inference. As he writes elsewhere, "[d]eduction is really a matter of perception and of experimentation, just as induction and hypothetic inference are; only, the perception and experimentation are concerned with imaginary objects instead of with real ones."[57]

Peirce was, therefore, perfectly willing to follow the empiricists and admit "that *experience* is the only source of any kind of knowledge";[58] provided we make a few caveats. First, we need to carve out a processual understanding of experience as *"personal history,* life" (again, the processualism I have explored

---

reasoning is a misnomer; it is as much as to say analysis with nothing to analyze? Analysis of what? I ask. Of those ideas which no man is without."
55 See CP 4.88.
56 CP 4.86. Cf. 6.595 (1893): "[M]athematics brings to light results as truly occult and unexpected as those of chemistry; only they are results dependent upon the action of reason in the depths of our own consciousness, instead of being dependent, like those of chemistry, upon the action of Cosmical Reason, or Law. Or, stating the matter under another aspect, analytical reasoning depends upon associations of similarity, synthetical reasoning upon associations of contiguity." See also W2, p. 315 (1869), where Peirce, quoting Gauss, calls algebra a "science of the eye."
57 "Reply to the Necessitarians," CP 6.595 (1893).
58 CP 4.91.

in Chapter 3).⁵⁹ Second, we need to admit the existence of inner experience and the possibility of experiencing with diagrams.⁶⁰

Finally, a third distinction that Peirce advances as a replacement of the Kantian terminology is the entirely psychological one between innate ideas and ideas that we get from experience. He insists, however, that this distinction is far from being clear-cut. This is, indeed, one of the major disagreements Peirce had with Locke: "Locke failed to see that learning something from experience, and having been fully aware of it since birth, did not exhaust all possibilities."⁶¹

But what, then, are the alternatives? Peirce suggests that we might know something innately, but obscurely. Although innate, this cognition would still need to be clarified, to be articulated by dint of an a posteriori process of inquiry: "that may be innate which is very abstruse, and which we can only find out with extreme difficulty."⁶² Moreover, a similar argument can be made if we move from the opposite starting point, namely a posteriori experience or the manifold of sense, and show that it, too, needs a gradual process of articulation. As Peirce claims in an earlier text, "the first impression has no parts, any more than it has unity or wholeness; yet it may be allowed to be potentially a manifold, if we say that all that the intellect evolves from it lies involved within it."⁶³ Or in yet other words:

> Kant gives the erroneous view that ideas are presented separated and then thought together by the mind. This is his doctrine that a mental synthesis precedes every analysis. What really happens is that something is presented which in itself has no parts, but which neverthe-

---

59 CP 4.91. Cf. EP2, 47 (1898): "For what is observation? What is experience? It is the enforced element in the history of our lives."
60 Around 1901 to 1902, Peirce would further elaborate on this point by introducing the distinction between corollarial and theorematic deduction in mathematics. See NEM4, p. 38 (1902): "*Corollarial deduction* is where it is only necessary to imagine any case in which the premisses are true in order to perceive immediately that the conclusion holds in that case. [...] *Theorematic deduction* is deduction in which it is necessary to experiment in the imagination upon the image of the premiss[.]" The distinction between explicatory and ampliative reasoning in mathematics may now be mapped onto this new distinction.
61 CP 4.92. Cf. a similar remark in CP 5.612 (1901): "The word 'experience,' however, is employed by Locke chiefly to enable him to say that human cognitions are inscribed by the individual's life-history upon a tabula rasa, and are not, like those of the lower animals, gifts of inborn instinct. His definition is vague for the reason that he never realized how important the innate element of our directest perceptions really is."
62 CP, 4.92.
63 W5, 299 (1886).

less is analyzed by the mind. That is to say, its having parts consists in this, that the mind afterward recognizes those parts in it."[64]

"Facts about Men": The Challenge of Psychologism

A last point we should consider in order to have a complete picture of Peirce's take on a priori and analytic cognition is something I anticipated when talking about his criticism of Kant, namely the distinction between logic and psychology, or what we would call today the problem of psychologism. In the period in which Peirce was writing, the debate over psychologism had acquired a truly paradigmatic significance in discussions about the status of philosophy vis-à-vis the empirical sciences.[65] This paradigmatic significance was not alien to Peirce: his classification of the sciences not only places logic fully within philosophy but takes psychology to be a major sub-division of idioscopy, or empirical science. It is therefore legitimate to consider Peirce's arguments about the relation between psychology and logic as a blueprint for thinking about the relation between philosophy and empirical knowledge at large.

Approximately coeval with Husserl and Frege, Peirce can be associated with them in a sort of canonical anti-psychologistic trinity.[66] This would not be wrong: Peirce was adamant that the kernel of logic should be preserved from any reduction to psychological observations. The aim of developing a thoroughly "unpsychological view of logic"[67] was one of his earliest, most pressing urges, and would remain so throughout his life.

Yet, his take on the problem was nuanced. To begin with, Peirce was keenly interested in the empirical study of mind. In fact, he was one of America's first experimental psychologists: the paper he co-authored in 1884 with his Baltimore student Joseph Jastrow, which rejects Gustav Theodor Fechner's hypothesis of a perceptual threshold, has come to be regarded as pathbreaking work.[68] Even more to the point, the kind of logic Peirce was busy developing did not rule

---

64 "A Guess at the Riddle," W6, p. 449 (1887–1888).
65 See Kusch 1995.
66 See Stjernfelt 2014, p. 24.
67 See W1, p. 305 (1865). For a late statement, see, e. g., the "Minute Logic," CP 2.39 (1902): "Nobody will do injustice to the present treatise by describing its position as extremely unfavorable to the use of psychology in logic."
68 See "On Small Differences of Sensation," W5, p. 122–135. Hacking 1988, p. 427–451 has defined this paper as a "milestone" in the history of associative psychology, in particular because of its original employment of statistical methods. See also Cristalli 2017.

out altogether – at least not in a first phase – the possibility of dialogue with the empirical sciences. In "The Fixation of Belief," he described Darwin's "immortal work" as revolving on issues "in which questions of fact and questions of logic are curiously interlaced."[69] In the 1885 review of Royce, he claimed that "formal logic in its new development" should "draw nutriment *from physiology and from history* without leaving the solid ground of logical forms."[70] In fact, he went back to this problem throughout his life, repeatedly trying to correct his older positions, which he even charged with being themselves overly psychological. This alone would be enough to show that what we actually face, more than a steadfast conviction, is a problem, a theoretical urgency, an insight that was particularly important to him but which he was hard-pressed to settle once and for all. Perhaps the reason for this difficulty was that Peirce also felt the weight of the other side of the matter, namely the role of empirical observations in the study of logic. In other words, his anti-psychologism is everything but the result of a lack of interest in psychology.

In an attempt to lay out Peirce's most significant arguments against psychologism, we should also make a preliminary remark: neither "psychology" nor "logic" can be taken as monolithic concepts in his work. In particular, logic can be broken down into three sub-disciplines, namely "speculative grammar," "critic" and "speculative rhetoric" (or "methodeutic"). Moreover, the purely formal side of logic, or what we would today call 'mathematical logic,' is not really logic but, rather, mathematics.[71] Given this diversification, we should expect that the problem of logic's relation to psychology may be put in different terms depending on which sub-branch of logic we are focusing on.

Furthermore, the very idea of a relation between logic and psychology can be understood in at least two different senses. In one sense, it hinges on what it is customary to call the genetic or naturalistic fallacy: is it legitimate to reduce questions of essence, or norms, to questions of facts? (Norwood R. Hanson has claimed that even *that* question can be broken down into a multitude of layers).[72] In another sense, it relates to the debate between internalism and externalism in our conception of our mental states. Is it legitimate to explain mental and cognitive phenomena in terms of what happens inside our heads? Although we are

---

69 W3, p. 244 (1877).
70 W5, p. 225 (1885). My emphasis. Peirce links this remark directly to his observations about the outward clash: "Besides the lower consciousness of feeling and the higher consciousness of nutrition, this direct consciousness of hitting and of getting hit enters into all cognition and serves to make it mean something real. It is formal logic which teaches us this [...]."
71 See the second classification scheme in Ch. 2.
72 See Hanson 1967.

mostly concerned with the first issue, it should be noted that part of Peirce's antipsychologistic preoccupations was fueled by the second issue, namely by his staunch aversion to all purely internalist conceptions of thought.[73]

In the main, Peirce provided two criteria to keep logic apart from psychology and other "descriptive" or empirical sciences. The first criterion is the Comtian notion I have repeatedly evoked: logic is more general and abstract than all descriptive sciences. The second and more important criterion concerns, in particular, the sub-discipline of logic that Peirce called "critic," that is, the normative theory of sound reasoning. Critic hinges on the phenomenon of self-control. Hence, only those inferences and beliefs that we can control fall within the competence of logic. This reference so self-control introduces a normative component into logical theory – what we ought to believe – which is irreducible to empirical observation. In fact, Peirce took self-control to be one of the chief aspects of this chapter's topic, namely intellectual autonomy.[74]

This seemingly clear-cut picture, however, is immediately made more complex by a relatively simple remark. Especially if we focus on logic in the broadest sense of the term, as encompassing all three branches mentioned above, we find that there are indeed some concepts that are pivotal to the discipline but are not definable without some reference to experience. These are concepts like 'doubt,' 'belief,' 'inquiry,' 'habit' – and indeed, the very concept of 'self-control.' If we examine these concepts' foundational role for Peirce's formulation of logical truths, it becomes tempting to say that logic depends on at least a minimum of psychological knowledge. Indeed, these are precisely the concepts Peirce felt most insecure about: in his mature years, he considered his own earlier characterization of the pragmatic maxim to lapse into psychologism.[75] But even then, he kept thinking that concepts such as doubt or belief make logic ultimately rest "on certain facts of experience among which are facts about men."[76]

The latter quote shows us a way out of the predicament we seem to have fallen into. Peirce speaks about "facts of experience." But it would be incorrect to think that this can only refer to empirical facts about human psychology. Indeed, a fact of experience is not necessarily a fact that falls within the domain of the empirical sciences. To see why, just think once again of the distinction between

---

[73] However, this anti-internalist attitude applies not only to philosophy, but to all the sciences, hence to psychology as well. Peirce thought that psychology too, like philosophy, should stop focusing exclusively on consciousness and study the broader phenomena of habit-taking. See CP 7.367 (1902); Colapietro 2003b, p. 170–171.
[74] Cf. Hampe 2006, p. 69–70.
[75] See EP2, p. 139–140.
[76] EP2, p. 189 (1903). See Colapietro 2003b, p. 158, 169.

idioscopy and cenoscopy. As the words themselves say, both are "observations." But only the first characterizes the observations of the empirical sciences. The second points to a different kind of observation, one that is exemplified by phenomenology, logic and other philosophical disciplines. Thus, in the entry on "Logic" written in 1902 for James Baldwin's *Dictionary of Psychology and Philosophy*, Peirce explicitly sought to

> discriminate between facts of [psychology] which are supposed to be ascertained by the systematic study of mind, and facts the knowledge of which altogether antecedes such study, and is not in the least affected by it; such as the fact that there is such a state of mind as doubt, and the fact that the mind struggles to escape from doubt.[77]

These different kinds of observation, however, are similar in making all sciences depend on looking at what happens outside of us. Let us recall what we have seen in the preceding section about the experimental/experiential aspect of mathematics: Peirce believed that all sciences, including philosophy, rely on experience and "observation." However, this reliance on experience is itself internally differentiated:

> All knowledge whatever comes from observation; but different sciences are observational in such radically different ways, that the kind of information derived from the observation of one department of science (say natural history) could not possibly afford the information required of observation by another branch (say mathematics).[78]

To sum up: logic does draw from experience, because, like all sciences, it is observational. To escape psychologism, it only has to pitch its basic notions at the correct level of generality and abstraction. This conclusion is compatible with what we have seen in the preceding pages. A strong reliance on observation and experience pervades all kinds of cognitive enterprises. Therefore, the distinction between philosophy and empirical sciences cannot be drawn on that basis. Rather, it has to be drawn on the basis of the different qualitative kinds of observation, as well as on the aforementioned phenomenon of self-control.

Finally, there is a last, methodological comment I would like to make on Peirce's general anti-psychologistic attitude. Even when we choose to focus on the cenoscopic level of experience as opposed to the idioscopic level, we cannot neglect genuinely empirical observations. This can be shown by looking at Peir-

---

[77] CP 2.10 (1902). Peirce adds that "[e]ven facts like these require to be carefully examined by the logician before he uses them as the basis of his doctrine."
[78] CP 1.238 (1902). On the internal differentiation of the concept of observation, cf. RLT, p. 182–187 (1898), to which I return in Ch. 6.

ce's own method of research. Precisely when he thought that it was necessary to disentangle the observation of logical essences from the observation of contingent facts, Peirce resorted to empirical inquiries. In doing so, he aimed to discriminate the *variable* aspects of a phenomenon from its *invariant* traits.

The best case in point is Peirce's attitude toward a problem that is cognate with psychologism. I mean the question of the influence of historical languages on thought, and therefore the relation between logic and linguistics. In his lifelong quest for the right method to investigate logical and metaphysical questions, Peirce came to be increasingly convinced that the tendency to project the grammatical features of Indo-European languages onto logical considerations is a mere variation of the psychologistic fallacy: it amounts to unduly absolutizing a contingent, empirical fact. However, avoiding this fallacy did not mean abstaining from linguistic studies. In fact, Peirce intensified these studies, broadening the spectrum of his interests to include a good number of non-European languages.[79] In turn, these empirical studies led him to confirm one of the basic tenets of his speculative grammar, or general semiotics. The real universal elements of language are not to be found in specific grammatical categories but, rather, in the general classifications of signs, such as the division between icons, indices and symbols.[80] Once again, the danger that empirical information overly encroaches on logic is not avoided by shutting one's eyes to experience, but rather, by widening the scope of our observations. The attempt to strip reality of its inessential accidents is no reason to stop looking at the variety of the world.

---

[79] This attitude is well captured in EP2, p. 309 (1904): "How the constitution of the human mind may compel men to think is not the question; and the appeal to language appears to me no better than an unsatisfactory method of ascertaining psychological facts that are of no relevancy to logic. But if such appeal is to be made (and logicians generally do make it; in particular their doctrine of the copula appears to rest solely upon this), it would seem that they ought to survey human languages generally and not confine themselves to the small and extremely peculiar group of Aryan speech." This passage is a good illustration of how enlarging the basis of linguistic study may help undermine precisely logicians' reliance on linguistics. See also RL 75, memoir 15 (1902): "In this memoir, I show by careful analysis that psychological truths are not relevant to the theory of cognition, but on the contrary that the establishment of those truths depends upon special points of the doctrine of logic. I undertake to show what a theory of cognition becomes when it is stripped of everything irrelevant and inadmissible, and that it then becomes a sort of grammatica speculativa. I then examine universal grammar as it is generally conceived, and show that most of its propositions are merely matters of certain special languages, some of the indo-european languages, with such others as happen to resemble them."
[80] See Bellucci 2017, Ch. 6.

History and Ampliative Reasoning

Can we now translate this depiction of the relation between logic and psychology (or linguistics) to the relation between logic and yet another empirical discipline, namely history? The answer to this question is more complex than we might expect. On the one hand, the same texts that we have been considering above show Peirce's willingness to use his anti-psychologistic argument as a blueprint to assess the relation between logic and history. But on the other hand, history does occupy a peculiar place within the domain of empirical disciplines. Thus, when he talks about the relation between logic and history Peirce appears slightly less resolute than when he talks about psychology or linguistics.

Let me start with the aforementioned 1902 dictionary entry on "Logic." In this text, Peirce is preoccupied with arguing that logic does not depend on those disciplines that philosophers have now and again chosen as their basis, such as psychology, linguistics, metaphysics and history. When he talks about psychology, his argument follows the theses I summed up in the preceding section.[81] When he talks about linguistics, he rehearses the idea that, in order to escape the contingent constraints of language on thinking, "it would be necessary to look beyond the small and very peculiar class of Aryan languages."[82] As for history, his argument runs as follows:

> Logicians occasionally appeal to the history of science. Such and such a mode of reasoning, it is said, for example, was characteristic of mediaevalism or of ancient science; such another produced the successes of modern science. If logic is to be based upon probable reasonings, as some logicians maintain that it must be, such arguments, if critically examined, must be admitted to have great weight. They will naturally be out of place in a system of logic which professes to demonstrate from certain initial assumptions that the kinds of reasoning it recommends must be accepted.[83]

Peirce is thus distinguishing two cases. Claiming a foundational role of history for logic is altogether misplaced if one focuses on the deductive part of logical reasoning. Things, however, may change if one admits that logic is based on "probable reasonings" as well.

By "probable reasoning," Peirce meant both non-necessary deductions (such as statistical inferences) and, more importantly, "ampliative" (or synthetic) inferences, namely abductions and inductions. As we read in the 1883 paper, "A

---

81 See CP 2.210.
82 CP 2.211.
83 CP 2.213.

Theory of Probable Inference," one major difference between these kinds of inferences and deductive or "demonstrative" reasoning is their being underdetermined with respect to the "facts laid down in the premises." To draw the correct conclusion of a probable reasoning, those facts are not sufficient, "but account has to be taken of various subjective circumstances – of the manner in which the premises have been obtained, of there being no countervailing considerations, etc."[84] It is therefore, we might surmise, precisely to fill the gap left by this underdetermination that historical observations may aspire to a more foundational function. However, Peirce's passage above only hints at this argument, without giving it too much credit.

But if we turn to the "Minute Logic," things look slightly different. In fact, the "Minute Logic" proves once again to be an invaluable document for the study of Peirce's ideas about history's bearing on philosophy. Peirce discusses at length the different methodologies that have guided logicians' inquiries in the course of history and proceeds to take a stand on them.[85] In this context, he also discusses the historicist logic of Hegel (see Chapter 3).[86] The bottom line of his reflections – if there is one – is that Hegel, whatever his demerits, was right in stressing the processual and historical nature of symbols; their "life-history." (Moreover, Hegel invites us to adopt a historicized version of experience in order to assess the tenability of his own claims: "I call in the data of experience, not exactly the every-minute experience which has hitherto been enough, but the experience of most men, together with the history of thought."[87]) Peirce then goes on to discuss the same issue that he had taken up in the dictionary entry, namely, the possibility that the study of logic may be based on an empirical study of history. However, he now makes explicit who these logicians are, who have "occasionally" appealed to history. And somewhat to our surprise, we discover that he is talking about his great source of inspiration, William Whewell.

> Appeal is often made by logical writers to the history of science as supporting their views of right reasoning. Whewell placed his *Novum Organum Renovatum*, a work of high logical value, almost exclusively upon the basis of this method. As a source of secondary evidence upon such general doctrines of logic as may need such help, and even of primary evidence

---

84 W4, p. 410.
85 See CP 2.18–2.77.
86 See CP 2.32–34; 2.111–118.
87 CP 2.115.

as to the value of special modes of reasoning, this method has been (it would be disgraceful to deny it) occasionally of no little service.⁸⁸

The tone, again, is very cautious. But Peirce's mentioning the man he so admired forces us to take his remark as seriously as possible. Indeed, there is a sense in which the "Minute Logic" itself tries to follow in the footsteps of Whewell, by constantly referring to the history of science as a source of insight for the logic of science.

The first and most important example thereof is provided by Peirce's conviction that the history of science may strengthen our faith in the power of abduction:

> The reasonings of the present treatise will, I expect, make it appear that the history of science, as well as other facts, prove that there is a natural light of reason; that is, that man's guesses at the course of nature are more often correct than could be otherwise accounted for, while the same facts equally prove that this light is extremely uncertain and deceptive […].⁸⁹

As Francesco Bellucci and Ahti-Veikko Pietarinen have shown, Peirce seems indeed to bestow a crucial role on the history of science in his mature justification of abduction. The validity of this mode of inference rests on a sort of meta-abduction, namely the abduction that we have the ability to perform sound abductions. This meta-abduction is in turn justified inductively, that is, by gathering a plurality of historical illustrations of successful scientific abductions.⁹⁰ (Note that, in the continuation of the passage on Whewell just cited, Peirce explicitly refers to historical arguments as a kind of induction.⁹¹)

So, the history of science provides inductive proof that abductions are a justified mode of reasoning. This might be a way to give a less timid interpretation to the aforementioned 1902 entry on "Logic": "If logic is to be based upon prob-

---

88 CP 2.74. My emphasis. See Whewell 1858b. The passage continues: "In making use of it, it will be necessary, of course, to take good care that the history is open to no doubt. But there are great numbers of facts of scientific history about which it is as impossible for any sane man to entertain any real doubt (unless, indeed, we include German 'higher critics' among that number) as about any item of the multiplication table. We also have to ask whether the facts are sufficiently numerous to lend any great certainty to an induction." I will return to this epistemological and methodological remark in Ch. 7.
89 CP 2.25.
90 See Bellucci/Pietarinen 2020; Bellucci 2018. Bellucci and Pietarinen speak about "*ur*-abduction." But I prefer the more straightforward term "meta-abduction," originally used by Eco 1983. I return to this issue in the following chapter.
91 See fn. 88.

able reasonings [i.e., abductions and inductions], [...] such arguments [i.e., historical arguments], if critically examined, must be admitted to have great weight."[92] This argument revives an insight as old as the 1877–78 essays on pragmatism: "How to give birth to those vital and procreative ideas which multiply into a thousand forms and diffuse themselves everywhere [...] is an art not yet reduced to rules, *but of the secret of which the history of science affords some hints.*"[93]

A second example of history's relevance to logical and philosophical questions in the "Minute Logic" is Peirce's critical discussion of the "criterion of inconceivability." We have already encountered this point while examining critical common-sensism. We are constantly tempted to reject a philosophical idea because it is inconceivable. Yet, Peirce observes that what seems evidently inconceivable today may appear in a completely different light in the future, and vice versa. "As J. S. Mill puts it, the history of science teems with inconceivabilities which have been conquered."[94] (Compare an earlier formulation: "The history of science affords illustrations enough of the folly of saying that this, that, or the other can never be found out."[95]) The same point can be made against those critics of Hegel who quickly dismiss his historicist conception of thought:

> There are minds who will pooh-pooh an idea of this sort, much as they would pooh-pooh a theory involving fairies. [...] I wish I had the leisure to place before those gentlemen a work to be entitled The History of Pooh-pooh-ing. I think it would do them good; and make room in their minds for an essay upon the Logic of Pooh-pooh-ing.[96]

Finally, a third example of history's relevance to logic might be taken from a text Peirce wrote a few years after the "Minute Logic." In the 1908 manuscript entitled "Amazing Mazes," Peirce observes that the history of science may provide an

---

92 There is, however, an additional difficulty. In other texts, Peirce seems determined to defend the idea that the rationales of abduction and induction are purely deductive. See, e.g., CP 5.146 (1903): "While Abductive and Inductive reasoning are utterly irreducible, [...] yet the only rationale of these methods is essentially Deductive or Necessary. If then we can state wherein the validity of Deductive reasoning lies, we shall have defined the foundation of logical goodness of whatever kind." This is perhaps the reason why, in CP 2.74, Peirce talks about the history of science as a "source of secondary evidence."
93 W3, p. 276. My emphasis.
94 CP 2.29. Cf. CP 2.49. A favorite example of Peirce's is Lobachevsky's refutation of Euclid's axioms: see CP 8.91 (1892).
95 W6, p. 64 (1887). Cf. also CP 1.404; 5.215; 8.45.
96 CP 2.111. The two titles of Peirce's imaginary works, "History of Pooh-pooh-ing" and "Logic of Pooh-pooh-ing," might be loosely inspired by Whewell's *History of the Inductive Sciences* (Whewell 1837) and *Philosophy of the Inductive Sciences* (Whewell 1840).

empirical survey of inferential reasoning, on the basis of which the logic of science can build its classifications.

> I wish a historical study were made of all the remarkable theoric steps and noticeable classes of theoric steps. I do not mean a mere narrative, but a critical examination of just what and of what mode the logical efficacy of the different steps has been. Then, upon this work as a foundation, should be erected a logical classification of theoric steps; and this should be crowned with a new methodeutic of necessary reasoning. My future years [...] shall, I hope, somehow contribute toward setting such an enterprise on foot.[97]

All this does not mean that Peirce was willing to overcome completely his reservations about logicians' appeal to history. The "Minute Logic" itself is adamant in this respect. "Considering how very, very little science we have attained, and how infantile the history of science still is, it amazes me that anybody should propose to base a theory of knowledge upon the history of science alone."[98] But it does mean that history is one essential component of the logician's toolkit – a tool among many, which can be used in a plurality of ways. As we know, a comprehensive assessment of history's bearing on logic and philosophy ought to take into account not only this plurality of uses, but also Peirce's explicit rationales for a history of science (see Chapter 2) and his concrete historical inquiries (see Chapter 6).

An Exchange with Dewey

I will close the chapter by looking at a particularly significant document of Peirce's complex stance toward history, namely the exchange he had with his ex-student, John Dewey, after the publication of the latter's *Studies in Logical Theory* (1903).

In that book, Dewey made extensive use of the idea that logic should be a "natural history" of thought. Any clear-cut distinction between "origin" and "nature," "genesis" and "analysis," "history" and "validity," according to Dewey, reflects a state of thought that does not pay enough heed to the actual import of

---

97 CP 4.615 (1908).
98 CP 2.150 (1902). This remark is made in the context of a critical discussion of those theories of scientific progress that, unlike Peirce's agapastic model, claim that science evolves "by complete cataclysm[s]" which "sweep away old theories and replace them by new ones." For a further discussion of this point, see Chs. 5 and 6.

evolutionism.⁹⁹ Peirce reacted with a review, in which the tone of respect for the newly-founded "Chicago school" of pragmatism does not conceal sharp criticism.¹⁰⁰ Dewey's argument, Peirce argues, obscures the fact that logic is necessarily "more than a mere natural history," precisely because it is normative ("inasmuch as it would pronounce one proceeding of thought to be sound and valid and another to be otherwise.")¹⁰¹

In a contemporaneous and rather stern letter to Dewey, Peirce further articulated his misgivings.¹⁰² Logic cannot be reduced to natural history, he maintained. First, because it does not deal with actualities; and second, because its object is "Moral, or Self-controlled, thought."¹⁰³ He then took up his criticism of those arguments that make logic depend on disciplines like "Metaphysical Philosophy, Psychology, Linguistics [...] History." These arguments, Peirce claimed, are fallaciously circular – or better, "would be circular if they rose to the degree of correctness necessary to that kind of fallacy."¹⁰⁴

Peirce did not deny that a genetic method in logic might be profitable (to characterize Dewey's methodology, he used the phrase "anatomy of thought," which, as we know from Chapter 2, he had used earlier to describe his own work).¹⁰⁵ What he denied, however, was the idea that the normative aspect of logic may derive from genetic considerations. The normative character of logic cannot come from the observation of historical regularities, but must spring from the phenomenon of self-control. As is easy to see, this argument brings us back to Peirce's strategy against psychologism. For all his esteem for the history of science, this was the point on which Peirce was not willing to negotiate.

But what also contributed substantially in triggering Peirce's polemic was, I believe, Dewey's appropriation of a concept that was extremely important for Peirce: namely, the concept of "natural history." Let us recall what we already know about this concept. Peirce had been educated in natural history and natural classification under Louis Agassiz. Throughout his life, he retained a very high esteem for Agassiz's teaching, while feeling dissatisfied over the latter's dis-

---

99 Dewey 1903, Ch. 1 and 2.
100 CP 8.188–190 (1904).
101 CP 8.190.
102 CP 8.239–242 (1904).
103 CP 8.240.
104 CP 8.242.
105 CP 8.239. See also CP 8.244: "What you had a right to say was that for certain logical problems the entire development of cognition and along with it that of its object become pertinent, and therefore should be taken into account. What you do say is that no inquiry for which this development is not pertinent should be permitted."

missal of Darwinism (see Chapter 1). So, the concept of natural history was perfectly positioned to become the main theatre of a tension between a more ahistorical naturalistic methodology and a thoroughly historical, evolutionary one. This can, in part, explain why Peirce talked about "natural classification" as a sort of intermediate stage between a historical and a conceptual investigation of reality. As we know from Chapters 2 and 3, the "genealogy" through which we identify natural classes is historical but looks to final, rather than to efficient, causes.

However, the exchange with Dewey brings to the fore a slightly different nuance. Natural history, Peirce argues, is unable to penetrate the "essence" of logic because that essence is of a normative kind. This point may seem to introduce a tension with what I have said in Chapter 3. For in that case, the "essence" of signs, and of natural classes, was tethered to their final causes, hence to a genealogical method of inquiry. We can somewhat appease this tension by keeping the essence of teleological phenomena such as natural classes separate from the essence of the normative, demonstrative kernel of logic.

The further we go toward the end of Peirce's career, the more we find evidence of his thinking drifting toward an emphasis on an essentialist conception of logic as against natural history. In a 1906 manuscript on phenomenology, for instance, we find once again a denunciation of psychologism and of those scholars "who know no other logic than a 'Natural History' of thought."[106] The best way to represent essences "free from psychological or other accidents" is the observational method of graphical logic. As opposed to that, a natural history is a merely "descriptive science," which classifies objects while

> still remain[ing] ignorant of their essences and of the ultimate agencies of their production [...]. Thus a logic which is a natural history merely, has done no more than observe that certain conditions have been found attached to sound thought, but has no means of ascertaining whether the attachment be accidental or essential; and quite ignoring the circumstance that the very essence of thought lies open to our study[.][107]

The opposition between the methods of graphical logic and the "observations" performed by natural history brings us back to my suggestion that we distinguish between different kinds of observation. As we learn from a very late manuscript, one kind of observation is the one that characterizes mathematics and diagram-

---

106 CP 4.8 (1906).
107 CP 4.8.

matic logic; another is that of natural history.[108] In order to spell out the differences between these two approaches, Peirce quotes the teacher of his youth, Louis Agassiz. But somewhat to our surprise, Agassiz is not, here, a champion of natural history. Rather, he epitomizes the attempt to study nature from an overly a priori standpoint. In his *Essay on Classification*, Peirce argues, Agassiz described "relatively well [...] what a classification of animals ought to be." But "subsequent zoölogists" found out that "when he came to adjusting his idea to the facts of the animal kingdom, it did not seem to be a good fit." This is so because Agassiz tried to grasp directly "the ideas of the Creator," instead of classifying them "according to the course of evolution." The latter method is more adherent to science, because it ascertains "precisely the genealogy of species. Now genealogy is not at all the same thing as logical division."[109]

---

108 See CP 1.570 (1910): "[T]here is a world-wide difference between the divisions that one recognizes in classes whose essence one can comprehend, and the varieties that one observes from the outside, as one does those of objects of natural history, without being able to guess why they should be such as they seem to be[.]"
109 CP 1.571–572.

5 Sociality, Dialogue, Disagreement

The Problem of Peirce's Social Thought

In the last two chapters, we explored two main aspects of philosophy's relation to history. Chapter 3 was devoted to the issue of "historicity," that is, the question whether, and to what extent, considerations about the past are relevant to the understanding of the present. I showed that Peirce's semiotic and metaphysical processualism has the consequence of making diachronic considerations relevant across a wide spectrum of philosophical and scientific problems, although in degrees and modalities that must be specified case by case. Then, in Chapter 4, we broached a second aspect. The main question there was not the relation between past and present, but the role of experience, learning and tradition for philosophical understanding. Peirce, I argued, was at pains to defend the autonomy of philosophy without making the observation of historical and empirical reality irrelevant.

The present chapter closes the central part of the book by tackling the problem of sociality. In doing so, it seeks to develop the two themes just mentioned along new lines. For one thing, the social nature of thought and action provides us with yet another perspective from which we can appreciate their historicity. For another, the problem of autonomy is enriched by taking into account the social and dialogic nature of philosophical understanding. Are philosophers allowed to articulate their ideas privately? As I will maintain, Peirce's answer is negative: philosophical and scientific *Selbstdenken* should go hand in hand with the effort to take seriously the informed and reasonable opinions of others.

As soon as it is mentioned, however, this new aspect of our discussion gives rise to a difficulty. When compared with the painstaking depth of his logical, semiotic or epistemological inquiries, Peirce's treatment of the social dimension of human life may appear meagre. Although his definition of signs as social and public entities plays a crucial role in pragmatist rejections of solipsism, Peirce did not concern himself with the concrete details of social interaction or with the historical or sociological factors that shape it. And even when he made forays into social or political considerations, his remarks remained fragmentary and unsystematic, thus betraying a certain reluctance to tackle the field of social philosophy with full argumentative force. The same reluctance is visible in the later period of his career, when Peirce explicitly advocated a separation between "theoretical" and "practical" matters, according to which the latter should be left to the "conservatism" of instincts and common sense, and ought not to be affected by theoretical investigations. The predictable outcome of this attitude is that even the most promising among Peirce's remarks about the social world are left in an inchoate state. What is more, his plea for conservatism in the field of practice is not exempt from reactionary traits, even if it is at times oriented to social criticism and to a Christian-inspired defense of solidarity – most notably in his scathing depiction of free-market ideology as a "Gospel of Greed."[1]

In the present chapter, I will deal with these difficulties as follows. First, I will briefly consider the development of Peirce's insight about the role of sociality and dialogue in logical, metaphysical, and epistemological issues. This idea is bound up with his conviction that thought can only take place in a dialogic form. The immediate implication for the problem of autonomy is that we are compelled to take the opinions of other competent people seriously when articulating our ideas. "No mind can take one step without the aid of other minds."[2]

After that, I will suggest that the best place to look for Peirce's social philosophy is not so much in his fragmentary social criticism or his remarks about politics, but rather in his analysis of the only social institution he studied at length: science. Peirce advocates a community-oriented understanding of scientific inquiry: a view of science as a community of scientists, as a social institution. The same applies to philosophy, which, as we already know, is part and parcel of science, although it displays some specificities that will have to be taken into account as well.

The conception of institution that reverberates in Peirce's epistemology has strong ties to the processualist and historicist ideas I investigated in Chapter 3. All social institutions are historical entities. This means, first, that their workings can only be understood as a historical development or growth: "Every institution should be a growth, because the adjustment of means to ends is beyond human calculation beforehand."[3] Second, the members of an institution should cultivate historical awareness in order to appreciate their own activity. As the young Peirce already claimed, history is "the only sound basis for any human institution – philosophy, natural science, government, church, or system of education."[4]

In closing the chapter, I will examine Peirce's remarks about conservatism and the separation between theory and practice. Notwithstanding the philosophical and political perplexities they raise, I will try to make sense of them as a

---

[1] W8, p. 189 (1892). See below.
[2] "The Ethics of Terminology," EP2, p. 263 (1903). I return to this text at the end of this chapter.
[3] R 1329 (undated), a draft of a letter to Francis Lathrop on issues regarding higher education. The passage continues: "Its first beginnings should have vitality and nothing to check its inherent power of growth; and this is more true of a university than of anything else."
[4] W2, p. 336 (1869). See Ch. 1.

contribution to a non-intellectualist understanding of human affairs. The relevance of history and tradition will come into view once again.

The Guiding Thread of Dialogue

The idea that thought and semiotic phenomena are irreducibly dialogic is one of the most characteristic motifs of Peirce's philosophy. We can already detect it in the early fragments examined in Chapter 1, which make use of the three English personal pronouns – I, IT and THOU – to refer to the metaphysical categories. The concept of THOU, which prefigures in many ways the later category of Thirdness, indicates the peculiar status of a second-person perspective, as something irreducible to the distinction between subject (I) and object (IT).

These fragments are also interesting from a methodological standpoint. We may recall from Chapter 1 that the young Peirce, steeped in the writings of Kant, put forth a definition of metaphysics as the "analysis" of our most fundamental conceptions. Peirce's writings on pronouns are related to that definition, because pronouns are among the most fundamental elements of language, both as a grammatical category and as a reverberation of the typical communicative situation between an utterer and an interlocutor. In this sense, Peirce's early work might be compared to that of another prominent post-Kantian thinker, namely Wilhelm von Humboldt. In his writings on language, Humboldt looked at personal pronouns as a universal element of language and one with significant theoretical implications, as it transformed the classical philosophical opposition between *Ich* and *Nicht-Ich* into a triadic distinction between I, Thou, and 'He' (*Ich, Du, Er*).[5] This focus on the second person was, moreover, accompanied by an emphasis on the pragmatic relation between speaker and interlocutor – between 'me' and 'you' – as a necessary condition of both language and thought.

During the 1860s, Peirce gradually abandoned the use of the pronouns as the name for his metaphysical categories. In its place, a more orthodox Kantian perspective was adopted: one in which the guiding thread for the deduction of the categories was no longer supplied by language, but by logic. As we saw in

---

5 See, in particular, Humboldt [1827] 1997 and Humboldt [1829] 1997. Peirce may have never read Humboldt, but there are many indirect links between the two figures. I have explored at greater length the connection between Peirce and Humboldt in Viola 2011. See Topa 2007, p. 152–156 for a comprehensive discussion of Peirce's sources. On the linguistic tradition initiated by Humboldt, see Trabant 2000. Among twentieth-century linguists, Roman Jakobson is probably the one who brought this tradition the closest to Peirce's semiotics. See, in particular, Jakobson [1961] 1971. See also Trabant forthcoming for Humboldt's treatment of dialogue.

Chapter 4, moreover, logic should be independent from the categories of language and grammar, and this applies to pronouns as well, notwithstanding their virtually universal character.[6] This, however, does not mean that the focus on dialogue and the second person was abandoned. In his anti-Cartesian essays, Peirce took up the classical Platonic thesis that thought is but an internalized form of dialogue, a "silent speech of the soul with itself."[7] He conceived this thesis as a corollary to his major claim, namely, that thought has a semiotic and inferential structure all the way down. There is no place for intuitive cognitions or for an intuitive power of self-consciousness. Rather, self-consciousness has social roots: we become self-conscious beings during our infancy, by reflecting on the painful clash between our experience and the testimony of other people.[8]

This argument has momentous epistemological implications. Using the highly polemical terms of a struggle between science and traditional philosophy, Peirce pointed out that scientists, unlike metaphysicians, do not hold individual certainty in high esteem. A scientific theory is first advanced as a hypothesis and is considered "on probation" until the whole community of scientists has accepted it. "[I]f disciplined and candid minds carefully examined a theory and refuse to accept it, this ought to create doubts in the mind of the author of the theory himself."[9] In this sense, disagreement acts as a prod for scientists to pursue their inquiries. However, this appreciation of disagreement as a source of inquiry runs in parallel with a robust emphasis on agreement and convergence as the paramount ideal of rationality. Peirce's early view of science is explicitly premised on a conception of reality as the plane of convergence of several individual perspectives.

> The real [...] is that which, sooner or later, information and reasoning would finally result in, and which is therefore independent of the vagaries of me and you. Thus, the very origin

---

[6] Peirce's interpretation of Aristotle's categories is revelatory of this transition from language to logic. On the one hand, Peirce thought that Aristotle was a precursor of the Kantian methodology of deducing metaphysics from logic (see W1, p. 302, 1865). On the other hand, he followed the German philosopher F. A. Trendelenburg in considering the Aristotelian categories to be heavily influenced by the Greek language. See, for instance, R 584 (1864), "[t]he opinion of Trendelenburg satisfies me"; HP, p. 864 (1894), "Trendelenburg in my opinion is the best." For Peirce's interpretation of Aristotle, see Oehler 1984-85. As for the supposedly universal nature of personal pronouns, cf. a very late remark, EP2, p. 484 (1908), where Peirce seems first to uphold this idea, then to discard it.
[7] W2, p. 172 (1868).
[8] See W2, p. 167–169; 201–203.
[9] W2, p. 212.

of the conception of reality shows that this conception essentially involves the notion of a COMMUNITY, without definite limits, and capable of an indefinite increase of knowledge.[10]

As we will see later, the pragmatist essays from 1877 to 1878 hinge on the same tension between an appreciation of disagreement and an emphasis on convergence. But they also display the continuing influence of Peirce's early insight about the dialogic nature of thought throughout the mid-phase of his career. In "The Doctrine of Chances" (1878), Peirce went as far as to assert that "[l]ogic is rooted in the social principle."[11] About a decade later, in one of the definitions he wrote for the *Century Dictionary*, he returned once again to the pronouns and coined the word *tuism*, meaning "[t]he doctrine that all thought is addressed to a second person, or to one's future self as a second person."[12] I believe we may take this definition as a sort of self-description. Peirce's attempt to articulate a "tuistic" position in logic and philosophy is one of the deepest and most enduring elements of his work.

In this respect, Peirce's late semiotic writings bear a number of similarities to his earliest philosophical reflections: "it is not merely a fact of human Psychology," he wrote, for instance, in 1906, "but a necessity of Logic, that every logical evolution of thought should be dialogic."[13] Or again:

> Thinking always proceeds in the form of a dialogue – a dialogue between different phases of the ego – so that, being dialogical, it is essentially composed of signs, as its matter [...]. Not that the particular signs employed are themselves the thought! Oh, no: no whit more than the skins of an onion are the onion. (About as much so, however). One selfsame thought may be carried upon the vehicle of English, German, Greek, or Gaelic; in diagrams, or in equations, or in graphs; all these are but so many skins of the onion. Its inessential accidents. Yet that the thought should have some possible expression for some possible interpreter, is the very being of its being.[14]

The metaphor of the onion (already encountered in Chapter 3) is here deployed to steer a middle course between a loosely Humboldtian belief in the influence of language upon thought and an insistence on the transcendence of logical forms. Logical or semiotic analysis, Peirce maintained, may help us strip off our con-

---

10 W2, p. 239. Cf. 6.610 (1893), where Peirce talks about his "social theory of reality, namely, that the real is the idea in which the community ultimately settles down."
11 W3, p. 284 (1878). On this basis, Apel [1967–1970] 1981, p. 86–99 has spoken of a "logical socialism" in the young Peirce.
12 CD, p. 6525. See Fisch 1982, p. xxix.
13 "Prolegomena to an Apology for Pragmaticism," CP 4.551 (1903).
14 CP 4.6 (1906).

ceptions of the vagaries of language; but it will not bring us anywhere *beyond* the sphere of signs. In this sense, "it is indifferent whether [logic] be regarded as having to do with thought or with language, the wrapping of thought, since thought, like an onion, is composed of nothing but wrappings."[15] Moreover, these wrappings, qua semiotic, are essentially structured in a dialogic form.

So, at the end of his career, Peirce articulated his "tuistic" insight in robust logical and semiotic terms. The dialogic nature of thought is not simply the consequence of the pragmatic conditions of linguistic communication, but it is rooted in the very condition of possibility of thought, regardless of its linguistic expression. In this perspective, it might be worth returning to a semiotic concept that we considered in Chapter 3, namely the concept of vagueness, because this concept, too, is tightly bound up with the dialogical nature of semiotic processes. "No communication of one person to another can be entirely definite, that is, non-vague. [...]. Much [...] must be vague, because no man's interpretation of words is based on exactly the same experience as any other man's."[16] This is one of the points where Peirce's philosophy takes on a most explicit hermeneutic tinge: processes of communication take the form of a dialogue between interlocutors who do not share exactly the same universe of experience.

Peirce never tired of stressing the idea that dialogue had a crucial importance in the way he did philosophy. A few month prior to his death, he wrote: "I address the Reader [...] in the second person, because I think of him as a real person, with all the instincts of which we human beings are so sublimely and so responsibly endowed."[17] It may seem a tragic irony that the dire circumstances of Peirce's life did not allow him to fully enjoy precisely this cultivation of dialogue. ("My having no second person to whom to appeal as to the reasonableness of my doubts prevents their being laid to rest."[18]) Nonetheless, Peirce kept steadily faithful to the idea that a necessary condition of rationality is its being able to take on a dialogic form; its being able to address a "thou."

This brings to completion one of the arguments I outlined in the preceding chapter: Peirce operated a decided rebuttal of epistemological solipsism, with crucial implications for the way philosophy and science should be understood.

---

[15] EP2, p. 460 (1911). On the relation between language and thought (with a reference to linguists Steinthal and Sayce), see CP 2.69 (1902).
[16] CP 5.506 (c. 1905). The passage continues: "It should never be forgotten that our thinking is carried on as a dialogue, and though mostly in a lesser degree, is subject to almost every imperfection of language." On vagueness, communication and dialogue, cf. Bergman 2009, p. 145–158.
[17] EP2, p. 463–464 (1913).
[18] EP2, 462 (c. 1911).

As he said in his review of Royce's *The World and the Individual*, philosophy is concerned with everyday experience, therefore it has to "set out from ideas familiar and complex [...] [it has to] begin with men and their conversation."[19] But even more importantly, "conversation with all sorts of people whom we do not altogether understand freshens the mind."[20] This conversation, moreover, includes people from the past, with whom we can hold a dialogue through "extensive reading" of their written works.[21] The history of science and philosophy is part and parcel of scientific rationality.[22]

Science: A Community in History

The social epistemology to which I briefly referred when discussing the anti-Cartesian papers from 1868 to 1869 has a number of notable implications for the problem of the historical nature of scientific inquiry. Not accidentally, Peirce started elaborating more explicitly on these questions from the early 1890s; that is, at the beginning of his most productive period as a historian of science. Let me quote a passage that is especially significant in this respect. Starting from the problem of how to define science, this passage ends up raising the crucial question of the relation between scientific progress and history.

> What is science? [...] Mere knowledge, though it be systematized, may be a dead memory; while by science we all habitually mean a living and growing body of truth. We might even say that knowledge is not necessary to science. The astronomical researches of Ptolemy, though they are in great measure false, must be acknowledged by every modern mathematician who reads them to be truly and genuinely scientific. That which constitutes science,

---

19 CP 8.112 (1900).
20 RLT, p. 192.
21 RLT, p. 192. Peirce also says that "[r]eal reading consists in putting oneself into the author's position, and assimilating his ways of thinking."
22 Cf. Houser 1998, p. xviii: "[N]o one can think in a vacuum – thought must necessarily relate to past thought, just as it must appeal to subsequent thought [...]. To Peirce this was obvious. Given his upbringing among mathematicians and experimental scientists he learned early that intellectual progress is always relative to knowledge already gained and that any successful science must be a cooperative endeavor. One of the reasons Peirce is so important for the history of ideas is that he approached philosophy in this way, knowing that if philosophy was ever really to amount to anything it would have to abandon the notion that great ideas arise ex nihilo – that one's ideas are wholly one's own. As a result of this understanding, and of his desire to help move philosophy toward a more mature stage of development, Peirce became a diligent student of the history of ideas and sought to connect his thought with the intellectual currents of the past."

then, is not so much correct conclusions, as it is a correct method. But the method of science is itself a scientific result. It did not spring out of the brain of a beginner: it was a historic attainment and a scientific achievement. So that not even this method ought to be regarded as essential to the beginnings of science. That which is essential, however, is the scientific spirit, which is determined not to rest satisfied with existing opinions, but to press on to the real truth of nature.[23]

The question with which this passage opens, "What is science?," is here answered in three consecutive steps. In a first step, Peirce rules out the possibility that the essence of science might be identified with a specific body of doctrines. For this would run counter to one of the most obvious results of both his fallibilist epistemology and his historical inquiries: namely, that all scientific theories are sooner or later destined to be substituted by better ones. So, in a second step, Peirce considers the possibility that science might consist not so much in a body of doctrines as in a specific method. But this idea, too, proves simplistic when put to the test of the history of science. For the scientific method is as much a product of history as the body of scientific doctrines. (Recall Peirce's reflections on the historical evolution of *logica utens*, as touched upon in Chapter 4.) Therefore, Peirce's third step is to try and solve the problem by pointing to yet another, more fundamental ingredient of science, which he calls the scientific "spirit." This alone, he claims, is "essential" to science. Elsewhere, Peirce similarly insists on the "necessity to consider science as living, and therefore not as knowledge already acquired but as the concrete life of the men who are working to find out the truth."[24]

We can interpret this argument as Peirce's attempt to reconcile two conflicting urgencies. On the one hand, the fallibilist, historically informed philosophy of science that he developed throughout his life gave him good reasons to reject the idea that there is something like an ahistorical essence of science, one detectable in all times and places. But on the other hand, Peirce wished to avoid the skeptical implications of this conclusion. He wished to stick to the idea that science has a number of essential features on which its validity is grounded, and that these features are the common trait that unite the scientific inquiries of the past with those of the present and the future.

His solution, however, would seem at first glance to raise more questions than it settles. It is not immediately clear how Peirce might characterize more precisely this scientific "spirit," so as to show that the inclination "not to rest sat-

---

23 CP 6.428 (1893).
24 CP 7.50. Cf. the Putnam History, HP, p. 307 (1898), where Peirce defends a definition of science as a "mode of life" against the outsider's definition of science as an "organized body of knowledge."

isfied with existing opinions" can really be considered a universal trait of scientific inquiries throughout the ages. Secondly, talking about a scientific spirit seems to make science depend on individual qualities or virtues; and it is not clear how this might be compatible with the social epistemology laid out in Peirce's early essays. Thirdly, and for us more importantly, it is not clear how we might reconcile two different conceptions of history that seem to derive from what Peirce says. On the one hand, scientific methods are a "historic attainment," and this suggests that historical contextualization is essential to the assessment of scientific theories. On the other hand, scientific doctrines of the past risk being relegated to "dead memory," as Peirce also says in the passage just quoted. From this viewpoint, the history of science becomes a cemetery of useless doctrines, no longer inhabited by their spirit.

To see whether Peirce was able to deal successfully with these challenges, let us begin by considering how he spelt out the most characteristic features of the scientific spirit. As I have suggested, Peirce insisted on the role of scientists' virtues or individual qualities. The most important among them is the disinterested passion to learn. "Our boundary line" – we read for instance in the Putnam History – "is run between the pursuit of knowledge for the sake of that knowledge alone, and the pursuit of knowledge for some ulterior motive."[25] Indeed, the ability to carry out inquiry in a fully disinterested manner is the trait of a specific "class of men."

> If we endeavor to form our conceptions upon history and life, we remark three classes of men. The first consists of those for whom the chief thing is the qualities of feelings. These men create art. The second consists of the practical men, who carry on the business of the world. They respect nothing but power, and respect power only so far as it [is] exercized. The third class consists of men to whom nothing seems great but reason. If force interests them, it is not in its exertion, but in that it has a reason and a law. For men of the first class, nature is a picture; for men of the second class, it is an opportunity; for men of the third class, it is a cosmos, so admirable, that to penetrate to its ways seems to them the only thing that makes life worth living. These are the men whom we see possessed by a passion to learn, just as other men have a passion to teach and to disseminate their influence.[26]

It is, of course, quite legitimate to see in this tripartition of human types a reflex of Peirce's ubiquitous categorial scheme. Artists follow a Firstness-driven mode of life (they attend to "qualities of feeling"); practical people deal with actualities

---

[25] HP, p. 307 (1898). See also HP, p. 477 (1896): "The history of the troubles of scientific men in their collisions with outsiders is no part of the life of science, and hardly touches it." On the concept of "outsiders" see below, fn. 29.
[26] CP 1.43 (1898).

or Secondness; scientists devote their life to rationality or Thirdness. We will have to wait until the next chapter to see in a bit more detail how this idea can be reconciled with the data of the history of science, which show all too often how scientific truths are the result of quite mundane and practical activities. For now, let us just note that Peirce seems to give no *prima facie* cogent reason why the disinterested passion to learn and to admire the workings of nature might be either a sufficient or a necessary condition for science, as a historical and social phenomenon, to exist.

A different and more promising approach to the notion of a scientific "spirit" can be found in Peirce's emphasis on precisely the topic of intersubjectivity and dialogue that I have considered in the previous section. In that case, the "essence" of thought was found in nothing but its semiotic and dialogic structure. In the same vein, Peirce equated the essence of science with its being not only the disinterested pursuit of truth, but a pursuit that can only be achieved through dialogue and collaboration. Science is, in other words, "*essentially* a mode of life that seeks coöperation."[27] This has the immediate consequence of making it necessary to have a certain relation with the past, which Peirce described in terms of a progressive and cumulative dynamic. "[I]n storming the stronghold of truth one mounts upon the shoulders of another who has to ordinary apprehension failed, but has in truth succeeded by virtue of the lessons of his failure. *This is the veritable essence of science.*"[28]

This also goes some way toward solving the tension between a community-oriented and an individualist conception of science, that is, between science as a community of inquiry and the scientific spirit as an individual quality. The individual quality or virtue that is essential to science is the very quality of seeking cooperation and dialogue; thus, to recognize that one's work is not the work of the individual alone but of a community. Indeed, no single person alone can ever produce science:

> I do not call the solitary studies of a single man a science. It is only when a group of men, more or less in intercommunication, are aiding and stimulating one another by their understanding of a particular group of studies as outsiders cannot understand them, that I call their life a science.[29]

---

27 CP 7.55. My emphasis.
28 CP 7.51. My emphasis. For yet another take on the concept scientific spirit, see Peirce's text on Peregrinus, HP, p. 59 (1893), to which I return in Ch. 6. There, the crucial hallmark of science is the ability to perform "experiments [...] with apparatus devised for the purpose."
29 R 1334 (1905), quoted in Ketner 2009, p. 37. Peirce's reference to "outsiders" (see also fn. 25) points to a problem Peirce does not seem to have reflected much upon, namely the sociological implications of drawing a boundary between insiders and outsiders. The community of science

Looked at from this perspective, the idea of a scientific spirit no longer looks sharply opposed to Peirce's social epistemology. Also, it entails a closer relation to history. If we understand the scientific spirit in terms of intersubjective cooperation, its history-transcending "essence" boils down to the minimal procedural criteria that we need to grant in order for communication to be in place. Moreover, working scientists need to stand on the shoulders of past scientists if they desire to make headway.[30] So they need to appreciate that their work is the product of a history.

In this sense, the idea of a scientific spirit allows Peirce to confer on science precisely the kind of historicity that I have explored in Chapter 3. Science is a "*living* historic entity."[31] (Recall my discussion of the concept of life in that chapter). It is endowed with a certain historicity; but a historicity that does not necessarily rule out the permanence of a transcendent element – the soul of the scientific body, as it were.

Finally, let me point out yet another issue that is involved in the passage quoted at the beginning of this section. Peirce says there that "[t]he astronomical researches of Ptolemy, though they are in great measure false, must be acknowledged by every modern mathematician who reads them to be truly and genuinely scientific." This passage is consistent with Peirce's agapastic model of scientific change (see Chapter 3): ideas grow by gradual approximation to an idea that was already divined – however imprecisely – at the beginning of the process of inquiry. Therefore, all truly scientific theories of the past, including those that now appear to be false, can be read as first approximations of truth. As Peirce explains with reference to the astronomical model of Hipparchus:

> Since this hypothesis was an inevitable and ineluctable step toward the truth, it was in fact true, although its truth was destined to be swallowed up in the completer truths first of

---

that Peirce envisaged can be interpreted as a "republic of letters." It is not the scientifically informed community, or the enlightened public opinion, that other pragmatist philosophers, such as John Dewey, were at pains to describe. Also for this reason, the problem of education, which plays such a paramount role in Dewey, remains very much in the background of Peirce's epistemology.

30 See, e.g., CP 1.7: "[I]n brief, my philosophy may be described as the attempt of a physicist to make such conjecture as to the constitution of the universe as the methods of science may permit, with the aid of all that has been done by previous philosophers."

31 CP 1.44 (1898). My emphasis. In the same passage, we find yet another rendition of Peirce's polemical contraposition of science and philosophy: "Science and philosophy seem to have been changed in their cradles. For it is not knowing, but the love of learning, that characterizes the scientific man; while the 'philosopher' is a man with a system which he thinks embodies all that is best worth knowing."

Ptolemy's bisected equant, and then of the hypothesis of Coppernicus [sic], and then of Kepler's ellipse [...]. This is something like Hegel's *Aufheben*.[32]

In a similar way, an 1896 text for the *American Historical Review* warns that "history will not bear [...] out" the image of "the typical scientific man as a sort of nominalist, pooh-pooh-ing every proposition not plain, intelligible, definite." What history does bear out, Peirce goes on to argue, is that "a thinker can win no ground in any department if he be afraid of harboring ideas which, as they first come to him, are *vague and shadowy*."[33] A scientific theory is first born as a vague and poorly articulated idea, which is then progressively refined over time.[34]

This argument has notable consequences for a traditional question of the history and philosophy of science, namely whether scientific change takes place more by means of revolutionary changes or by means of a gradual evolution. As we shall better see in Chapter 6, Peirce was on the lookout for a balance between these two ideas. His agapastic model clearly pushed him toward a continuistic and evolutionary understanding of scientific change, but he also wished to take into account the role of intellectual revolutions. In the "Minute Logic," we find a significant statement in this respect. Peirce criticizes the cataclysmic theory of evolution; that is, the opinion in "vogue among men of science,"

> that we cannot expect any physical hypothesis to maintain its ground indefinitely even with modifications, but must expect that from time to time there will be a complete cataclysm that shall utterly sweep away old theories and replace them by new ones.
>
> As far as I know, this notion has no other basis than the history of science. Considering how very, very little science we have attained, and how infantile the history of science still is, it amazes me that anybody should propose to base a theory of knowledge upon the history of science alone. [...] The only really scientific theory that can be called old is the Ptolemaic system; and that has only been improved in details, not revolutionized. The most unhappy of physical theories has been that of Phlogiston; and even that was not altogether false, since something *is* lost from a burnt body; namely, energy.[35]

---

32 HP, p. 354–355 (1898).
33 HP, p. 478 (1896). My emphasis. This is a less technical use of the word "vague" than the one I have explored in Ch. 3. However, there is a slight resemblance between the two senses. In both cases, Peirce is giving a strong heuristic value to vagueness and he is recognizing its role in the growth of scientific ideas.
34 See EP2, p. 263 (1903), where Peirce refers to the "increasing value of precision of thought as it advances." An idea should be vague and shadowy when it is born, but the more thought advances, the more it needs to be made precise.
35 CP 2.150 (1902). See Ch. 4.

We know by now that one important use of the history of science in Peirce's oeuvre is as a basis to test the validity of ampliative reasoning and the criteria of justification of scientific knowledge. In the preceding chapter, I argued that the history of science supplies many cases of successful abductions, which in turn have the power to support inductively Peirce's hypothesis about the validity of abduction. But if considered attentively, that argument was exposed to a rather dangerous objection, one that we left unanswered. Why are we allowed to look at the scientific discoveries of the past as cases of successful abductions, if we now consider them to be wrong or obsolete? The arguments just examined provide an answer to that objection. Even if they now appear obsolete, past scientific discoveries drew their validity from two facts. First, they followed the criteria of scientificity and were therefore perfectly valid relative to the specific historical situation in which they were formulated. Second, they were steps toward a better truth. At the same time, Peirce's position also implies that the scientific truths of today will most likely be considered equally obsolete by future observers.[36] This means that we must resist the temptation to regard our own position as transcending the historical process.[37]

Philosophy: The Architectonic Principle

Can we apply Peirce's discussion of the nature of science to philosophy as well? Can we maintain that philosophy is just a special case of scientific inquiry – a dispassionate, cooperative pursuit of the truth – and therefore reproduces the same structural relation with history?

We know that Peirce conceived of philosophy as part and parcel of science. He repeatedly claimed that philosophy is doomed to remain in an "infantile condition,"[38] to be "a humbug"[39] or "balderdash,"[40] if it does not adopt a scientific

---

36 Peirce's argument may appear similar to the "pessimistic meta-induction" theorized by Larry Laudan and others. See Laudan 1981; Wray 2015. However, I would argue that Peirce avoids the skeptical implications of the pessimistic meta-induction thanks to what we may call an "optimistic meta-abduction," namely the hypothesis that we have a power to guess rightly at nature, as I described it in Ch. 4.
37 Colapietro 1998, p. 259–262, talks in this sense of a "historical proviso" to Peirce's view of science. From another pragmatistically oriented perspective on the same problem, see Joas [2011] 2013, p. 121, who talks about the "inevitable self-positioning" of the historian within the historical process.
38 RLT, p. 107 (1898): "In my opinion, the present infantile condition of philosophy, – for as long as earnest and industrious students of it are able to come to agreement upon scarce a single principle, I do not see how it can be considered as otherwise than in its infancy, – is due to the

methodology. This seems to entail that philosophy should conform to the cumulative, community-oriented, and fallibilist attitude that is proper to science. However, things are slightly more complex than that. Peirce did recognize that the question of philosophical method cannot be reduced to a mere application of what he said about science. Philosophy has some distinguishing features that set it apart from other scientific disciplines. It is a "cenoscopic" mode of inquiry, displaying an indissoluble relation to common sense, drawing on different kinds of observations, and placed on a higher level in the general scheme of the classification. Do these features affect in any significant manner the picture of scientific inquiry that I have sketched in the previous section?

To answer this question, we should go back to the Kantian idea of the "architectonic" nature of philosophy, which Peirce started discussing in the late 1880s. The title of Peirce's 1891 essay, "The Architecture of Theories," is the most explicit reference to this motif.[41] However, at least as interesting for the purposes of the present chapter is another text, in which Peirce read the Kantian idea quite literally, as suggesting a parallel between philosophy "and a piece of architecture."[42] We know that Peirce had been fascinated by the analogy between philosophy and architecture since his youth. In the text I am referring to, Peirce insisted on the anti-individualistic rationale of this analogy. Unlike a painting or a piece of sculpture, he argued, a building

> is meant for the whole people, and is erected by the exertions of an army representative of the whole people. It is the message with which an age is charged, and which it delivers to posterity. Consequently, thought characteristic of individual [...] is too little to play any but the most subordinate rôle in architecture.[43]

Understanding the "message" of a piece of architecture is thus analogous to grasping the purport of a philosophy and of its architectonic principle: that "deliberate logical faculty" whose "sole function [...] is to grind off the arbitrary and

---

fact that during this century it has chiefly been pursued by men who have not been nurtured in dissecting-rooms and other laboratories, and who consequently have not been animated by the true scientific Eros, but who have on the contrary come from theological seminaries [...]."
39 From a 1902 letter to Josiah Royce, in CP 8.117n10.
40 From a 1909 letter to William James: "philosophy is either a science or is balderdash." See Colapietro 1998, p. 34.
41 See W8, p. 84–110.
42 CP 1.176–179 (c. 1896).
43 CP 1.176. At 1.177 Peirce adds that "historical painting is one of those exceptions which go to prove the rule that in works which aim at being secular, rather than individualistic, the preliminary business of planning is particularly important and onerous."

the individualistic character of thought."⁴⁴ While Kant gave expression to this anti-individualistic strain through his idea of "cosmic philosophy," Peirce went on to remark, the words "*secular* or *public* would have approached nearer to the expression of his meaning."⁴⁵ The architectonic model can thus be read as a further elaboration of the community-oriented theory of scientific inquiry. Peirce sought to grasp the specificities of philosophical reason without giving up philosophy's general allegiance to science. This conclusion has two corollaries, which we can relate to the two main axes of our discussion about history: the theme of autonomy and the theme of historicity.

With regard to autonomy, Peirce took the architectonic model to entail that empirical inquiries do not limit themselves to filling up the general scheme laid out by philosophy. Rather, they provide the latter with its preparatory material. In this sense, there is an important difference between Peirce's and Kant's use of the concept of architectonic, despite Peirce's laudatory tone toward that "celebrated and splendid chapter of the Methodology, in the *Critic of the Pure Reason*."⁴⁶ The two thinkers agree in conceiving of philosophy as the organizing agency of our cognitions. They also agree in claiming that philosophy should advance more by "fission" than by "accretion."⁴⁷ However, in Peirce there is a stronger continuity between the mode of inquiry of philosophy and that of the other sciences. As a consequence, empirical cognitions have a larger bearing on philosophy than Kant would have maintained: they are "the conceptions out of which a philosophical theory may be built."⁴⁸

> That systems ought to be constructed architectonically has been preached since Kant, but I do not think the full import of the maxim has by any means been apprehended. What I would recommend is that every person who wishes to form an opinion concerning fundamental problems, should first of all make a complete survey of human knowledge, should take note of all the valuable ideas in each branch of science, should observe in just what respect each has been successful and where it has failed, in order that in the light of the thorough acquaintance so attained of the available materials for a philosophical theory and of the nature and strength of each, he may proceed to the study of what the problem of philosophy consists in, and of the proper way of solving it.⁴⁹

---

44 CP 1.178.
45 CP 1.176.
46 CP 1.176.
47 CP 1.177.
48 W8, p. 99. For Kant's distinction between philosophical reason and the sciences in his architectonic, see Ferrarin 2015, Ch. 1.
49 W8, p. 85. Cf. CP 5.5 (c. 1906).

To properly understand this passage, we need to recall Peirce's discussion of the classification of the sciences (Chapter 2), as well as his critique of psychologism (Chapter 4). The higher status that philosophy occupies in the classificatory ladder as compared with the empirical sciences does not entail that philosophy can do away with empirical observation. On the contrary, philosophers must embark on a study of the sciences "at least as deliberate and thorough as those that are preliminary to the building of a dwelling-house."[50] At the same time, they are on the lookout for "simple concepts applicable to every subject."[51] Philosophers may use the empirical material to support observations that have an independent logical or phenomenological basis. So, while the architectonic principle is not in contradiction with the classification of the sciences, it does qualify it, as it shows the sense in which the relation between philosophy and the empirical sciences runs in both directions.

Remember, also, that in the "autobiographical account" published in *The Monist* for 1893 (see Chapter 4),[52] Peirce pitted his architectonic method against two opposite philosophical attitudes. The first attitude, "positivism," was the tendency to avoid all "originality" by attempting to ground philosophical reflection on pure experience, or else on ideas "that have been handed down from the good old times." The second attitude, "constructionism," was the tendency to "take ideas at haphazard," without any guidance "from observation or accepted facts." As against these two opposite extremes, philosophers ought to look to experience, though only through the filter of a conceptual apparatus that is not the outcome of a mere "brain-spinning," but is structured along systematic principles.

The second implication of the architectonic principle for our argument has to do with historicity. More precisely, it has to do with the historical character of philosophy itself. Peirce remarks that the philosopher's task is to erect "a philosophical edifice that shall outlast the vicissitudes of time."[53] However, precisely on account of philosophy's relationship with the particular disciplines that both inhabit and compose it, this edifice cannot be considered eternal. At best, it can lay foundations that are so "deep and massive"[54] as to stand for centuries. But in the long term, deep renovations of the edifice will be unavoidable. The "Guess at the Riddle" makes this point clear:

---

50 W8, p. 85.
51 "A Guess at the Riddle," W6, p. 169 (1888). This is another key text in Peirce's development of the architectonic metaphor.
52 CP 6.604.
53 W6, p. 168.
54 W6, p. 168.

> The undertaking which this volume inaugurates is to make a philosophy like that of Aristotle, that is to say, to outline a theory so comprehensive that, for a long time to come, the entire world of human reason, in philosophy of every school and kind, in mathematics, in psychology, in physical science, in history, in sociology, and in whatever other department there may be, shall appear as the filling up of its details.[55]

Note that Peirce says "for a long time to come." He does not say "for eternity." The best he was hoping for while writing these lines was to have the same destiny as Aristotle. The latter supplied "solid" and "unshakable" concepts; and this explains why his system has survived for centuries, penetrating deeply into common sense. This, however, has not prevented modern scientists and philosophers from gradually realizing that "the old structure will not do for modern needs."[56]

Once again, we must be careful to distinguish the several layers of Peirce's argument. If we look at the very foundations of philosophy, namely its logical, metaphysical and phenomenological structure, the changes brought about by the mere passing of time are minimal at most. This holds true, in particular, for the categories. In fact, Peirce's insistence that other philosophers, such as Aristotle or Hegel, had come very close to discovering his three categories, may be read as a clue to his conviction that this foundational element of his system really has the stamp of eternity. But if we go up a level – or a "floor," to remain with the architectonic metaphor – Peirce is indeed suggesting that there is a point at which the cumulative results of new experiences will call for a careful restructuring of the edifice.

Disagreement and Convergence

We may interpret the architectonic model as a way of making Peirce's community-oriented conception of science more sophisticated and inclusive. This model takes into account some of the specificities of philosophy without relinquishing the continuities with scientific inquiry at large. Through this move, Peirce made his view much more plausible than it would have been if he had said that philosophy is just science. Also, the architectonic model is in line with science from

---

55 W6, p. 168–169.
56 W6, p. 168. For a slightly different perspective on the historical nature of philosophy, see CP 1.12 (c. 1897): "The development of my ideas has been the industry of thirty years. I did not know as I ever should get to publish them, their ripening seemed so slow. But the harvest time has come, and to me that harvest seems a wild one, but of course it is not I who have to pass judgment. It is not quite you, either, individual reader; it is experience and history."

the viewpoint of the relation to history. Like scientists, philosophers ought to look at the work of past authors as the "shoulders" on which they stand. They ought to accept the consequence of fallibilism, namely the idea that all our ideas are subject to revision in the course of time. And they ought to keep in mind that historical contextualization is a powerful tool to assess the scientificity of a given doctrine.

This idea goes hand in hand with Peirce's emphasis on agreement and convergence as a mainstay of rationality. "[T]he pendulum of dispute may swing long; but we must hope it will at last come to rest."[57] If a philosophical or scientific inquiry is genuinely rational, we must hope that it will ultimately yield a result upon which all competent people will be able to converge. This is not to say that disagreement and controversies do not play a pivotal role in science and philosophy. I already remarked on the productive role of disagreement in Peirce's early writings (see Chapter 1). In particular, the 1869 lecture on William Whewell points out that scientific theories develop through "controversies," the function of which is to render the mind "so much clearer as to make a vast difference in the progress of science."[58] But this appreciative understanding of controversies pairs with the conviction that disagreement must ultimately be overcome. Controversies fulfill their positive heuristic function when they instill doubt into the minds of scientists, or when they prompt them to clarify their conceptions, thereby clearing the way for the attainment of a more widely shared opinion.

A similar coexistence between the appreciation of the epistemic power of disagreement and a normative emphasis on convergence is at work in the 1877 to 1878 essays on pragmatism. It will be recalled that the whole argumentative machinery of "The Fixation of Belief" hinges on the existence of a powerful "social impulse" (see Chapter 1).[59] Precisely the fact that people disagree with my opinions compels me to call those opinions into doubt, and all pre-scientific methods of fixing beliefs turn out to be unable to deal rationally with such doubts. For instance, in the a priori method (which is the method of traditional philosophy) there is plenty of pleasant, mundane conversation going on. However, it is a conversation that merely indulges in the differences among conversants. It is, therefore, ultimately irrational.[60] Only the scientific method, thanks to its reference to an external reality which is "caused by nothing human,"[61]

---

57 CP 8.118 (1902).
58 W2, p. 341 (1869). See also p. 340: "[C]ontroversies [...] resulted in the establishment of clear conceptions." I return to Whewell's conception of scientific controversies in Ch. 7.
59 W3, p. 250 (1877).
60 See W3, p. 252.
61 W3, p. 253.

is successful in setting aside disagreement, because it forces our different opinions to eventually converge toward the best possible description of that reality. In other words, the scientific method rests on the idea that consensus in the long run is the goal of rational inquiry. "The opinion which is fated to be ultimately agreed to by all who investigate, is what we mean by the truth, and the object represented in this opinion is the real."[62]

Later in his life, Peirce relaxed his emphasis on final agreement as a regulative ideal of scientific inquiry, to accentuate instead the role of the "outward clash," that is, the brute influence that external reality exerts on our explanatory hypotheses (see Chapter 4).[63] But the main thrust of his argument did not change because of that. Indeed, in the very same text in which Peirce introduced his concept of the outward clash, the 1885 review of Josiah Royce, he reiterated his conviction that disagreement must be taken seriously precisely because we want to overcome it.

> When I meet with an opinion held by sane and instructed men, which is so radically different from my own that it seems strange and incomprehensible to me how men can believe such a thing, I for my part [...] am always tempted to examine the grounds of that opinion with a good deal of care, and am not satisfied until I have either become a convert to it or at least can fully understand and feel how it is that others hold to it.[64]

We might sum up Peirce's position by saying that disagreement has an ontological and epistemological status that is akin to the status of doubt. Both are indispensable to inquiry, but they are so precisely because they call to be replaced by a belief.[65] Two questions might be asked at this point. First: is this conception of disagreement plausible as a general depiction of our processes of inquiry? Second: is there really no qualitative difference between the role of disagreement in science and the role of disagreement in philosophy? There is no need to say that even a minimally satisfactory answer to these two questions would require another book. I will therefore confine myself to remarking that Peirce's emphasis on the importance of overcoming disagreement is of a piece with his tendency

---

62 "How to Make Our Ideas Clear," W3, p. 273 (1878).
63 However, in "The Fixation of Belief," Peirce had already prefigured the idea of the outward clash when defining reality as "something upon which our thinking has no effect" (W3, p. 253). The difference, as Gava 2014, p. 100–101 suggests, lies in Peirce's later emphasis on indexicality, which has the potential to deprive the idea of final opinion of any foundational role.
64 W5, p. 221.
65 See, e.g., EP2, p. 337 (1905): "Doubt [...] is not a habit, but the privation of a habit. Now a privation of a habit, in order to be anything at all, must be a condition of erratic activity that in some way must get superseded by a habit."

to foreground the cumulative and progressive dynamics of inquiry both in science and in philosophy. While this has the great benefit of dictating high standards of rationality for philosophical disputes, it risks losing sensitivity to the fact that the dynamics of cumulation and convergence in philosophy are not the same as in science. This has, in turn, remarkable implications for the problem of philosophy's relation to history.

A concrete example may help us better understand this point. In the Introduction, I briefly mentioned the name of Walter B. Gallie. His notion of "essentially contested concepts" was aimed precisely at grasping the kind of non-cumulative dynamics that we might be forced to recognize when looking at the history of philosophical disputes. Claiming that some philosophical concepts are essentially contested is tantamount to saying that disagreement in philosophy cannot be eliminated even when discussants abide by strict criteria of rationality. Furthermore, essentially contested concepts have a robust historical dimension. In the face of our inability to overcome disagreement by dint of purely argumentative strategies, we need to make recourse to history in order to better understand the semantic purport of the concepts we are using, or to back up what we take to be their best use.[66] In other words, the existence of essentially contested concepts – or more generally, of irreducible disagreement – forces us definitively to abandon the idea that the only relation philosophers may have with their past is to stand on its shoulders.

As we saw in the Introduction, Gallie was also a Peirce scholar.[67] Although, as a philosopher of history, he greatly admired Peirce's "historical mindedness,"[68] his work on essentially contested concepts was precisely aimed at pushing his reflections on history in a direction that Peirce was not willing to take. His book on the philosophy of history, *Philosophy and the Historical Understanding* (1964), is quite explicit in this respect. It says that an appreciation of essentially contested concepts depends on answering in the negative the question whether the possibility of "agreement in the long run" should be accepted as a necessary criterion of rationality. Therefore, "those, e.g. Peirce, who have urged us to accept an affirmative answer on this issue have entirely neglected the existence of essentially contested concepts."[69]

The issue I am discussing finds application even beyond the special case of the relation between science and philosophy. Take Peirce's attitude toward reli-

---

66 See Gallie 1956a, in particular p. 197–198; Gallie 1956b.
67 I have analyzed in more detail the relation between Peirce and Gallie in Viola 2019.
68 Gallie 1964, p. 146.
69 Gallie 1964, p. 83.

gion. Peirce often pitted scientists against "theologians": the first animated by their passion for learning, the second by their zeal for teaching; the first fallibilist, the second dogmatic; the first educated in laboratories, the second in seminaries.[70] At the same time, he was a profoundly religious man (see Chapter 1). Quite similarly to what he did for philosophy, he attempted to take seriously the specificity of religion while insisting on the importance of science as a paradigmatic model of rationality. He was therefore interested in articulating a conception of Christianity more in line with his own community-oriented and fallibilist ideal of scientific inquiry. "[R]eligion cannot reside in its totality in a single individual. Like every species of reality, it is essentially a social, a public affair. It is the idea of a whole church [...] an idea having a growth from generation to generation."[71] To reach this ideal, "religious thought should abandon that extravagant absoluteness of assertion which is proper to the state of intellectual infancy."[72]

Conservatism and Sentimentalism

Finally, the question of disagreement inevitably leads us to confront issues of moral, political and social philosophy. Let me address them by going back for the last time to "The Fixation of Belief." Taking agreement in the long run as a criterion of truth, Peirce argued there, amounts to defining reality itself as the object of our final opinion. In other words, everything we can agree upon – that is, everything we can rationally talk about – has a robust metaphysical underpinning, a reality toward which it tends. But while it is relatively easy to grasp what that means in the case of the empirical sciences, the case of morality and politics is harder to make sense of. When confronted with moral values or with normative political ideals, it is philosophically more demanding – although by no means impossible – to defend a strong realistic conception of epistemic convergence.[73]

---

[70] See, e.g., CP 1.128 (c. 1905) for a contraposition of "laboratory-philosophy" versus "seminary-philosophy." See also fn. 38 above.
[71] "The Marriage of Religion and Science" (1893), CP 6.429.
[72] "Reply to the Necessitarians" (1893), CP 6.603. Recall that Peirce attributed "infancy" to philosophy as well. See fn. 38.
[73] See Misak 2000 for an account of moral and political inquiry premised on a Peircean understanding of epistemic convergence; Frega 2012, Chs. 6 and 7 for a reply to Misak on the basis of a Deweyan conception of moral and political inquiry as the solution of problematic situations.

Peirce's own solution to this problem is rather surprising. Especially from the late 1890s onward, he insisted on a radical separation between theory and practice. Whereas theoretical inquiry should obey the pragmatist criteria of inquiry, practical matters should be left to instincts. Whereas theory embodies a progressive stance, practice is inherently "conservative" and "sentimentalist." Whereas theory deals with eminently "useless things," practice deals with the useful.[74] These ideas have been commented upon many times, because of the great interpretive difficulties they present and of the many questions they raise – both theoretically and politically.[75] Here, I will limit myself to suggesting one (admittedly insufficient) way of making sense of Peirce's ideas: what Peirce said about the "sentimentalist" and "conservative" nature of practice can be taken as a symptom of a more general attitude toward institutions, an attitude that straddles the theory-practice divide and can tell us something revealing about our fundamental question, namely the question of Peirce's approach to history.

The first thing to note is that, at the moment when the topic of sentimentalism entered stage in Peirce's philosophy, it was connected to a tendency to wed philosophy and social criticism. The 1892 essay on "Evolutionary Love" is one of Peirce's few attempts (although quite an idiosyncratic one) to play the role of the public intellectual, linking sophisticated philosophical arguments to a critical assessment of social issues. The nineteenth century, Peirce claimed, was intoxicated by the false generalizations philosophers have drawn from political economy. The idea that self-interest might be the engine of society, and that public benefits may derive from private vices, overshadowed solidarity and love. Darwinism is part of the same picture:

> The *Origin of Species* of Darwin merely extends politico-economical views of progress to the entire realm of animal and vegetable life. [...] As Darwin puts it on his title-page, it is the struggle for existence; and he should have added for his motto: Every individual for himself, and the Devil take the hindmost! Jesus, in his Sermon on the Mount, expressed a different opinion.[76]

Note that Gallie 1956a looks at the sphere of moral and political discourse as a particularly important repository of "essentially contested concepts."

74 See CP 1.76 (c. 1896); Cf. Bergman 2010, p. 23.

75 On Peirce's distinction between theory and practice, see Misak 2004; Atkins 2016. For a defense of Peirce's conservatism in politics, see Short 2001. Among the many insightful attempts to build a progressive social agenda out of Peirce's philosophy, see Bernstein 1981.

76 W8, p. 189 (1892).

With a rhetorical move that may remind us of Christian socialism, Peirce pitted the "Gospel of Christ" against this treacherous "Gospel of Greed." The latter is "materialist," while the former is "sentimentalist." However, Peirce made clear that sentimentalism cannot be unrestrained either. It must have a counterweight, lest it lapse into as flawed an ideology as that which it hinders.

> The economists accuse those to whom the enunciation of their atrocious villainies communicates a thrill of horror of being *sentimentalists*. It may be so: I willingly confess to having some tincture of sentimentalism in me, God be thanked! Ever since the French Revolution brought this leaning of thought into ill-repute, – and not altogether undeservedly, I must admit, true, beautiful, and good as that great movement was, – it has been the tradition to picture sentimentalists as persons incapable of logical thought and unwilling to look facts in the eyes. […]. But what after all is sentimentalism? It is […] the doctrine that great respect should be paid to the natural judgments of the sensible heart. […] [T]he nineteenth century has steadily contemned it, because it brought about the Reign of Terror. That it did so is true. Still, the whole question is one of *how much*. The reign of terror was very bad; but now the Gradgrind banner has been this century long flaunting in the face of heaven, with an insolence to provoke the very skies to scowl and rumble.[77]

The tone of social criticism that pervades "Evolutionary Love" became much less prominent in subsequent years. Concurrently, Peirce put more emphasis on the idea that "Sentimentalism implies Conservatism."[78] The most important document in this respect is the first of the 1898 Cambridge lectures, in which Peirce depicted theory as the locus of pure reason and rational progress, and as absolutely opposed to practice, which is instead governed by sentiment and natural instincts.[79]

---

[77] W8, p. 188. The "Gradgrind banner" is a reference to Charles Dickens' *Hard Times* (Dickens [1854] 2008). The mention of the French Revolution should be placed alongside Peirce's reading of Rousseau. See the entry "sentimentalism" that Peirce wrote for the *Century Dictionary*, CD, p. 5497: "Tendency to be swayed by sentiment; […] specifically, the philosophy of Rousseau and others, which gave great weight to the impulses of a susceptible heart." See also Peirce's review of Thomas Huxley's political essays, CN2, p. 22 (1894): "Of course, Rousseau was a sentimentalist by conviction, and it is quite true that, since he wrote, the world has received terrible proof of the evil of exaggerated sentimentalism. Still, civilization rests, and must rest, mainly upon sentiment."

[78] RLT, p. 111 (1898).

[79] See RLT, p. 105–122. This lecture has often been interpreted as a provocative reply to William James. See, e.g., Misak 2004, p. 163. But the role of James as a polemical objective of Peirce's should probably not be overestimated. Girel 2011, for instance, suggests taking into account a larger picture, which includes Peirce's relation to Royce. Be that as it may, Peirce in that lecture went as far as to expunge from theoretical life the very linchpin of his epistemology, namely the concept of belief. See RLT, p. 112: "There is thus no proposition at all in science which answers to the conception of belief." Misak 2004, p. 162 has insightfully noted, however, that Peirce himself,

These peremptory assertions, however, conceal a more complex scenario: one in which rationalism and sentimentalism are not separated by a watertight boundary but represent two polarities that permeate both reasoning and practical conduct. In an 1899 book review, for instance, Peirce claimed that we should not give too much weight to the "pretensions of individual reason to solve the great problems," but he also added that "after all, it is our nature to reason, and we have to make the best of it." So, "the whole question is how far we are to carry rationalism, and at what point to check it."[80] The same applies to conservatism: in the 1898 Cambridge lectures, Peirce described it as the refusal "to push any practical principle to its extreme limits, – including the principle of conservatism itself."[81] What is more, Peirce admitted that both sentimentalism and conservatism are themselves theoretical positions and that they are, therefore, adopted on rational, theoretical grounds. "If I allow the supremacy of sentiment in human affairs, I do so at the dictation of reason itself."[82] Thus, theory does play a role in practice. Specularly, sentiment plays a role in theory; for there is a structural affinity between the instincts that guide practical conduct and the instinctive ability to guess at the right hypothesis, the *lume naturale*, which lies at the very core of scientific reasoning.[83]

Here, Peirce's concepts of sentiment and reason appear as ubiquitous polarities of both theory and practice, each oriented toward curbing the excesses of the other. In this sense, conservatism and sentimentalism are not simply the label of Peirce's political opinions. They are the mark of his lifelong attempt to develop a conception of human thinking, of human action and of social institutions which shuns the excesses of rationalism and atomistic individualism. (The concept of *habit*, which Peirce and all subsequent pragmatists took to be the keystone of both rational inquiry and practical conduct, should be regarded as a central piece of this conception. See Chapter 3.)

In a 1904 letter to Victoria Welby, moreover, Peirce explicitly linked his conservatism to a number of philosophical convictions that have momentous impli-

---

just a few years later, would say something more profound about the role of belief in science. "A scientific investigator is in a double situation. As a unit of the scientific world, [...] he can wait five centuries, [...] before he decides upon the acceptability of a certain hypothesis. But as engaged in the investigation which it is his duty diligently to pursue, he must be ready the next morning to go on that hypothesis or to reject it." (RL 75, 1902, as quoted by Misak).

80 CN2, p. 201 (1899). In the same text, Peirce also explicitly addresses the shortcomings of "religious spirit" as a counterpart to rationalism.
81 RLT, p. 111.
82 RLT, p. 112.
83 See RLT, p. 111; Misak 2004, p. 158–160.

cations for the philosophy of history.⁸⁴ First, "the past cannot be reformed," and its consequences on the present have, therefore, to be carefully scrutinized. Second, "we never can foresee all the consequences of a great change." Indeed, some of these consequences "are sure to be corrupting. [...] Reason blunders so very frequently that in practical matters we must rely on instinct & subconscious operations of the mind." In other words, all forms of human association have to face up to the existence of unexpected consequences of action; the future cannot be perfectly foreseen. Finally, traditions exert a legitimate influence on our thought and action.⁸⁵

The Ethics of Terminology

A consequence of the interpretation just advanced is that Peirce's conservatism is, first of all, a philosophical attitude toward social life that is neither necessarily reactionary nor necessarily opposed to a more rationalistic tendency to reform. Rather, the two attitudes may coexist in our handling of social institutions. A corroboration of this reading comes from Peirce's work on a quite peculiar

---

84 See S&S, p. 19–20 (1904). See also the following section, where I comment on this text.
85 With regard to this emphasis on the unexpected consequences of action, cf. the aforementioned review of Thomas Huxley, which seems to undermine the distinction between theory and practice, as Peirce here derives from his epistemology a form of political liberalism. CN2, p. 22-23: "The pretence that one can see no meaning in the statement that all men are born free and equal, would hardly have been patiently tolerated by our Revolutionary fore-fathers. [...] [Huxley] even goes so far as to sneer at the principle of toleration. Where would Huxley, or any other evolutionist who lived in the sixties, have been without that principle? The Principle of toleration is intimately connected with the fundamental principle of science, for it can have no rational basis except the acknowledgement that nothing is absolutely certain [...] Now the scientific man will not shut off any question whatever as too sacred or too well known for further investigation, and therefore he must tolerate every opinion. But, further, in regard to questions of politics and the like, the scientific man must admit that not only can the true alternative not be certainly named, but also that no formula can be framed all whose possible consequences shall be just; and for that reason it is most desirable that, alongside of the formula which is less erroneous, the opposite formula which is more erroneous should constantly have its advocates, so that it may not be forgotten when the moment comes at which it is to be preferred to the other. In this point of view, what Huxley calls 'the pet doctrine of modern liberalism, that the toleration of error is a good thing in itself,' appears to be not, after all, out of harmony with the ideas of science."

form of social institution, namely scientific terminology.[86] Once again, we observe that Peirce's interest in the traditional problems of social philosophy tends to be displaced onto issues that concern scientific inquiry and the use of symbols. Science and scientific symbols are the social institutions that Peirce most cared about.

Historically, Peirce's work on terminology can be construed as a prosecution of his extensive lexicographic research, as well as of his work for the Office of Weights and Measures, a department of the United States Coast Survey (see Chapter 1). As with all the activities he undertook, Peirce explicitly reflected on the logical and epistemological principles underlying his occupation.[87] In this case, the leading question was precisely how to manage a system of symbols in such a way as to strike a rational balance between conservation and innovation.[88] Many years later, in the "Syllabus" of 1903, this question became the object of a genuine philosophical study, which Peirce labelled the "ethics of terminology."[89] He meant in particular the terminology of philosophy, with all the complexities related to this term that we have already discussed. On the one hand, philosophy is a scientific discipline like all others and ought, therefore, to rest on a technical vocabulary (which Peirce saw best exemplified in the terminology of Scholasticism). On the other hand, it needs to retain a strong relation with ordinary language and common sense, in virtue of its "cenoscopic" nature.

The philosophical assumptions behind Peirce's ethics of terminology are a set of ideas about thought and meaning that we have already encountered in Chapter 3. For one thing, symbols are not a mere clothing of thought, but its essence. Hence, a sound use of symbols dovetails with sound thinking. For another, symbols find themselves in a state of constant change.

---

[86] This interest is related to Peirce's willingness to develop "speculative rhetoric" as a branch of semiotics. Rhetoric is defined as "the science of the essential conditions under which a sign may determine an interpretant sign of itself and of whatever it signifies." (EP2, p. 326, 1904).

[87] See, e.g., the "Theses on the proper functions of the 'National Office of Weights & Measures'" (1899), HP, p. 619–629.

[88] Peirce was quite explicit in linking this kind of preoccupation to some typical problems of social philosophy. See, as an instance, HP, p. 621: "The constitution and government of this country, while acknowledging the supremacy of certain universal truths, are yet distinguished from those of the first French Republic in being in every respect adapted to the circumstances of place and time. The force of contrary considerations is recognized; and adjustment is made so as to assign to each its due measure of effect under existing conditions, without assuming that these are to remain forever unchanged."

[89] EP2, p. 263–266 (1903). Cf. RLT, p. 229–232 (1898).

[E]very symbol is a living thing, in a very strict sense that is no mere figure of speech. The body of the symbol changes slowly, but its meaning inevitably grows, incorporates new elements and throws off old ones. But the effort of all should be to keep the *essence* of every scientific term unchanged and exact; although absolute exactitude is not so much as conceivable. Every symbol is, in its origin, either an image of the idea signified, or a reminiscence of some individual occurrence, person, or thing, connected with its meaning, or is a metaphor.[90]

These assumptions, Peirce argued, are sufficient to bring about a sort of obligation toward symbols, which consists in taking as seriously as possible the tension between change and stability. But if we add the social nature of symbols to this picture, it becomes clear that the obligation of which Peirce spoke cannot be dealt with on a private, individual basis. On the contrary, we have to find a "general agreement" on scientific terminology. Moreover, such general agreement cannot be brought about by "arbitrary dictation," but rather by the "power of rational principles."[91]

Here is further confirmation – if we still needed one – of something I said at the beginning of this chapter. One of the basic insights of Peirce's semiotics is that individual autonomy can only be exerted with social and public tools, because no symbol is private. Conversely, Peirce's willingness to lay out a number of ethical precepts to regulate the use of symbols testifies to the indispensable role of reason in practical matters. But the exercise of reason needs to go hand in hand with a sensitivity for history and tradition. When we want to introduce a new word in science, we need both general principles and "acquaintance with [...] history."[92] Knowledge of what has been established in the past, together with the awareness of how difficult it is to change it, act as a counterweight to the abstractness of rational stipulation.[93] Elsewhere, Peirce deployed the concept of conservatism to express precisely this point. "I am a great conservative and am usually opposed to reforms of well-established practices, especially of expression."[94] The reason for that is laid out in the same letter to Victoria Welby upon which I have commented above:

---

90 EP2, p. 264.
91 EP2, p. 263–264.
92 EP2, p. 264.
93 Similarly, an office of measures should carry out historical research, "both documentary and inductive." See HP, p. 625.
94 HP, p. 365 (c. 1898). Compare CN3, p. 158 (1904), where Peirce says that a "healthy conservatism" is the best tool we may deploy against "the follies to which unmeasured rationalism in regard to weights and measures [...] may lead."

> [Y]ou are a rationalistic radical, while I am a conservative on rationalistic & experiential grounds. [...] Besides all these considerations which apply to all reforms, in regard to proposals for changing modes of expression it has to be remembered that the past cannot be reformed; and consequently, its memory and records subsisting still, no prevalent mode of expression can be annihilated. The most you can do is to introduce an additional way of expressing the same meaning. Now the multiplication of equivalent modes of expression is itself a burden [...]. There are some evils that, once embraced, had better be adhered to.[95]

What is admittedly a bit paradoxical is that, notwithstanding his conservative precepts, Peirce was by no means shy to introduce a great number of neologisms in his philosophy. In a sense, the conservatism he professed in theory was constantly contradicted in practice. Peirce was aware of this tension; but his attempts to ease it are not completely convincing. He argued, for instance, that only the utter novelty of a given subject matter or conceptual connection can justify the use of a new term.[96] But if we look at how many times he made recourse to this rule, it is legitimate to suspect that he abused it, if judged by his own conservative principles. As a matter of fact, the idiosyncratic nature of his philosophy is, in part, due precisely to his adoption of a technical terminology that was not shared by anyone else. Here, we face a predicament analogous to the "tuistic" epistemology considered at the beginning of this chapter: it was vehemently professed by a thinker who, in his daily life, was profoundly alone.

---

[95] S&S, p. 19–20 (1904).
[96] See EP2, p. 266. There is also a second argument, which however is even more problematic, because it draws on a sort of immediacy (maybe a form of sentimentalism?) in the creation of a word. See HP, p. 366: "There is nothing more detestible [sic] than a brand new word, never yet handselled. But when it slips off the pen before one thinks, then when one stops to think, it may plead that *now* it has already been used."

Part III

6 Peirce the Historian

The Scope of Peirce's History of Science

We have now concluded the book's central part. What we have hopefully achieved is a comprehensive view of the many senses in which Peirce allowed history to have a bearing on science and philosophy. Chapters 3 and 4 looked at this problem along two axes, which I labelled the axis of historicity and the axis of autonomy. Chapter 5 sought to enrich that picture, by asking in which way a serious consideration of the social nature of science and philosophy influences their relation to history. Overall, these three chapters have followed a largely reconstructive strategy. I have aimed to piece together Peirce's arguments and to critically assess their significance for the central problem of my book, even when that significance was not made explicit by Peirce.

The final part of the book adopts a more descriptive approach. As in Chapters 1 and 2, it goes back to taking into primary consideration Peirce's explicit conception of history. In particular, we will be concerned with examining Peirce's mature writings on the history of science. This chapter is devoted to his concrete work as a historian. The next and final chapter will be devoted to his methodological reflections on the writing of history. But the narrative of the two chapters will intertwine at many junctures, as Peirce's methodology cannot be neatly separated from the concrete subject matter of his historical works.

My goal will not be to offer a complete survey of all the relevant issues touched upon in Peirce's history of science. Nor can I hope to put forth an exhaustive contextualization against the background of nineteenth-century historiography and of the many sources that Peirce relied upon. Rather, I will select some topics that seem to me particularly revealing of the tight relation between historical and philosophical interests in Peirce's work. On the one hand, this means showing that Peirce's historical inquiries are the prosecution of his philosophical preoccupations on a new terrain. This can be easily accounted for if we follow Peirce's own classificatory scheme (Chapter 2): history borrows its research questions and its methodological principles from philosophy. But on the other hand, I will show that the relation also holds the other way around. This is less easily accountable if we rely on the classification alone but is quite understandable in light of the results we have achieved in Chapters 3 to 5.

In the following pages, I will focus in particular, though not exclusively, on the 1892–93 Lowell Lectures on the history of science and on what I have been calling the 'Putnam History,' written around 1898 (see Chapter 2). In these texts, Peirce is almost exclusively occupied with the history of science, although this label has to be understood in an extremely broad sense. For the history of science encompasses the history of philosophy (philosophy *is* a science, although a *sui generis* one). Moreover, Peirce makes occasional forays into broader issues of cultural and political history as a way of shedding light on the history of science and philosophy. This may look like a hopelessly broad enterprise; but Peirce balances the breadth of his conception of history with a rather narrow choice of subject matters.

The first subject matter is a comparative study of ancient civilizations. Peirce considers, in particular, ancient Egypt, Babylonia and classical Greece, with China, India and other civilizations occasionally added to the list. The second subject matter is a set of more specific investigations into the history of European science from the Middle Ages onward. The period that most drew Peirce's attention is the scientific revolution of early modernity – "from Copernicus to Newton."[1] However, Peirce did try to cover other historical epochs as well. In particular, he focused on the late Middle Ages and on the nineteenth century. The latter period is especially relevant, on account of the theoretical and methodological novelties represented by scientists such as Darwin, Faraday or Mendeleev.

Before starting, let me recall that in Chapter 2 I investigated the plurality of rationales through which Peirce justified his interest in the history of science. At least three ideas were of pivotal importance. First, history is a "specimen of how the laws of growth apply to the human mind."[2] It offers an empirical test of the general account of intellectual evolution that Peirce laid out in his more philosophical writings. Second, history is a repository of "practical lessons"[3] on which scientists themselves may draw whenever they have to reflect on their own methodology. Third, history helps us discover how "the truths we are familiar with got found out."[4] This third rationale, I have also suggested, is related to Peirce's critical philosophy of common sense: history is a crucial tool to understand the real scope and purport of our beliefs, to contextualize them, to put them into perspective. Finally, in the book's central part, we witnessed the emergence of some new rationales, the most important among which is the idea that the history of science may offer an inductive justification of the validity of ampliative reasoning. We will need to keep in mind this plurality of rationales as we turn now to the concrete details of Peirce's work as a historian.

---

[1] W9, p. 78 / HP, p. 149 (1892). See the commentary to the Lowell Lectures in De Tienne forthcoming.
[2] W9, p. 141 / HP, p. 202.
[3] HP, p. 557 (1892).
[4] W9, p. 97 / HP, p. 143.

The Origins of Science

Let me begin with the chronological beginning: with Peirce's inquiry into the history of ancient civilizations. One main reason why Peirce was interested in ancient civilizations was the possibility of exploring the very origins of science. Peirce wished to gain a better grasp of the conditions that bring human communities to devote their energies to scientific inquiry. He did so by identifying a small number of "instincts" that lie at the basis of our cognitive activities.

If we concentrate in particular on the Lowell Lectures, it becomes clear that Peirce's focus on instincts was a way to take up Whewell's thesis about each science's relation to a distinctive "idea" (see Chapter 2), and to give it an even more radically historical tone. Ideas evolve over time out of the primitive instincts; and science is the gradual development and refinement of those instincts. Indeed, this is the paramount reason why Peirce chose to start his Lowell Lectures with a diagram of the classification of the sciences (see, again, Chapter 2). In providing his audience with such an overview, he was in effect offering a guiding thread to follow his historical narrative about how the different human instincts, or primitive ideas, brought about the different domains of scientific knowledge. In one passage, for instance, Peirce remarks that "the most fundamental division of the sciences," namely the division of physical and psychical sciences, is the outcome of the distinction between the instinct of nutrition and the instinct of reproduction.[5] But in another passage, he identifies the two fundamental instincts as, first, the instinct toward the construction of a rational image of nature; and second, the social impulse, which is the necessary condition of social life.[6]

From an epistemological viewpoint, Peirce's talk about instincts aligns well with an idea we have already touched upon in the book's central chapters. "[K]nowledge gained by instinctive processes and not deliberately"[7] is the necessary antecedent of critical, self-controlled thought, although it cannot, as yet, be called rational, precisely because it is not subject to the normative constraints of logic. Peirce puts forth the hypothesis that these instincts are already at work in prehistoric times. Later on, they gradually develop into self-controlled beliefs.

---

5 W9, p. 74. See De Tienne forthcoming.
6 See W9, p. 202–203 / HP, p. 239–240. It is tempting to relate these two instincts to the two criteria for the scientific fixation of belief set forth in the 1877 essay (see Ch. 1): the sense of reality and the social impulse.
7 W9, p. 80 / HP, p. 151. The passage continues: "Among the remains of the Stone Age we find various implements fashioned into shapes upon which a modern engineer could not easily improve. But all that was knowledge gained by instinctive processes and not deliberately or with a full consciousness of making an investigation."

"[I]n [...] instinctive knowledge, geometry and mechanics are really *wrapped up*. Man has nothing to do but to render his instinctive ideas abstract and precise, to correct their errors, and to follow them out." And again: "These instincts are of the nature of knowledge; or at least, they only require to be reflected upon to become knowledge."[8]

If we recall the argument of Chapter 3, we may notice a problem that looms large in Peirce's account of the development of science from instincts. I mean the problem of teleology. To say that scientific disciplines like geometry and mechanics are "wrapped up" in instinctive knowledge seems to suggest that the development of these sciences follows a teleological pattern. But does this, in turn, mean that the result of the historical process is unavoidable and predetermined?[9] Earlier on, I claimed that Peirce's treatment of teleology suffers from a slight ambiguity. On the one hand, Peirce wished to marry an appreciation of teleological processes with an overall non-deterministic metaphysics. Indeed, the whole point of his theory of evolution is to reconcile teleology and contingency. On the other hand, there are moments in which his own account of the development of science seems to veer toward what he would have himself called an anancastic (that is, deterministic) account of the historical process.

This ambiguity notwithstanding, Peirce's concrete work on ancient civilizations seems explicitly aimed at preserving some non-deterministic aspects of the passage from instincts to science. For the basic human instincts of which Peirce speaks do not always or necessarily lead to scientific knowledge. And this is so for at least two reasons.

First, the scientific mode of life is not the only way humans may go about cultivating their instincts. As we saw in Chapter 5, there are other classes of people who use their cognitive faculties in quite different ways, such as "artists" and "practical men." However, while the opposition between scientists and practical people is very sharp, that between scientists and artists admits to some degree of interaction. This difference is mirrored in two quite different "practical lessons" that Peirce drew from his historical studies. On the one hand, ancient history teaches us that "Greek Science [was] ruined by their mixing moral, practical with scientific purposes."[10] On the other hand, the history of early modern Eu-

---

[8] W9, p. 202–203 / HP, p. 239. My emphasis.
[9] Let me note the terminological similarity between the passage I am discussing and another passage that I have discussed in Ch. 3: "It is what the man is destined to do, what of the future is *wrapped up* in him, that makes him what he is." (CP 7.666, 1903. My emphasis).
[10] HP1, p. 408. Cf. CP 1.576 (1902): "History does not tell of a single man who has considerably increased human knowledge [...] having been proved a criminal, unless theology be knowledge." On Peirce's account of the relation between theory and practice, see Ch. 5.

rope ("from the Renaissance to the French Revolution") teaches us that there is a "reciprocal influence of Art and Science."[11]

A second reason for upholding a non-deterministic view of scientific progress is that not all ancient civilizations reached the same degree of scientific development. This is due to the fact that the birth of science is dependent not only on the immanent evolution of primordial instincts, but also on the appearance of favorable circumstances in both the natural and the social environment. The Putnam History says that the populations that were most likely to initiate a veritable scientific activity were those that lived in territories "annually flooded by the rivers," like Egypt, Babylonia or northern China. For they were able to develop an agricultural system that "depended on irrigation." This, in turn, made necessary "strong governments," able to manage infrastructure and curb occasional outbursts of famine by concentrating political power and ruling with authority. Out of necessity, the government would direct "great operations of engineering." These would almost unavoidably necessitate scientific investigations. "When a civilization has reached this stage, we might hope to find the birth of science; for engineering must at least have trained men to exactitude and definiteness of conception."[12]

However, the comparative cases of Egypt and Babylonia show that not even these environmental factors can predict which of the ancient civilizations would end up developing the highest degree of scientificity. This is the point where Peirce's account becomes most problematic, because it betrays a racist conviction that the different peoples of antiquity had unequal intellectual and moral powers. In particular, the Egyptians, who certainly had agriculture, a strong government and the ability to preside over colossal works of engineering, were nonetheless not scientific people. They showed an interest in science that was entirely centered on the practical outcome of their results and had no sensitivity toward scientific generalizations as such. By contrast, "the Babylonians were an infinitely more scientific people than the Egyptians [...]. In fact, they had much more of the spirit of research than the Greeks." Their scientific results, and astronomy in particular, show a "natural disposition to make systematic inquiries."[13]

The comparison between the Egyptians and Babylonians, however, has a more interesting aspect as well. Peirce asked what "the oldest scientific book"

---

[11] HP, p. 404.
[12] HP, p. 310 (1898). Note the similarity between this account of the role of governments and Peirce's depiction of the "method of authority" in the "Fixation of Belief." See Ch. 1.
[13] W9, p. 138 / HP, p. 152. Cf. HP, p. 310–311 (1898). On Peirce's acquaintance with Egyptian language and culture, see Kammerzell/Lapčić/Nöth 2016.

was. But he recognized that there are at least two ways of answering that question. We may try to identify "the oldest book which conveys *truths*." Or we may look for the oldest book that betrays a genuine spirit of "research," a "conscious prying into things."[14] I think it is legitimate to see a relation between this distinction and Peirce's reflections on the definition of science (see Chapter 5): science may be defined either as a systematized body of knowledge, or as a specific mode of life; and we know that Peirce chose the latter definition over the former. It may, thus, become more understandable why the oldest scientific book, according to Peirce, is Egyptian if we follow the first definition, and Babylonian if we follow the second.[15]

The Egyptian work is the text known today as Ahmes Papyrus, or Rhind Mathematical Papyrus. Discovered in 1858, it is not a theoretical treatise but rather a list of problems and of their solutions with a view to immediate practical application. (I will return to this text later on.)[16] The Babylonian work, by contrast, is a mythological tale of creation, which Peirce believed to have influenced the book of Genesis as well.[17] And though this mythological tale is, by today's standards, nothing but a "wild dream" (as Peirce puts it), it does betray a sincere attempt to understand the workings of nature. After all, "wildest dreams *are* the necessary first steps toward scientific investigation." (Recall what we saw in Chapter 5: "[A] thinker can win no ground in any department if he be afraid of harboring ideas which, as they first come to him, are vague and shadowy."[18])

In conclusion, let me note yet another significant aspect of Peirce's reflections about the origin of science. Peirce saw the natural disposition toward scientific inquiry as going hand in hand with an interest in the study of the past. Indeed, this is another piece of evidence that he considered historiography to be on a line with scientific inquiry at large. The Babylonians, for instance, were not only the most scientific people of antiquity. They were also "great archaeologists; and it is to the diligence with which some of them searched out their own history, that the chronological accuracy of our knowledge about it is

---

[14] W9, p. 110 / HP, p. 157.
[15] See W9, p. 110 / HP, p. 157.
[16] See Robins/Shute 1987. Cf. the review of J. N. Lockyer's *The Dawn of Astronomy*, HP, p. 439 (1894): "The mathematical papyrus is a marvel of inaptitude."
[17] In all likelihood, Peirce was referring to the *Enûma Eliš:* a Babylonian text that bears some notable similarities to the biblical story. In the early twentieth century, the relations between Babylonian culture and the Bible would give rise to the so-called *Babel-Bibel-Streit*. See Talon 2013; Gebauer 2015.
[18] HP, p. 478 (1896).

due."¹⁹ The Egyptians, on the contrary, had no talent for the dispassionate study of the past, and lapsed into an "excessive reverence for the antiquity."

> [W]hy are there no records? Simply because, for the Egyptian, the Past, as being something he could not influence, was something with which he had no concern [...]. This readiness to accept the wisdom of the ancients show how little impulse there was toward independent investigation; while it betrays the decadence of the intellect of the Egyptian race.²⁰

This passage supports an idea that I discussed in Chapter 4. For Peirce, an interest in the study of the past is not tantamount to a placid acceptance of tradition. Quite on the contrary, the cultivation of historical inquiries go hand in hand with the cultivation of intellectual autonomy. It is precisely an over-estimation of the past, a lack of critical distance with the past, that prevented the Egyptians from studying it scientifically. "To their mind what was old and what was true were indistinguishable; but *to veracious history they were indifferent*."²¹

The Laws of Growth: Evolution versus Revolutions

Peirce's interest in the origins of science slides seamlessly into a second issue, namely, the question of how science has evolved. In investigating this second question, the first rationale for a history of science that I mentioned above becomes paramount. History is, first and foremost, a "specimen of how the laws of growth apply to the human mind." Therefore, it is tied to the theory of evolution that Peirce laid out in "Evolutionary Love." Let us briefly recall what Peirce did in that paper. He presented three models of evolution in general, and of intellectual evolution in particular: tychasm, anancasm, and agapasm (see Chapter 3). While Peirce leaned toward agapasm, he never ruled out the possibility that some phenomena follow a tychastic or an anancastic pattern. It is the task of the historian of science to look more closely into the "the historical development of human thought"²² and measure it against the general theory.

In turn, this issue is bound up with further theoretical and methodological questions. To make clear what I mean, let me cite a long passage from "Evolutionary Love":

---

19 HP, p. 439.
20 HP, p. 314–315.
21 Cf. HP, p. 439 (1894). My emphasis.
22 W8, p. 196 (1892).

> Students of the history of mind there be of an erudition to fill an imperfect scholar like me with envy edulcorated by joyous admiration, who maintain that ideas when just started are and can be little more than freaks, since they cannot yet have been critically examined, and further that everywhere and at all times progress has been so gradual that it is difficult to make out distinctly what original step any given man has taken. It would follow that tychasm has been the sole method of intellectual development. I have to confess I cannot read history so; I cannot help thinking that while tychasm has sometimes been operative, at others great steps covering nearly the same ground and made by different men independently, have been mistaken for a succession of small steps, and further that students have been reluctant to admit a real entitative "spirit" of an age or of a people, under the mistaken and unscrutinized impression that they should thus be opening the door to wild and unnatural hypotheses. I find, on the contrary, that, however it may be with the education of individual minds, the historical development of thought has seldom been of a tychastic nature, and exclusively in backward and barbarizing movements.[23]

This passage makes clear that the problem of finding the right balance between the three models of historical development is related to at least three different but interdependent questions. First, what is the role of chance, causal determinism and teleology in the evolution of ideas? Second, is intellectual progress gradual or is it the outcome of revolutions and cataclysms? Third, is it legitimate to postulate the existence of collective entities, like the Hegelian "spirit of an age," or can all intellectual phenomena be investigated from an individualistic perspective? We have already dealt with the first question in Chapter 3. This section and the next will thus focus on the other two questions: what is the balance between gradualism and revolutions in intellectual progress? And is there something like a spirit of an age?

On the whole, the tychastic model emphasizes gradualism. But it is a specific kind of gradualism: one that is dominated by chance alone. By contrast, the agapastic model marries gradualism and teleology. If read through the lenses of agapasm, the history of science appears as a seamless, gradual approximation toward the truth. This is the model Peirce preferred, because it aligns very easily with his processualism in metaphysics, in semiotics and in epistemology. However, this does not mean that he stopped taking seriously the possibility that revolutionary moments, too, may have a role to play. He linked the revolutionary aspect of intellectual history to "external" anancasm, i.e., to the force of external circumstances on the development of ideas.

Let us look at the historical examples Peirce presented in "Evolutionary Love" in order to make his view more plausible. Tychastic development is exem-

---

[23] W8, p. 197–198. For a commentary, see Topa 2016.

plified by two historical phenomena.[24] The first is "the history of Christianity from about its establishment by Constantine to say the time of the Irish monasteries." The second, "a hundred times swifter," is the history of the French Revolution. Peirce did not say a single word on the latter example, so the reader is left wondering what exactly his point was. (Perhaps he merely wanted to remark that there is no intelligible pattern to be found in the events of revolutionary France.) As regards the former, his explanation – rather intricate and unclear – seems to be that there has been a conflict, going on for centuries, between the gradual affirmation of the universalistic claims of Christianity and a constant relapsing "into a party spirit." To state that this process was tychastic amounts to saying that it has proceeded "by insensible or minute steps; for such is the nature of chances when so multiply as to show phenomena of regularity."[25]

Turning to anancasm, and in particular to external anancasm, things become a bit more complicated. It will be recalled from Chapter 3 that Peirce considered external anancasm to be virtually ubiquitous in intellectual history, although always in combination with other elements. In this respect, Peirce quoted Whewell once again, "whose masterly comprehension of the history of science critics have been too ignorant properly to appreciate."[26] The British scholar, he argued, teaches that "[n]ever are external influences the only ones which affect the mind."[27] Rather, there is an interplay between the internal development of the mind and the impact of external circumstances. One of Peirce's examples is particularly telling: "In the rise of medieval thought, scholasticism and the synchronistic art developments, undoubtedly the crusades and the discovery of the writings of Aristotle were powerful influences."[28] However, the development of Scholasticism and of the arts cannot be entirely explained as a reaction to these circumstances.

Finally, Peirce considered agapasm. As will become clearer in the next section, he looked for the proof of the actual existence of this model of evolution, and indeed of its primacy over the other two models, in all those phenomena in

---

24 See W8, p. 198–199.
25 W8, p. 197.
26 W8, p. 200.
27 W8, p. 199.
28 W8, p. 200. On the same page, Peirce criticizes the German historian Karl von Prantl on precisely this point: "[F]ew men have thumbed more books than Carl Prantl. He has done good solid work, notwithstanding his slap-dash judgments. But we shall never make so much as a good beginning of comprehending scholasticism until the whole has been systematically explored and digested by a company of students regularly organized[.]" As a possibly purer form of anancasm, the text also mentions "the recent Japanese reception of Western ideas." On Prantl, cf. CP 4.26 (1893).

which an intellectual change cannot be accounted for by the power of the individual but appears influenced by a collective agency. But it should also be noted that Peirce's emphasis on agapasm was largely due to its being in accordance with a processualist understanding of intellectual development. Scientific truths are first formulated in a vague manner; and only in the course of inquiry do they become more precise, general, and true. Agapastic evolution dictates that even the influence of external circumstances is directed toward a new generalization, toward the establishment of a new habit. So, for instance, the introduction of a new instrument is, in a sense, an external fact; yet it is of a kind that has a huge bearing on our cognitive habits.

The Lowell Lectures from 1892 to 1893 present a picture that is similar to the *Monist* series, but not identical. Peirce did not use his three technical terms of tychasm, anancasm and agapasm but referred, nonetheless, to "three ways by which Human Thought grows, by the formation of habits, by the violent breaking up of habits, and by the action of innumerable fortuitous variations of ideas [...]."[29] This time, he explicitly identified the second model of evolution – the mechanical, cataclysmic and deterministic one – with the theory of Spencer: "I group all these manifold theories under three grand classes, to which I attach the familiar names of Darwin, Spencer and Lamarck."[30] The first of these models, the Darwinian, is dismissed rather quickly. It can be "a considerable factor in individual thinking, – yet in the history of science it has made [...] no figure at all, except in retrograde movements." When it did play a role, its influence can be discerned by the two "symptoms of proceedings by insensible steps and of proceeding in a direction different from that of any strivings."[31]

Setting aside Darwinism, Peirce put more emphasis than in "Evolutionary Love" on the oscillation between a gradualistic and a cataclysmic model of intellectual development. He differentiated between the two in a way that may recall Thomas Kuhn's now-classical distinction between normal science and revolutionary periods. The model of evolution that insists on "growth by exercise, or by direct efforts in the direction of the growth" (i.e., what Peirce elsewhere called agapasm) is "certainly the method of the ordinary successful prosecution of scientific inquiry." On the other hand, "the great and startling advances in scientific

---

[29] W9, p. 256 / HP, p. 287.
[30] W9, p. 94. Cf. W9, p. 84; 92. For Peirce's attitude toward Spencer in the early 1890s, see also W8, p. 242–244 (1891); Houser 2010, p. 25.
[31] W9, p. 256 / HP, p. 287.

thought" follow a different pattern. They depend on the "violent breaking up of certain habits."[32]

From the viewpoint of concrete historical inquiry, this led Peirce toward making some comparative remarks about the great turning points, renaissances, and revolutions of intellectual history. In all the cases considered, what ignited the revolution, according to Peirce, was the contact between two different intellectual or cultural contexts. So, in the case of Greek thought, the revolution that caused the commencement of a "great original life" was the "extension of commerce" which brought Greece into contact with other civilizations. Similarly, in medieval times, "the ideas of the Dark Ages was rudely shaken up by contact with the more civilized Saracens."[33] Even the Italian Renaissance, Peirce maintained, can be explained by looking at the influence of "foreign ideas." However, in that case, the revolution was less abrupt than in the other cases.

> The renaissance in Italy was of slower growth, because foreign ideas had been slowly filtering in since the thirteenth century uninterrupted. However, after the fall of Costantinople in 1454, there was a much more rapid movement. That movement was first strongest in the direction of art, which I take to be a mark of rapidly growing minds, of minds receiving nutrition too rapidly to be packed down into the forms of science. But the scientific development came later. Galileo was born the very day of Michelangelo's death.[34]

This passage is significant for yet another reason. It addresses an issue we have considered earlier in this chapter, namely Peirce's conviction that there is a "reciprocal influence of Art and Science,"[35] one that became especially visible in early modern Europe. In turn, this has further implications for a question I started discussing in Chapter 5: the relation between science and other domains of

---

32 W9, p. 256–257 / HP, p. 287–289. For a discussion of Kuhnian elements in Peirce, see Skagestad 1995; Pencak 1991.
33 W9, p. 257 / HP, p. 287–288.
34 W9, p. 257 / HP, p. 288. What about Peirce's apparently bizarre remark that "Galileo was born the very day of Michelangelo's death"? Peirce was here tapping into a quite engrained legend about the coincidence of the two dates. Galilei's biographer, Vincenzo Viviani, had already dwelt on it. See Segre 1991, p. 116–122; Bredekamp 2001. However, the legend was false: Galilei was born three days before the death of the Roman artist. But the noteworthy point here is another one. By the time Peirce penned these lines, the legend had already been refuted. Still, Peirce was not only unconvinced by this refutation. He also spent a considerable amount of energy on elaborating complex calculations aimed at showing that the coincidence was in fact true and its refutation wrong. (See, e.g., W9, p. 235 / HP, p. 267.) To Peirce, the idea of the coincidence of the two dates was too attractive to let go so easily. Why? Because it perfectly epitomized his general conviction about the historical transition between arts and science.
35 HP, p. 404.

human culture. We saw that Peirce was inclined to consider both philosophy and religion as being in a state of "intellectual infancy" as long as they did not adopt a more scientific form. By contrast, art is, here, depicted as a sort of prelude to science. So, on the one hand, we encounter once again Peirce's conviction that science is, in a sense, the *telos* or paramount goal of human culture. But on the other hand, Peirce did not believe that the arts themselves should become more scientific. Rather, he said that they tend to produce a more scientific mode of reasoning. Arts grow into science; they foreshadow it. (On other occasions, Peirce said something similar about "the arts," not so much in the sense of the fine arts as in the sense of the arts and crafts.)[36]

At the same time, Peirce's view of the relation between art and science is yet another symptom of his willingness to use his metaphysical and semiotic conceptions as a blueprint for his historical theory. As related to Firstness, art may evolve into science, which is dominated by Thirdness. And as we have seen in Chapter 3, Peirce's sparse remarks about the historical evolution of language from iconic to symbolic structures express a similar insight, though couched in a semiotic terminology.

Yet another picture comes out of the historical manuscripts written around 1898. This time, Peirce reiterated (although with slightly different arguments) his objections against Darwinian evolution;[37] but he placed more emphasis than in 1892 on the possibility that science progresses by leaps and discontinuities. "[T]he impulse for each leap is either some new observational resource, or some novel way of reasoning about the observations." Examples such as Pasteur, "who began by applying the microscope to chemistry," show us "new

---

[36] RLT, p. 119: "The art of medicine grew from the Egyptian book of formulas into physiology. The study of the steam engine gave birth to modern thermodynamics. Such is the historical fact. The steam engine made mechanical precision possible and needful. Mechanical precision rendered modern observational precision possible, and developed it. Now every scientific development is due to some new means of improved observations. So much for the tendency of the arts. Can any man with a soul deny that the development of pure science is the great end of the arts?"

[37] The Darwinian model is at work whenever a judgment "in regard to some [...] delicate questions" is almost imperceptibly changed over time, "so that the next recall would be influenced by this fortuitous modification," and so forth (CP 1.107). This, however, is not the way science develops, because science "is controlled and exact." If at all, then a sort of Darwinism is at work whenever scientists test "[v]arious tentative explanations" until they find the right one. Also, Darwinian evolution is not the kind of evolution that governs established social conventions. The reason thereof is that "human communities are exceedingly conservative." We need an external event such as "the despotism of a modern government with a modern police" to change the course of a socially established convention (CP 1.106).

ideas connected with new observational methods and a fine example of the usual process of scientific evolution. It is not by insensible steps."[38]

To sum up, throughout his career as a historian of science Peirce struggled to hold together the two sides of the coin: evolution and revolutions; gradualism and cataclysm. Perhaps one of the clearest expressions of this effort can be found in a review of F. Cajori's *A History of Mathematics* (1894). In scientific evolution, "there is no absolute breach of continuity." However, it is crucial that "great, startling, and revolutionary discoveries from time to time get made."[39] Or to put it in different terms: even when agapastic gradualism has the upper hand in history, it must be admitted that the process of gradual articulation of ideas is interspersed with sudden ruptures, which bring about both new scientific discoveries and a number of fundamental changes in the *logica utens* of scientists.

The Laws of Growth: Individuals versus Collectives

Let us now move on to the second problem mentioned above: the "spirit of an age" and the balance between individual and collective agencies as engines of historical change. For Peirce, accepting the agapastic model meant to accept the presence of collective, ideal entities that have a real and irreducible force over individuals. On the contrary, the Darwinian or tychastic model is decidedly individualistic. As in the case examined above, Peirce was at pains to reconcile his espousal of agapasm with the insights that may come from the opposite idea, namely the emphasis on individual agency.[40]

"Evolutionary Love," in particular, cites two reasons why the agapastic model is not individualistic. First, it stresses the role of ideal purposes that orient individual action. Second, it postulates the existence of a continuity of minds (which Peirce, as we know, investigated in another essay of the *Monist* series, namely "The Law of Mind"). Indeed, all three versions of the agapastic model entail that ideas develop through the minds of individuals but are not confined to individual minds. It is, therefore, possible to talk about the existence of a supra-individual existence of ideas. "If it could be shown directly that there is

---

38 CP 1.109.
39 HP, p. 443–444. See p. 444 for a reference to Whewell.
40 Let us keep in mind that Peirce construed his pragmatism as an inherently anti-individualistic philosophy. See, e.g., CP 5.504 (1905): "It is impossible rightly to apprehend the pragmaticist's position without fully understanding that nowhere would he be less at home than in the ranks of individualists."

such an entity as the 'spirit of an age' or of a people, and that mere individual intelligence will not account for all phenomena, this would be proof enough at once of agapasticism and of synechism." Peirce professed himself "unable to produce a cogent demonstration of this."[41] However, he found some evidence thereof in two related phenomena. Both phenomena have to do with the historical character of ideas, that is, with the notion (quite possibly stemming from Whewell) that not all ideas are available to individuals at all times.

The first such phenomenon is the existence of simultaneous scientific discoveries. This, Peirce remarked, is not the exception in the history of science, but the rule. A few example he brings up are "the prediction of a planet exterior to Uranus"; "the principle of the conservation of energy"; "the mechanical theory of heat."[42] These facts, he went on, can only be explained by taking seriously the possibility that scientific ideas grow on a collective or social level, so that they become accessible to many individuals at the same time. In a much later text, we read that one task of the historian is to ascertain "whether, at a given stage of intellectual development, a given generalization was within the reach of a whole class of minds or only of one hero, and what form it would take in different minds."[43]

The second phenomenon is the development of artistic styles. Again, we face the existence of ideas that appear very easily accessible in certain periods but are completely out of artists' reach in other epochs. Not surprisingly, Peirce's example in this case is the history of Gothic architecture (see Chapters 1 and 5):

> The pointed Gothic architecture in several of its developments appears to me to be of such a character. All attempts to imitate it by modern architects of the greatest learning and genius appear flat and tame, and are felt by their authors to be so. Yet at the time the style was living, there was quite an abundance of men capable of producing works of this kind of gigantic sublimity and power. In more than one case, extant documents show that the cathedral chapters, in the selection of architects, treated high artistic genius as a secondary consideration, as if there were no lack of persons able to supply that; and the results justify their confidence.[44]

With regard to both phenomena (simultaneous discoveries and artistic styles), Peirce's argument is based on a dilemmatic alternative – mere coincidence or zeitgeist? – which may appear a bit simplistic today. Peirce failed to consider the many social and psychological factors that can explain the influence of cul-

---

[41] W8, p. 203 (1892).
[42] W8, p. 204.
[43] HP, p. 486 (1901).
[44] W8, p. 203–204.

ture on the individual without any need to postulate super-individual entities.[45] Moreover, his argument can be charged with being dangerously inclined toward transforming the spirit of the age into the spirit of a people, or even of a race.

On the whole, however, it is fair to say that Peirce did not so much wish to advocate an unrestrained collectivism as he wished to allow for a dialectical oscillation between universal and individual forces. Granted, ideas are not limited to the minds of individuals, and there is a sense in which individuals are the products of ideas rather than their producers.[46] But we should not forget what we saw in Chapter 3 about the balance between ideal and real causation, or teleology and determinism. The two poles complement each other; they cannot exist without one another. The question of the relation between individuals and collective entities can be conceived as a corollary of that more general metaphysical fact. This, by the way, tallies with the mitigated linguistic relativism I have outlined in the previous chapter. A super-individual entity par excellence, language does hold sway on how individuals think. Still, individuals can reshape the constraints of language. In fact, "to trace the mental characters of a people in their language is a most delicate task."[47]

Another argument through which "Evolutionary Love" explores the scope and limitations of individual agency hinges on the question of historical periodization. Peirce asked whether history can be partitioned in an objective way. If it can, then "there should be an approximate period at the end of which one great historical movement ought to be likely to be supplanted by another."[48] He outlined a few examples of such supposedly natural periodization. Let me report one of them, which concerns the "history of thought" in Europe.

B.C. 585   Eclipse of Thales. Beginning of Greek Philosophy
A.D. 30   The crucifixion
A.D. 529   Closing of Athenian schools. End of Greek Philosophy.
A.D. 1125 (Approximate) Rise of the universities in Bologna and Paris.
A.D. 1543 Publication of the *De revolutionibus* of Copernicus. Beginning of Modern Science.[49]

---

45 Just to take an example, Gombrich [1974] 1979 suggested looking at social dynamics, such as fashion and competition for prestige, instead of postulating the existence of a spirit of the age.
46 Wiener 1949, p. 20 remarks that Peirce himself spoke of his great philosophical idea, namely pragmatism, as the product of a group of people, because "it is almost self-evident that simply to assign the idea to an individual can give little account of what the process was that actually took place."
47 W9, p. 260 / HP, p. 349 (1893).
48 W8, p. 202.
49 W8, p. 202. Bloch [1949] 1992, p. 153 would later scoff at this kind of calculations as "Pythagorean dreams."

The interval from an event to another being roughly 500 years, Peirce concluded that "perhaps there may be a rough natural era of about 500 years. Should there be any independent evidence of this, the intervals noticed may gain some significance."[50] The tone here is very cautious, and with good reason: the evidence gathered is only anecdotal, and no rationale whatsoever is given for Peirce's choice of historical events, so that the danger of vicious circularity is all too obvious.

Setting apart its shortcomings, this passage is just one of many texts in which Peirce expressed interest in the theoretical problems involved with historical periodization. Another example is a text on "Great Men" from 1901, in which Peirce admitted that "[e]very possible dissection of history is more or less butchery." Yet, this should not prevent historians from indicating the real contours of historical epochs, however vague these contours may be. Indeed, Peirce claimed that periods of "two to five hundred years or longer" are the most natural partition of human affairs. And the natural generations of people, succeeding themselves in intervals of about thirty years, may be identified as the atoms of intellectual history.[51]

Periodization touches on a mathematical and logical problem that had a great importance for Peirce: how can we trace boundaries within a continuum, granting a certain vagueness to the boundaries themselves, but without going as far as to deny their reality? Peirce was positive that the solution of this general problem could be applied to the specific case of history. "To conclude," he argues in the text just mentioned, "that because the point of separation between one part of a continuum and another has no definite location, therefore the division itself has no objective existence," amounts to a logical fallacy. "You can only define the boundary of the branch of a tree or of a river in a purely arbitrary way; but the fact that there are just so many branches does not depend upon our definitions."[52] It does not matter if we do not know where, exactly, to trace a boundary between two areas, or the point at which they divide: the areas remain objectively distinguished all the same.

We might ask ourselves if Peirce was not going too fast here. For in the analysis of historical processes, we are confronted with an opposite argument that is at least as important. It is the points themselves – the individual human actions and events of which history is constituted – that may be taken as most real, no matter how we construct the broader areas, or historical periods, to which they

---

50 W8, p. 203.
51 HP, p. 872 (1901).
52 HP, p. 872.

may be said to belong. Historians do not limit themselves to identifying and describing a given partition of the historical process. They also study what events have been instrumental to the emergence of that partition. As far as I can see, Peirce did not explicitly reflect on this discrepancy between his general mathematical argument about boundaries and the specific case of history.

Still, his historical writings are traversed by the awareness of precisely such an ambivalence between a focus on individual agency and a focus on collective entities. On the one hand, he was very sensitive to the macro-dynamics of historical epochs and to the paths of civilizations. But on the other hand, he was attracted by a microscopic approach, one that zooms in on the biographies of individuals, on their power to bring about change, as well as on the apparently trifling details that may veer the course of history. This focus on individuals is in turn related to Peirce's fascination with the "great men" of history, as well as to his conviction that we can draw "practical lessons" from the history of science (see Chapter 2). The inferential processes pursued by great individuals may enlighten us on the way future inquiry should be carried out.

For all these reasons, Peirce devoted many pages of his history of science to such outstanding figures as Pythagoras, Plato and Aristotle for ancient history (see Chapter 7); and Galilei, Newton, Mendeleev and others for early modern history. But it is, in particular, Johannes Kepler who stands out as the great hero of Peirce's history of science. Kepler is "the greatest reasoner who ever lived,"[53] whose logical abilities may teach us more than those of anybody else. In particular, Peirce described very thoroughly the inferential process on which Kepler's *De Motibus Stellae Martis* is based.[54] The argument of that book, Peirce argues, is "the greatest piece of Retroductive reasoning ever performed." Also, it is particularly instructive because it can be followed step by step. ("Kepler shows his keen logical sense in detailing the whole process by which he finally arrived at the true orbit."[55]) Moreover, Peirce was eager to show that great scientific discoveries, such as Kepler's, have actually been reached according to a pattern that complies with his theory of abductive inference.[56]

---

53 HP, p. 141 (1891).
54 See, e.g., W9, p. 228–233; W9, p. 227 / HP, p. 290 (1892); CP 1.70–74 (1898).
55 CP 1.74.
56 See HP, p. 354 (1898): "We have made some study of the history of astronomy. One purpose which I had in view, in doing this, was manifest at the time. Namely, I wanted to examine whether the actual reasoning of Kepler accorded with my hypothetic inference or whether it had the very different nature which Mill attributes to it when he says, with his intense nominalism, that it was not inference at all but merely framing a description of admitted facts." For a classic account of Peirce's work on Kepler, see Hanson 1958, Ch. 4.

Looking at Art, Artifacts, Architecture

We know that the example of Gothic architecture presented in "Evolutionary Love" comes out again a number of times in Peirce's work. I have insisted on the paradigmatic status this example had, not only for Peirce but, more in general, for nineteenth- and twentieth-century scholars who were interested in the hypothesis of a "spirit of the age" (see Chapter 1). A given cultural phenomenon – in this case, an architectural style – is read as the symptom of a more general intellectual attitude that reverberates in other cultural domains. Peirce deployed this methodological strategy repeatedly in his historical writings. That may be read as one of the main strategies he adopted to negotiate the tension I have already mentioned between collective forces and individual agency. A single object or artifact is taken to be the expression of general cultural traits of an epoch.

In the "historical notes" placed at the beginning of the "Grand Logic" (1893), for instance, Peirce takes up the example of Gothic architecture and does so with stunning attention to detail. He first claims that there is a general "synchronism between the different periods of medieval architecture, and the different periods of logic." Then, he mentions the different architectural styles that have succeeded one another over the course of time: the period of "round-arched churches"; the "early pointed architecture with one plate-tracery"; the "Decorated Gothic"; and finally, the "flamboyant period of architecture in France, the perpendicular in England." For each of these architectural styles, Peirce argues, it is possible to pinpoint some formal features (such as the greater or lesser complexity of the buildings) that have a strict counterpart in the formal features of logical or philosophical writings.[57]

Moving forward a bit in time, the Putnam History deals once again with Gothic churches and with their ability "to embody that intense yearning for something higher." The "Gothic arch" and "its logical conclusion, a lofty roof," can be interpreted as the solution to the new "problem" faced by those architects who wanted to have "wider aisles" and "oblong compartments." "What a wonderful train of thought this was!" Peirce comments. "How strong and simple in every step!"[58]

This is one of the few places in which Peirce consciously stepped out of the history of science and tried to speak the insider's language of another historical discipline, namely the history of art and architecture. (The model here, as we al-

---

[57] CP 4.27–4.29.
[58] HP, p. 351.

ready know, was once again Whewell).⁵⁹ Moreover, the analogy between art and philosophy lends itself to Peirce's quite ambitious attempt to understand architecture itself as a "train of thought." Like logical reasoning, architecture is the result of an inferential process; one that, given a certain expressive problem, looks for its expressive solution. This idea might represent an original way to discuss Peirce's contribution to a pragmatist aesthetics. All the more so as the use of logical analogies and a vocabulary of problem-solving is a trait that Peirce shares with other nineteenth-century professional art historians. It could therefore represent a new link between philosophy and art history that still awaits to be explored.⁶⁰

Nor is Gothic architecture the only cultural expression of the Middle Ages that Peirce sought to compare to philosophy. In a particularly impressive passage from 1905, Peirce mentioned a renowned work of fourteenth-century English literature, namely the Prologue of Chaucer's *Canterbury Tales*. What seems to have catalyzed his attention, in this case, is Chaucer's ability to reconcile the general and the particular in his vivid description of characters.

> I ask, can anybody who has seen Westminster Abbey, who has read the Prologue to the *Canterbury Tales*, and who stops to consider that the metaphysics of the Plantagenet age must have more adequately represented the general intellectual standing of that age, when metaphysics absorbed its greatest heuristic minds, than the metaphysics of our day can represent our general intellectual condition, can any such person believe that the great doctors of that time believed that generals *exist*? They certainly did not so opine, but regarded generals as modes of determination of individuals; and such modes were recognized as being of the nature of thought.⁶¹

Finally, ancient Egypt was yet another period with regard to which Peirce was fond of suggesting a relation between specific artifacts and the general cultural

---

59 See Peirce's reference to the British scholar in HP, p. 350, already discussed in Ch. 1: ""Whewell was right. [The Gothic] was simply forced upon the architects by their desire to open large spaces, and in order to do that to use compartments that were oblong not square."
60 Just to give an example, see Michael Podro's interpretation of German art historian Karl Schnaase, in Podro 1982, Ch. 3. On pragmatist aesthetics, see Shusterman 1992.
61 CP 5.503. Cf. W9, p. 86 (1892): "Five hundred years ago [...] Geoffrey Chaucer was writing the *Canterbury Tales*. Now, I hope most of you have read, at least, the prologue of that collection. We see there that those five hundred years have sufficed to radically transmute a nation's character. There is no personage among the 32 described in that unapproachable painting that resembles or suggests a modern Englishman." Wimsatt 1996 put forth a comparison between Chaucer and Scholastic Realism using Peirce's reading of the latter, but without being aware of Peirce's mentioning Chaucer himself.

trait of the people. A first case in point is the Great Pyramid of Giza. One of the most impressive achievements of a people that Peirce did not consider well versed in science, the pyramid was "standing as a monument of the forgotten scientific skill of those who built it." Peirce went on: "the fitting of the stones is far more perfect than the leveling, though this is good. This shows that scientific precision apart from utility was not made a great object."[62]

A specific problem Peirce encountered in the case of the Great Pyramid was the sheer amount of over-interpretation it was undergoing during the nineteenth century, when people attempted to draw all kinds of hypotheses on Egyptian culture from the wondrous aspect of the monuments. In this sense, the pyramid too, exactly like the Gothic cathedrals, was a paradigmatic case for the study of the "spirit of the age." Moreover, it showed in which sense historians urgently needed the help of logicians. All popular interpretations of the Great Pyramid, Peirce argued, forget that "it is bad reasoning to conclude that because a curious approximate relation exists between two magnitudes therefore it must have been intended." Good historical work is done "not [...] by fishing in the infinite sea of relations, but by trying the one kind of relationship which positive testimony requires us to confine ourselves to."[63]

A second, very different, Egyptian artifact that was the object of Peirce's scrutiny is the Ahmes Papyrus, which I have already discussed in connection to the question of the origins of science. To Peirce's eyes, the papyrus was yet another source of evidence of the Egyptian way of thinking and of its difference from ours. In particular, the papyrus's cumbersome way of representing fractions and additions provoked Peirce's – racist – bewilderment. "The language of a people is the mirror of its thought. A race which remains for six thousand years unable to invent any form of expression for a conception urgently requiring expression, cannot be capable of apprehending that conception very clearly."[64]

---

[62] W9, p. 80–82 / HP, p. 151–154 (1892). Cf. W9, p. 101: "To understand the pyramid, the first thing is to study the old Egyptian mind as it appears in those ages of which we have abundant monuments."

[63] W9, p. 82 / HP, p. 154 (1892). This also means that some relations are accidental. See HP, p. 323 (1898): "The great diversity in the angle of slopes of different pyramids of the Old Kingdom goes to show that, while religious ideas governed these structures in their general mode of construction, yet this particular feature was left to fancy; just as in a Gothic cathedral, while it must be cruciform, with its great door to the west, and must have a nave and a choire, a triforium and a clerestory, yet might or might not have a lady-chapel, or chapels in the east side of the transept, or a lantern, or a hundred other features."

[64] HP, p. 331 (1898). Cf. W9, p. 260 / HP, p. 349 (1893), where Peirce is more prudent ("[t]o trace the mental characters of a people in their language is a most delicate task"), but nonetheless

An "Extraordinary Little Book"

Peirce's most consequential philological work on a scientific text, however, is not the study of the Ahmes Papyrus. Rather, it is the work he started in 1883–84 on the *Epistula de Magnete*, a medieval text written by Petrus Peregrinus de Maricourt (see Chapter 1). Written in 1269, the *Epistula* is the first treatise of which we are aware that deals with the physical properties of magnets. It is also the first to describe freely pivoting compass needles, as were later used in navigation. It was an important source for Roger Bacon and heavily influenced William Gilbert's *De Magnete* (1600).[65]

As I recalled earlier, Peirce somehow became convinced that his work on the *Epistula* would help him soothe the financial difficulties he had started facing in the late 1880s. But this is certainly not enough to explain the enthusiasm he invested in this philological work. Carolyn Eisele reports that, during his 1883 European trip, he spent many weeks studying the manuscript of the *Epistula* conserved in Paris.[66] Peirce himself tells us that he "carefully collated" it with a number of other manuscripts (the most important of which were in Geneva, Leiden, Augsburg).[67] This work stemmed, in part, from his dissatisfaction with the 1838 edition by Guglielmo Libri, which had been conducted on one single manuscript.[68] After putting it temporarily aside, Peirce again took up the *Epistula* in 1893, ten years after his Paris sojourn. He wrote a "Prospectus" to the edition of the text, which he planned to append to his announced, but never completed, work on the "Principles of Philosophy."[69] In the same period, he reviewed for *The Nation* a new edition of Gilbert's work on magnetism and took that occasion to insist on the historical importance of Peregrinus.[70]

Both in 1883 and in 1893, Peirce's interest in Peregrinus shows two faces. These two faces are in turn tied to two different rationales that underlie Peirce's historical work. The first is the possibility of drawing from that medieval treatise a number of practical lessons about scientific methodology. The second is its

---

goes on to speculate that the "tendency to personification" of the Egyptian language "might indicate a sense of the reality of things."
65 See Eisele 1985b; Dauben, 1995 p. 174–176; de Lourdes Bacha/Vannucci 2014. The actual critical edition of the text is in de Maricourt 1995.
66 Eisele 1985b, p. 39–41.
67 HP, p. 60 (1893).
68 See HP, p. 60–61. Cf. Eisele 1985b, p. 40–41; Libri 1838, p. 487–505.
69 See HP, p. 58–61. This is the moment in which he most strongly hoped that the project would "pay well." See the letter to his brother James, HP, p. 45 (1893).
70 HP, p. 124–137 (1894).

relevance to an inquiry into the historical and evolutionary nature of our conceptions.

To begin with, Peirce was struck by the fact that the *Epistula*, a text long predating the scientific revolution in Europe, nonetheless breathes "more of the spirit of science than is found in Bacon himself."[71] This remark opens up a slightly new perspective on a question I have been considering in this and the previous chapter, namely the question of the origins and essence of science. The 1893 "Prospectus" on Peregrinus states that the "quintessence" of science consists in the "spirit of experimental inquiry" with which it is carried out. This means making experiments "for the simple purpose of learning the truth"; devising "a piece of apparatus [...] for the purpose of obtaining an experimental answer to a question"; conducting those experiments "in one connected series"; and finally drawing from these experiments a number of "laws and general propositions."[72] According to Peirce, Peregrinus was the first to have consciously followed this methodology. He understood that scientific inquiry cannot take place in the unaided mind of the investigator, but ought to be carried out through a constant interaction with the experimental equipment. "[A] given piece of apparatus quickly teaches us all it can teach, so that to make new progress new apparatus is required."[73] This is the fundamental reason why "this little book must be considered one of the most important monuments of human progress."[74]

As a matter of fact, Peregrinus did insist on experiment and manual work as a fundamental aspect of scientific investigation. From this angle, he appears as one of the most important pre-modern theorists of the experimental method, alongside Robert Grosseteste and Roger Bacon.[75] To cite Peirce's own translation of Peregrinus, the investigator "ought to know the natures of things. Nor should he be ignorant of the celestial motions. But above all he ought to be assiduous in handiwork [*sed oportet ipsum esse industriosum in opere manuum*], to the end that he may see his performances bring wonderful results to light."[76] Peirce saw in this thesis a perfect counterpart to his views about the tight interrelation of thinking, observation and experiment. As the 22nd "practical lesson" of the Putnam History teaches us, "Means of observation create science."[77]

---

[71] HP, p. 31 (1883).
[72] HP, p. 59.
[73] HP, p. 46.
[74] HP, p. 60.
[75] See, e.g., Freely 2013, p. 194–196. On Peregrinus and Roger Bacon, see HP, p. 31; 46.
[76] HP, p. 65. For the Latin, see HP, p. 68.
[77] HP, p. 410 (1898).

There is a second point, however, which Peirce cared much about. The existence, in the mid-thirteenth century, of such a sophisticated scientific treatise shed new light on the whole history of science. For it indicated that the scientific revolution of the sixteenth century had not come abruptly. "The idea of inductive science" did not spring "full grown from the brain of Francis Bacon." It had some precedents. What is more, these precedents were the work of a community. "Thoughts of that comprehensive kind do not start up in the mushroom-beds of individual brains. They require the broader fields of societies; and generations must pass by before they can acquire any maturity or strength."[78] This is precisely why the *Epistula*, as Peirce wrote to his brother, while being of "only historical interest," is "more than a curiosity": because it is no "sporadic fact." It is the expression of something that "must have more than one man's brain to grow up in."[79]

The study of Peregrinus showcases Peirce's conviction that the philosopher who is willing to grasp the actual dynamic of intellectual growth should delve deep into intellectual history. Peirce dwelt with philological scruple on the words used by Peregrinus (*manualis industria, instrumentum, manifestus*),[80] also with an eye to unearthing the vocabulary of a whole community of scientific inquirers. Moreover, he focused on the specific links that relate Peregrinus to his prior and subsequent sources. And he mused once again on that delicate balance between evolution and revolutions, between individuals and their communities, between bringing about an epochal change and reflecting it.

> What we chiefly want to know about Petrus Peregrinus is whether those germs of science we find in his treatise really had any social and dynamical continuity with the living science of today; and then, if this be so, [...] then we would like to know with what earlier researches his were connected, and in short, how this experimentation which in great measure makes our life, took its first beginning.[81]

Lastly, we find yet another reference to Peregrinus and to the experimental method in a manuscript[82] that is particularly significant for us, because it deals explicitly with the analogies between the process of inference, as investigated by the logician, and the history of science, as investigated by the historian.

---

78 HP, p. 60.
79 HP, p. 46.
80 See HP, p. 46–47; 64.
81 HP, p. 66.
82 CP 7.276–278 (undated, but probably 1896–1900).

The manuscript starts by breaking up the process of inference in "three chief steps." First comes "the putting together of facts which it had not occurred to us to consider in their bearings upon one another"; then comes "experimentation, observation, and experimental analysis"; and third, "the generalization of experimental results."[83] At this point, Peirce turns "to the history of the physical sciences, as the most perfect example of the successful application of thought to the external world," and remarks "that they have all gone through five stages." The first stage is the observation of an interesting phenomenon. The second stage is the invention of "an instrument or a method by means of which the elements of the phenomenon can be subjected to experiment." Then comes the experimental process, "resulting in the ascertainment of a law." The fourth stage consists "in the exact measuring of the constants concerned." Finally, "mechanical theories" that explain the causes of the phenomena are devised. Peregrinus is introduced as illustrating the crucial passage between second and third step in the science of magnetism. He did not discover the lodestone, but rather "invented a new method of experimentation. Namely, he shaped the lodestone into a terella [sic] or ball, and then applied to it short pieces of iron needles. With this apparatus he at once discovered the poles of the magnet and their properties."[84]

Peirce's thesis is that these five historical stages can be loosely brought into agreement with the logical analysis of the process of inference. This lends further credence to a thesis I have discussed in the book's central part. While logic cannot be based on the history of science alone, the history of science does provide logical analysis with supplementary evidence. It is not by accident that the manuscript evokes Peirce's paramount source of inspiration in the history and philosophy of science, William Whewell, by referring to the latter's concept of "colligation":

> Comparing the teachings of the history of science, on the one hand, with those of logic, on the other, we notice a certain agreement between the two. The interesting phenomenon which gives the first impulse to scientific thought corresponds with that interesting colligation of facts, which is the first step of the inferential procedure. Experimental analysis plays a great part in both. Finally, the generalization of the experimental result which completes the inference is represented in physical inquiry by speculation into the mechanical causes of the phenomenon. [...]

---

[83] The three steps loosely correspond to the abductive, inductive and deductive phase of reasoning. But see also RLT, p. 182 (1898), where Peirce talks about observation, experimentation, and habituation.
[84] CP 7.276.

Perhaps, just as the study of a physical phenomenon must depend upon applying such instruments as we can find, so in our attempt to enumerate the processes of thought, we cannot do better than to begin by laying hold of the suggestions that are offered by these analogies between the process of inference and the history of physical science.[85]

Observation of Lives

I would like to close the chapter with a brief analysis of yet another thread of Peirce's historical inquiry, namely the work on the biography of "great men" which he initiated while at Baltimore (see Chapter 1). This segment of Peirce's work showcases once again his methodological eclecticism and his reliance on different rationales to bring historical inquiry to bear on his philosophical interests. Moreover, it should be kept in mind that the question of "great men" – that is, what factors can explain great human achievements or personalities – had an important status in nineteenth-century science and philosophy. Here, we cannot but repeat something we have already said with regard to Peirce's analysis of Gothic architecture or his interest in the pyramids of Egypt: Peirce was willing to pick the objects of his historical inquiry among those that were already laden with a robust theoretical significance.

Two main reasons seem to have initially motivated Peirce's curiosity about "great men" during his Baltimore years. The first was the attempt to apply a rigorous mathematical technique to as fleeting a subject as the impression that biographies exert on the observer.[86] I have already hinted at the fact that Peirce wished to carry out his inquiry through statistical means. He demanded that his students survey a good deal of biographies of historical figures, formulate a subjective statement about their greatness, and then gather further data through a questionnaire about family background, biography, physical abilities, social milieu, work, daily habits, "genius," moral and religious character. On the basis of these data, it should have been possible to obtain a ranking of "greatness" of those people.[87] It is worth remarking that this method did not aim at using mathematics to silence the more impressionistic component of inquiry. On the contrary, Peirce wished to channel that component into a proper scientific methodology, with an eye to showing how the latter may be fruitfully applied even to such apparently impalpable objects as the greatness of a given historical

---

85 CP 7.277–278.
86 Cf. Peirce's later reminiscences about the 1883 to 1884 study, in CP 7.256–266 (c. 1900), and in particular par. 257, which stresses the "impressionist" character of the list of great men.
87 See W5, p. 25–106 (1883–1884); Houser 1993, p. xxiii-xxiv.

personality. In a sense, therefore, this method sought to strike a balance between the two kinds of observation, mathematical and qualitative, which Peirce was starting to differentiate.

The second reason is more implicit but no less important. It bears on the same issue I discussed earlier in this chapter, namely the balance between the role of individuals and the role of collectives in shaping historical progress. In fact, this is precisely the reason why the debate about "great men" occupied a central position in the nineteenth century.

A milestone in that debate – at least as far as the English-speaking world is concerned – was Thomas Carlyle's 1841 treatise *On Heroes, Hero-Worship, and the Heroic in History*.[88] That book emphasized the role of great personalities as the real subjects of history. Three decades later, Herbert Spencer countered Carlyle's position from a socially deterministic standpoint. Human greatness, he maintained, has little to do with innate individual qualities and must instead be ascribed to the influence of external circumstances. Before a man "can remake his society, his society must make him."[89] Concurrently, Francis Galton's *Hereditary Genius* (1869) sought to provide the study of greatness with a scientific foundation, by linking it to a study of the inheritance of cognitive traits. This idea was, in turn, bound up with his eugenic project.[90]

William James replied to all these positions in an 1880 lecture, entitled "Great Men, Great Thoughts, and the Environment." The Spencerian position, he contended, risks annihilating individual agency. This is not only unacceptably deterministic. It is also epistemologically untenable, as it amounts to calling upon the whole causality of the universe to explain the tiniest individual fact. Historians should, rather, learn from Darwin and make a distinction between the causes that randomly produce great individuals and those that maintain, sponsor or obstruct them – that is, environmental forces. Since, however, the latter may in turn be influenced by individuals' actions, we should conclude that environment and great personalities hold a mutual influence on one another.[91]

---

[88] Carlyle [1841] 2013.
[89] Spencer [1873] 1966, p. 34.
[90] Galton [1869] 1892. On Galton's eugenics see, e.g., Ginzburg 2004.
[91] James later republished the lecture with a slightly different title: "Great Men and their Environment" (James [1880] 1979). Another name worth mentioning is Frederick A. Woods. In 1913, Woods wrote an influential book, *The Influence of Monarchs* (Woods 1913), which used the neologism "historiometry" to refer to the statistical study of individual achievements. Woods was in contact with Peirce, who, to quote Houser 2010, p. lxv, "contributed a promotional comment, as did Royce, to support sales [of the book]. Peirce told Woods that 'biometry' would have been a better word." On the significance of the great man theory among pragmatists see also Wiener

We know that Peirce read Galton and James with his Baltimore students.[92] But to get a glimpse of what views he held of them, we must wait a few years. For after his dismissal from Johns Hopkins, Peirce temporarily set aside his work on great individuals. Among the several reasons behind this choice, we may spot a certain discontent with the results it led to. When he returned to it, in an 1891 review on a history of mathematics, he wrote: "The only history of much interest is that of the human mind. Tales of great achievements are interesting, but belong to biography (which still remains in a prescientific stage) and do not make history, because they tell little of the general development of man and his creations."[93]

But his ideas were not settled yet. Exactly one month after writing that review, he published another one, this time on Locke, which displays his interest in precisely those "tales of great achievements" that he had dismissed the month before. Peirce's opinion here goes decidedly against Galton. The latter, Peirce argued, insisted on the family inheritance of greatness. But if we restrict our focus to "the truly great" individuals, this relation no longer holds. Moreover, not even the truly great individuals "rise above other men as a man above a race of intelligent dogs." Random circumstances have a great weight in deciding over their successes or failures.[94]

In the same period, Peirce wrote a few more short texts on the topic, such as a comment on Comte's "positivist calendar" of great individuals, and a review of Lombroso's *Man of Genius*, in both cases sharply criticizing the two authors.[95] More significantly, while preparing his 1892–93 Lowell Lectures on the history of science, he suggested to his employer two possible topics: "the history of science from Copernicus to Newton," or the "comparative biography of Great Men." And he added that he was not so much interested in Galton's "eminent men," as in describing men of a higher order – in presenting "a sort of scientific Plutarch."[96]

1949, p. 129–136. Finally, a much later defense of this theory from a pragmatist viewpoint is Hook 1943.
92 Houser 1993, p. xxiii.
93 W8, p. 36 (1890).
94 W8, p. 38 (1890).
95 W8, p. 267–270; 277–283 (1892). Cf. Houser 1993, p. xxiv.
96 HP1, p. 141–142 (1891): "The other subject is much lighter. It refers, not to the *eminent* men whom Galton has studied, but to a higher order, the *phenomena* of the history of mankind. A list of about 300 of such men would be formed and discussed and a method for the comparative study of them developed. Comparative lives of a few of them would be given, – a sort of scientific Plutarch, – scientific I mean in the treatment, not so exclusively as to the subjects. Finally, a

As we know, the lectures ended up dealing with the former topic. But the latter was resumed on many occasions. Peirce drafted a new list of three hundred individuals "who produce upon us the impression of greatness."[97] It is also probably at about that time that he penned short narratives about such outstanding individuals as Cola di Rienzo or Napoleon.[98] Unlike Peirce's work on the history of science proper, his inquiries into "great men" also encompass the other two classes of people that we have briefly mentioned in Chapter 5: practical men and men of "emotion" or "feeling." That is, politicians and artists.[99]

This enlargement of focus has implications at the level of method as well. Much more forcefully than in the 1880s, Peirce emphasized that writing the biography of great men is a rather peculiar intellectual activity, based on a qualitative, impressionist grasp of its object. In this sense, it is again significant that Peirce considered his work on biography as a possible alternative to the history of science for his Lowell Lectures. Going back to some terminology I introduced in Chapter 4, we might say that the two projects epitomize two quite different kinds of historical observation: a descriptive and inductive one, which takes history first and foremost as the empirical basis for theoretical generaliza-

---

large number of general questions relating to the nature, kinds, causes, and characters of greatness would be inductively considered." Cf. De Tienne forthcoming.

97 W8, p. 258 (1892).

98 See Pencak 1991. For Cola di Rienzo, see HP, p. 550–554. The title of Peirce's text, "Rienzi, last of the tribunes," echoes the 1842 opera by Richard Wagner (*Rienzi, der letzte der Tribunen*), as well as the novel by Edward Bulwer-Lytton from which Wagner's opera is taken (Bulwer-Lytton 1835). For Napoleon, see, in particular, R 1319. In a later text, Peirce called Napoleon a "stupendous charlatan [...] by far the greatest man of [his] times." See HP, p. 873 (1901).

99 The concluding remarks to the 1892–93 Lowell Lectures bear witness to the tight interplay between Peirce's history of science and his project on "great men." See W9, p. 258 / HP, p. 289 / CP 7.275: "I have done what lay in my power to present as much of the history of science as I have been able to treat in a lucid manner, and to show that it is governed by Law like other departments of nature. But this law is not of the nature of mechanical forces, such that the individual and the spirit of man is swallowed up in cosmical movements, but on the contrary it is a law by virtue of which lofty results require for their attainment lofty thinkers of original power and individual value. You cannot silence or stifle or starve a single one of them without a loss to civilization from which it never can wholly recover. It is not more certain that the inches of a man's stature will be affected all his life by an attack of fever as a baby, than that we are now less happy because of the many great geniuses whom untoward circumstances have put down. The country that can first find the means not to provide the million with miscellaneous reading matter, and elementary education, but to utilize its superior intellects for the general good, will experience a wonderful acceleration of civilization from which the benefit of the million, in much more valuable ways, will come about of itself." The "Law" that is "not of the nature of mechanical forces" should be read as a reference to the "Law of Mind," W8, p. 135–157. See Ch. 3.

tions; and a more impressionist or qualitative one, which dwells on narratives of individual biographies.

If we look at the rest of Peirce's writings during the 1890s, this interpretation comes out strengthened. In those years, Peirce became more attentive to narrative tools, not only as a way to account for the diachronic character of events, but as a rhetorical device on its own. He even experimented with the writing of fiction.[100] And in his 1898 Cambridge lectures, he devoted a few pages to the many shades of "observation," stressing the role played by the observation of qualities and by physical discrimination. As regards the latter, he mentioned literary sources as diverse as Teophrastus, Jean de La Bruyère, Lavater and Maupassant.[101]

His parallel work on "great men" bear the mark of these broad range of interests. Peirce claimed that qualitative observation makes it possible to approach the lives of great individuals not, in the manner of Comte, as mere "factors" in the achievement of a grand scheme; but as "concrete souls" to be investigated with "sympathy," "in all their living reality."[102] In the case of scientific men, this has a two-fold implication. On the one hand – as Peirce wrote with regard to Spinoza – "light may be thrown upon any doctrine from the life and personality of its author."[103] On the other hand, "the contemplation of the lives and character of great men is a salutary and invigorating spiritual exercise."[104] For instance, the life of Pythagoras, "the sublimest of all human biographies," is also "one of the most precious [ones]; because it inspires and inflames the heart of the reader with a great and lofty ideal of humanity."[105] This point gains significance if we recall, first, Peirce's insistence on the "practical lessons" that the logician can draw from history (see Chapter 2);[106] and second, his conception of agapastic evolution and the pre-cognitive intellectual "sympathy" it

---

[100] See "Embroidered Thessaly" (1892-c. 1897), W8, p. 296–340. See the long editorial note on W8, p. 655–663.
[101] RLT, p. 182–187, and in particular p. 184.
[102] W8, p. 267 (1892). See also the criticism Peirce makes of Comte on the following page: "Where is Jesus? [...] Jesus is omitted because he does not represent the sentiments which it is Comte's purpose to inculcate."
[103] CN1, p. 164 (1892).
[104] W8, p. 267. See also ibid.: "Washed-out accounts of Washington and Franklin have done incalculable injury to American characters. [...] [E]ngendered from the spirit of lies, how could these biographies bear living seeds of anything but hypocrisy and sordidness?"
[105] HP, p. 558–559 (1892).
[106] A sentence I cited in Ch. 2 serves as an introductory remark to Peirce's 1892 biographical piece on Pythagoras: "I shall beg leave to intersperse among these essays others relating to points in the history of human reason, treated mostly with special reference to the practical lessons they suggest" (HP, p. 557).

postulates (see Chapter 3). Through biography, Peirce was attempting to broach from yet another angle this fundamental problem of the force that ideas may exert upon us before they are fully articulated.

For similar reasons, Peirce started to mention with enthusiasm the work of the French writer Charles-Augustin Saint-Beuve. In 1895, a "scientific Saint-Beuve" substituted the "scientific Plutarch" as a paramount model of biographical inquiry.[107] In 1902 Peirce added: "Happy would be the reader who was not familiar with the 'Causeries du Lundi,' since he would have one of the joys of life still to taste."[108]

Analogous preoccupations move the third phase of Peirce's interest for "great men," around 1901 to 1902. The texts from this period provide a retrospective systematization of Peirce's inquiries on that topic.[109] Again, they insist on the peculiar kind of observation that is requested by biographical work. This time, however, the concept of observation can probably be put in relation to Peirce's growing interest in phenomenology and in the peculiar kind of observation that it entails.[110] "[T]he way to judge of whether a man was great or not is to put aside all analysis, to contemplate attentively his life and works, and then to look into one's heart and estimate the impression one finds to have been made."[111] Human greatness "afford[s] an admirable training in what I call 'pure observational power,' by which I mean the power of looking out of one's eyes and of estimating the impression made by some element of what one contemplates."[112] The natural sciences are a good training in experiment, "but the pure observational part in them," which is necessarily "subjective," "is rudimentary."[113] This "pure observation" is completely neglected by "men who overvalue reasoning."[114] Again, it is different from a "Sherlock Holmes's habit of making deductions from minor circumstances." Rather, it is something like an "artist-like" observation, directed at the qualities of feeling.[115]

---

107 See HP, p. 454.
108 HP, p. 536 (1902).
109 See, in particular, HP, p. 489–496; HP, p. 872–876; CP 7.256–266 (1901).
110 On phenomenology, see Atkins 2019.
111 HP, p. 490.
112 HP, p. 873.
113 HP, p. 873. The following sentence is worth quoting as well (ibid.): "Natural history exercises men in great alertness of observation; but the fact that work as fine as that of Huber on bees was conducted by a blind man suffices to show how small a part the power I have in view plays in such studies."
114 HP, p. 874.
115 CP 7.256. In this passage, Peirce also calls the artist-like observation "Lavaterian." I return to Sherlock Holmes in the next chapter.

Peirce went on to deduce from these remarks an emphasis on the power of external circumstances. For all their greatness, great men remain men after all: "while great men are of no ordinary native gifts, and very great men far from being so, yet, after all, their development depends mainly upon circumstances, to such an extent that wherever there is an effectual demand for them there is pretty sure to be a supply."[116] While the greatest among them "do somewhat partake of the nature of monstrous births in that their exceptional natures are largely due to causes that very rarely operate at all,"[117] human greatness as a general phenomenon is related to "circumstances" and may thus change with history. Moreover, it is in the power of human beings, by devising better institutions, to sponsor or obstruct that greatness.[118] The autobiographical tone of these remarks is easy to note.

---

116 HP, p. 874.
117 HP, p. 875. In the "Minute Logic," CP 2.32 (1902), Peirce, discussing Hegel, remarked: "It is the normal minds who are influential." Cf. Ch. 3.
118 HP, p. 875.

7 The Logic of Historical Inquiry

Peirce on Historical Method

In the mid-1890s, Peirce started working for the newly appointed secretary of the Smithsonian Institution, Samuel P. Langley, as a translator and research assistant. Around 1900, Langley asked him to write a short piece for the Smithsonian *Annual Report*, dealing with Hume's argument about miracles and his conception of the laws of nature. The drafts Peirce sent to Langley were never published. But the work Peirce conducted on Hume was instrumental in invigorating his interest in historical methodology and in the epistemology of testimony.[1] This led him to write one of his lengthiest texts overall (over a hundred pages), entitled "On the Logic of Drawing History from Ancient Documents, Especially from Testimonies" (1901).[2]

As the title makes clear, Peirce's treatise is explicitly devoted to the methodological and epistemological implications of the study of antiquity. However, it also contains a critical discussion of Hume's argument about testimony and one of the most comprehensive expositions of Peirce's theory of scientific inquiry. This text is, thus, the best evidence that Peirce's work as a historian proceeded in parallel with a methodological and meta-theoretical reflection on the logical underpinnings of his inquiries. This should not surprise us: from the very beginning of his intellectual career, Peirce understood himself primarily as a logician and looked at all his intellectual activities from the viewpoint of the logical problems they involved.

This final chapter is devoted to the logic and methodology of history. In the first part of the chapter, I will deal with the treatise on ancient history. It will become clear that the logical and methodological reflections that Peirce advanced in that text cannot be separated from a major epistemological problem that dominates the philosophy of historiography, namely the problem of historical truth and historical explanation.[3] But I will also try to link Peirce's treatise on ancient

---

[1] See HP, p. 869–912; Brent [1993] 1998, p. 276–277; Wiener 1947; Merrill 1991; O'Hara 2008. Hume's argument about miracles is in Hume [1748] 2000, section 10.

[2] The text (R 690) is published almost in its entirety in HP, p. 705–800, with the exception of a section on Aristotle, which is published in CP 7.232–7.255. A related logical digression (from R 691) is published in NEM4, p. 1–12. The most exhaustive commentary on this treatise is Liatsi 2006.

[3] Grigoriev 2017 similarly discusses Peirce's 1901 treatise within the framework of the philosophy of historiography. See also Huebner 2019, p. 22–24.

history to further methodological questions that are more or less explicitly formulated at other junctures of his oeuvre.

One major claim provides the guiding thread for the whole chapter. Peirce, I maintain, was primarily interested in formulating a realistic take on historical inquiry. This is not to deny that – as Joseph L. Esposito has claimed – his realism is sometimes in tension with a more constructionist position. Peirce may have failed fully to appreciate this tension,[4] although I believe that, in the end, his readiness to accommodate some constructionist or anti-positivist insights is not so much a shortcoming as, rather, an asset of his realistic philosophy of history.[5] Be that as it may, the 1901 treatise on the "Logic of Drawing History from Ancient Documents" shows us quite unambiguously that Peirce's primary concern was to articulate a conception of history as relying on the same inferential machinery and on the same realistic presuppositions as all other empirical sciences.

Indeed, I will be unveiling a number of points that may let us think of Peirce as a sort of scientifically-minded antiquarian.[6] These points are: the polemic against historical skepticism; the interest in empirical evidence and archeological research; the emphasis on non-textual material; the passion for erudition and minute details. As we shall see, Peirce pitted this methodological attitude against one of the most authoritative historical schools of his time, namely the German school of higher criticism. But he did so out of a stern conviction that what he was offering was a more scientific, realistic account of historical explanation than his adversaries could ever provide.

Documents and Monuments of Ancient History

The first paragraph of "The Logic of Drawing History from Ancient Documents" deserves to be cited in full because it provides a clear introduction to the text's main argument and to its polemical objectives.

> Ancient history is drawn partly from documents and partly from monuments. The last generation has afforded so many examples of the refutation by archeology of the conclusions of the critics of documents as to suggest the question whether the whole logical procedure of the latter class of students has not been radically wrong. The purpose of the present

---

4 See Esposito 1983, which I discuss in the Introduction.
5 See the Conclusion for a more articulate discussion of this point.
6 I am using the term "antiquarian" in the specific sense that was investigated, in particular, by Momigliano 1950.

paper is to show that this is the case; that the logical theory upon which the critics proceed is as bad as logic can be; to set forth and defend the true logical method of treating ancient historical documents; and to set this new theory in a clear light by applying it to two or three examples, including a case where the testimonies are comparatively strong and another where the testimony is at best very feeble.[7]

Several things are anticipated here. First, Peirce refers to his adversaries as the "critics of documents." What he meant by that phrase is the school of nineteenth-century German historical criticism. One of the most prominent among such historians, whom Peirce targeted often, was Eduard Zeller.[8]

More generally, Peirce's polemic fits well into his critical attitude toward German academia, an attitude that became particularly virulent (and sometimes slightly chauvinistic) in his later years. What Peirce found problematic about German scholars was their continuous relapse into subjectivism. Whatever the value of this judgment, it helps us understand a fundamental point: Peirce's claim that the logical procedure of the German critics is radically wrong is not animated by a skeptical intent, as though Peirce wanted to deprive historical inquiry of any objective foothold. Quite the contrary: Peirce found too little objectivity in German historical criticism. He charged German historians with wishing to "evolve history from one's *Ich-heit*."[9] And he wanted to substitute this approach with a better one.

Second, Peirce was adamant not only about his adversaries but also about his allies. His strategy was to pit the philological methods of historical criticism against the other major discipline that studies antiquity, namely archeology. The passage just cited goes as far as to claim that archeology has "refuted" the results of the critics of documents. Peirce had in mind, in particular, the archeological research of the Egyptologist William M. Flinders Petrie and of the German discoverer of Troy, Heinrich Schliemann. According to him, it was specifically Schliemann who imparted the first decisive blow to the method of higher criticism.[10]

A third important point is Peirce's use of a distinct piece of terminology, namely the binomial document/monument. This is an age-old conceptual distinction, which can be interpreted in different ways.[11] Peirce interpreted it in a

---

[7] HP, p. 705.
[8] See Liatsi 2006, p. 1–2. The criticism of Zeller began as early as in the 1892–93 Lowell Lectures. See W9, p. 148–157 / HP, p. 169–176. See also RLT, p. 105–106 (1898).
[9] HP, p. 367 (c. 1898).
[10] See CP 1.113 (c. 1896). On Flinders Petrie, see, e.g., CP 1.209–210 (1902).
[11] See Le Goff 1978; Ceserani 2019.

slightly idiosyncratic manner. For him, monuments are all the physical objects that are passed down to us from the past, including manuscripts and written artifacts. Documents, by contrast, are testimonies *about* that past. As we shall see, a good portion of Peirce's methodological preoccupations hinges on the question over the right balance between monuments and documents.

> In the case of ancient history, the facts to be explained are, in part, of the nature of monuments, among which are to be reckoned the manuscripts; but the facts in greater part are documentary; that is, they are assertions and virtual assertions which we read either in the manuscripts or upon inscriptions. This latter class of facts is so much in excess, that ancient history may be said to consist in the interpretation of testimonies, occasionally supported or refuted by the indirect evidence of the monuments.[12]

Peirce's treatise can be broken up into three sections. The first section is a critical discussion of the methodology of historical criticism. The second section, though very long, is only tangentially concerned with history. Rather, it is a detailed exposition of the logic of scientific inference. Only at the end of this section does Peirce stop to draw some methodological "rules" to be applied to the investigation of ancient documents. The third section closes the text with an illustration of three case studies, which Peirce intended to use as a test of his methodological precepts. The case studies come from the history of philosophy: they are about the biography of Aristotle, Plato, and Pythagoras. I will take these three sections in turn.

At the beginning of his treatise, Peirce asserts that historical criticism is based on the "method of balancing likelihoods." This method consists in assessing the "impressions" of likelihood that all testimonies leave on the subject, as a degree of probability of the testimony itself; and then in proceeding to sum up algebraically all these impressions into a final impression which sustains the historical judgment. This method, Peirce goes on, derives from Hume's argument about how to assess the authenticity of testimonies. But the historians have worsened this method:

> The principal difference between Hume and them is that the word 'proof' is continually in their mouths, a word which Hume scrupulously avoided in speaking of the minor facts of ancient history. [...] They seem to be discontented with mere probability; and are always in search of an argument that something 'must' be.[13]

---

[12] HP, p. 760–761.
[13] HP, p. 707.

The method of balancing likelihoods is combined with a second principle, which may sound like the opposite of the one just described but actually goes in the same direction. As Peirce put it, historians transferred into history the philological precept of the *lectio difficilior*, or the idea that "in general, the more difficult reading is to be preferred." This led them to hold that "that narrative which was least likely to be invented, owing to its improbability," is the one to which we should give more credence.[14] What the two methodological criteria have in common is a 'quintessentially German' reliance on subjectivism, which makes the individual opinion of the scholar the ultimate benchmark of judgment. In fact, the two criteria, once welded together, gave German historians two complementary "defences against historical testimony":

> If the story told appears to them in any degree unlikely, they reject it without scruple [*by the criterion of balancing likelihoods*]; while if there is no taint of improbability in it, it will fall under the heavier accusation of being too probable [*by the criterion of the lectio difficilior*]: and in this way, they preserve a noble freedom in manufacturing history to suit their subjective impressions.[15]

One basic objection Peirce leveled against this subjectivistic approach is its taking for granted that we should begin our inquiry with a skeptical and doubting attitude. Peirce argued, on the contrary, that we should begin from our natural impulse "to believe anything that one may hear said, until it is found that that assumption leads to difficulties."[16] In other words, critical inquiry only sets in once we stumble upon doubt. The scholar's attitude cannot be at complete loggerheads with "a deep and primary instinct, such as is the instinct to believe testimony, without which human society could not exist."[17] In fact, ignoring this instinct amounts to a methodological fallacy. "There is no surer mark of inexperience in dealing with witnesses than a tendency to believe they are falsifying, without any definite, objective, and strong reason for the suspicion."[18] We can recognize an affinity between this argument and Peirce's criticism of Cartesian epistemology (see Chapters 1 and 4), as well as with the way he conducted his own historical inquiries (see Chapter 6).[19]

---

14 HP, p. 707. Peirce pointed to Richard Bentley as the father of this idea. On Bentley's work on the New Testament and his standing in the history of philology, see Timpanaro [1981] 2005, p. 63.
15 HP, p. 707.
16 HP, p. 712.
17 HP, p. 761.
18 HP, p. 761.
19 See, e.g., W9, p. 110 / HP, p. 157 (1892): "The Egyptians were convinced that their early ancestors had knowledge far superior to their own. Since they thought so, I think we must allow it

This does not mean that the method of balancing likelihoods can never be employed. Peirce did admit that in some cases it is a useful method. However, there are at least three reasons why it should not be taken as a methodological foundation for the study of history and, in particular, of ancient history. First, ancient testimonies cannot be assessed singularly, as though they were independent of one another or of the "antecedent probability of the story."[20] Second, the very idea of assessing testimonies probabilistically is flawed. Probability is a mathematical concept; it means "a well-founded statistical generalization." But German historians used it as though it referred to a psychological fact, namely "the degree to which a hypothesis accords with one's preconceived notions."[21] Finally, applying the mathematical theory of chance to ancient history means overseeing the qualitative difference between mathematical reasoning (necessary, demonstrative) and empirical science, which is aimed at "enlarging" our knowledge. "[T]he staple of our reasoning in ancient history should not be of the demonstrative kind."[22]

Peirce goes on to present his alternative approach to the study of ancient history. The leading idea is simple enough: history is just a species of scientific knowledge and must, therefore, be based on the same combination of abductions, deductions and inductions on which all other sciences are based. More specifically, history consists in formulating hypotheses – or abductions – about the past; in deriving a number of consequences from them; and in putting these consequences to an experimental test.

It might be objected that the subject matter of history does not lend itself to any experimental test in the proper sense of the word. Peirce answered this objection by claiming that the inductive, empirical confirmation of historical hypotheses must occur in a slightly different way from that which happens in the natural sciences. Namely, it must occur by putting historical abductions to the test of archeology. As I already said, he cited in particular a few examples of Egyptian and Greek archeology that, in his opinion, have disproved the reconstructions of the higher critics.[23]

---

probably was so; for they were in a better situation to judge of the matter than we are." (But then he also commented: "Still, I grant that they might be deceived by the superior workmanship and the gigantic scale of the pyramids.")

20 HP, p. 713.

21 HP, p. 715. This however should not mislead us into thinking that Peirce rejected a priori all attempts to relate mathematical reasoning and subjective or "impressionist" beliefs. As we know from previous chapters, his research on "great men" was fueled by precisely that interest.

22 HP, p. 718.

23 See HP, p. 719.

We thus come to the very long central section of Peirce's treatise, which presents one of the most accurate expositions of his mature theory of scientific inference.[24] Peirce begins by discussing the concepts of scientific belief, explanation, and inference. He then presents the three modes of inference – abduction, induction and deduction – with their relative subdivisions, and discusses at length the concept of "random sampling" that is involved in the concept of induction. With regard to abduction, he also articulates the most significant criteria that should guide us when we attempt to formulate a new explanatory hypothesis of a hitherto unexplainable fact.

The upshot of this long digression is a list of methodological "rules" that will amend the method of historical criticism.[25] Rule one: "It is not sufficient to say that testimony is not true, it is our business to explain how it came to be such as it is." Two: "our first hypothesis should be that the principal testimonies are true; and this hypothesis should not be abandoned until it is conclusively refuted." Three: "slight probabilities" and "merely subjective likelihoods" should not play a decisive role in our hypothesis. The latter, in particular, are "merely expressions of our preconceived notions," and thus obstruct the discovery of new facts. (As Peirce also observed, "one of the main purposes of studying history ought to be to free us from the tyranny of our preconceived notions.") Four: complex hypotheses should be split into elementary components, "so as to test each one singly." Five: "when we are in doubt which of two hypotheses ought to have precedence, we should try whether, by enlarging the field of facts which they are to explain, a good reason will not appear for giving one of them a decided preference over the other." Six: it is convenient, for economic reasons, to give provisional preference to hypotheses that will have to be tested in any case over those that require extra work.

Three Case Studies: Aristotle, Plato, Pythagoras

Finally, the third part of the treatise is devoted to three case studies. These are meant to show the concrete functioning of Peirce's methodological rules and to put them to an empirical test. In accordance with those rules, Peirce presented the three case studies in the form of puzzles or surprising facts. These puzzles demand to be solved by explanatory hypotheses, the consequences of which can in turn be tested by the analysis of documents and monuments.

---

24 See HP, p. 720–760.
25 See HP, p. 761–762.

Three Case Studies: Aristotle, Plato, Pythagoras — 199

All three case studies have to do with the history of Greek philosophy. More particularly, they deal with the lives of three eminent philosophers: Aristotle, Plato, and Pythagoras.[26] This choice can easily be related to Peirce's interest in the biography of great individuals. But in addition to that, in the cases of Aristotle and Plato, the historical and biographical interest is bound up with a genuinely philological interest in the reconstruction of the two greatest philosophers of antiquity.

This might come as a surprise: as we have just seen, the more theoretical part of Peirce's treatise puts much emphasis on the importance of using archeological data as a test of historical hypotheses. When choosing his own examples, however, Peirce picked cases where archeology hardly plays a role, but philology is pivotal. The difficulty can be overcome if we keep in mind that the polemical target of Peirce's treatise on ancient history is not philology as such, but a certain kind of philology, which he saw embodied in German scholarship. After all, we know that Peirce had been cultivating philological interests from his youth. In the course of this book, we have watched Peirce embarking on philological inquiries at several junctures of his life: when he wrote the *Photometric Researches*; when he studied the scientific theories of Petrus Peregrinus; when he worked as a scientific consultant for George A. Plimpton; and so on.

The first case study concerns the reception of Aristotle's writings.[27] The point of departure is the relation of Aristotle's extant works with his lost works. As Peirce noted, there is a huge discrepancy between the writings we actually know and the ancient catalogues of Aristotle's works. Moreover, the unpolished style of the extant writings conflicts with ancient descriptions of Aristotle's style as "highly artistic."[28]

The decisive hypothesis Peirce advanced to explain this puzzling fact is derived from a story that originates with Strabo.[29] Upon Aristotle's death, his writings came into the possession of his pupil, Teophrastus. When the latter died, he bequeathed them to his friend Neleus, who brought the books to Scepsis (in the

---

26 In a new cycle of lectures Peirce gave at the Lowell Institute in 1903 (HP, p. 1011), he presented a slightly different list of case studies. He talked about "five occasions in [his] life, and five occasions *only*," in which he "had the opportunity of testing [his] Abductions about historical facts." He mentioned three of them: the life of Pythagoras; his study of ancient Egypt; and his conjectures about Babylonian science. He also recalled his study of the true identity of the alchemist Basilius Valentinus (see Ch. 2, and HP, p. 570–579, 1898), but added that "in that case, I reach what may be counted as a certainty." We can speculate that the two remaining cases are precisely the studies of Plato and Aristotle conducted in the 1901 treatise.
27 CP 7.233–255. See Liatsi 2006, p. 60–76.
28 CP 7.233.
29 See Strabo, *Geography*, 13.1.54. Cf. Lindsay 1997.

Troad, Asia Minor). The writings of Aristotle remained in a cellar in Scepsis for decades, until a wealthy Greek book collector, named Apellicon, purchased the library and brought it back to Athens. "The papers of Aristotle" – Peirce explained – "had suffered grievously, during their century and a half of incarceration, from damp and insects, and were in places illegible; but Apellicon [...] occupied himself with copying and editing them." When Sulla, the Roman consul, besieged Athens, he brought the papers to Rome. "Ultimately, the peripatetic scholiarch Andronicus of Rhodes undertook the arrangement of the papers, the correction of the text, and the publication of a new edition." While the papers were in Rome, it was found that "the editing of Apellicon was excessively bad."[30]

Peirce admitted this hypothesis "upon probation" and went on to "trace out its consequences."[31] Here begins a striking train of inferences, which I report only in its outline.[32] Peirce pointed out a regularity in the length of Aristotle's writings and of their sub-chapters as calculated from the Berlin edition. On this basis, he felt confident he could infer that Aristotle had a tendency shared by many writers, namely to "to write nearly to the end of his last sheet, often crowding a little at the end";[33] and that the sheets he was using could contain about seventy lines of text of the Berlin edition.

Further, Peirce put forward the hypothesis that these sheets had not been pasted together, but only rolled up, because they were considered works in progress. Therefore, there was a possibility that later copyists had changed the order of the sheets, transposed chunks of texts, or inserted spurious texts more or less at an interval of seventy Berlin lines. This is precisely the circumstance that needed to be verified in order to test the hypothesis; a circumstance that Peirce considered all the more likely as Apellicon, the first editor of Aristotle's papers, was a "stupid" and corrupt man. He had no understanding of Aristotle's philosophy and no scruple in meddling with the manuscripts.

Note that Peirce did not wish to express a final judgment about whether his predictions were correct. He tells us he did not have the time to make a systematic investigation into them. "It is, perhaps, just as well that I have not; because their predictive character is thus made manifest."[34] But he did pause on one point that was particularly important to him.[35] In the *Prior Analytics*, Aristotle

---

30 CP 7.234.
31 CP 7.239.
32 CP 7.239–245.
33 CP 7.239.
34 CP 7.245.
35 See CP 7.248–254. Cf. Kempski [1951] 1992; Kempski [1988] 1992; Flórez 2014; Bellucci 2019.

deals with the two concepts of *epagôgê* and *apagôgê*, which Peirce translated as "induction" and "abduction."[36] But Aristotle's dealing with the latter concept, Peirce believed, is made unclear by a textual corruption in one of the examples, a corruption that he hypothetically ascribed to Apellicon. Because of this textual corruption, *apagôgê* is reduced to "nothing but an ordinary syllogism of the first figure, when we are not sure of the minor premiss, but still are more inclined to admit it than we should be to admit the conclusion if the latter were not a necessary consequence of the former."[37] However, Peirce believed that Aristotle must have had in mind a conception of *apagôgê* much closer to his own conception of abduction, namely, a syllogism that derives hypothetically the minor premise from the knowledge of the major premise and the conclusion.

Peirce's dealing with Aristotle's writings raises at least two problems. First, Peirce moved from an assumption that other scholars of Aristotle have considered unjustified. Whether or not the story told by Strabo about the cellar of Scepsis can be trusted, it is by no means assured that this was the unique way that the Aristotelian papers were passed on to us. Indeed, it seems far more likely that the edition prepared by Andronicus of Rhodes made use of other sources as well.[38]

But even if we cast aside this specific issue, there is a more general methodological problem. The train of inferences on which Peirce based his reconstruction of the genesis of the Aristotelian manuscripts is replete with extremely speculative assumptions (for instance: that Aristotle rolled up his sheets instead of pasting them together; that he had a tendency to write to the end of his sheets; and so forth). Now, Peirce was perfectly aware of this. His method consisted in formulating historical hypotheses with a great degree of liberty, only to abandon them if they were not found to agree with other circumstances. It is precisely in this respect that he aimed at turning upside down the methodology of the historical-critical school. But I suspect he overestimated both his readiness to abandon hypotheses that were, after all, too feeble, and his ability to take seriously those pieces of evidence that ran contrary to his hypotheses.

One last point I would like to make has to do with Peirce's treatment of Apellicon, the alleged first copyist of Aristotle. Peirce was quite critical of him. He emphasized both Apellicon's intellectual and moral flaws. True, Apellicon was the one who brought Aristotle's writings back to Athens. But he did so only out of cupidity. His interventions into the text amounted to a series of mistakes

---

36 *Prior Analytics*, II, 23–25. The Loeb edition (Aristotle 1938) translates *apagôgê* as "reduction."
37 CP 7.251.
38 Liatsi 2006, p. 64–66.

and corruptions. Still, a noteworthy aspect of Peirce's dealing with the copyist of Aristotle's manuscripts is his willingness to treat him as a fully-fledged historical actor, endowed with his own personality and intellectual attitude. When we conduct our philological investigations, Peirce seems to tell us, we must take into account the biography of Apellicon, the kind of person he was and the kind of circumstances he went through, in order to make the correct inference about the kind of emendations that he may have carried out.

This tacit presupposition of Peirce's argument may be related to his criticism of the *lectio difficilior*. Some philologists have argued that one risk of too straightforward an application of that criterion is precisely to strip the figure of the copyist of historical concreteness. The criterion of the *lectio difficilior* allows copyists or witnesses to intervene in the text either as mechanical transcribers or as trivializers. Their only thinkable activity is mechanically to corrupt a source into a more banal one. If one version of the text is more complex, original, "difficult" than another, then it is more likely to stem directly from the author than the other one.[39] On the contrary, rejecting or at least qualifying the criterion of the *lectio difficilior* means accepting a continuity between the figure of the author and the figure of the copyist or witness. Both are historical actors, endowed with motivations, intellectual dispositions and implicit biases that may act as filters in the composition or in the transmission of a text.

I will examine much more cursorily the other two case studies. The second is about the chronology of the life of Plato.[40] The question is whether we can determine such a chronology taking Plato's own writings as our basis. This, Peirce presumed, is only possible under the assumption that the main turning points of Plato's life should have left some traces in his dialogues. Therefore, answering that question depends on whether we can establish a precise chronology of Plato's dialogues without in turn making use of data from Plato's life (for otherwise we would come up with a circular argument).[41] To achieve this task, Peirce embarked on a painstaking analysis of the scholarly literature on the dialogues, on

---

[39] The philologist Giorgio Pasquali articulated precisely such a critique in Pasquali [1934] 1952, Ch. 2. He also suggested two correctives to the criterion of the *lectio difficilior*. First, the philologist should pursue the quintessentially historical task of reconstructing the social and cultural context in which the copyists worked, in order better to understand what kind of emendations they were likely to make. Second, he or she has to take into account the varying relationship between the likelihood of the event and the possibility that the copyist took it to be likely. See Ginzburg 2019.

[40] HP, p. 763–791. See Liatsi 2006, p. 77–97.

[41] See Liatsi 2006, p. 98.

the basis of which he suggested his own chronology.[42] Similarly to the case of Aristotle, where he had taken pains to calculate the number of lines of text of every chapter, he paid particular attraction to quantitative and stylometric methods.[43] Moreover, he stressed once again the possibility of making "predictions" about the relation between Plato's life and his writings based on his calculations. ("I wish to say that these were genuine predictions written out verbatim as here given long before I had any idea how the calculations were to be made or how they would turn out."[44])

Finally, the last case study is a reconstruction of Pythagoras's biography.[45] In this case, I am less interested in the concrete results of Peirce's investigation than in the motivations lurking behind his choice of examining the life of Pythagoras. We already know about Peirce's interest in Pythagoras from his study of "great men." But even more compelling was a methodological motivation. From 1892 onward, the life of Pythagoras represented to Peirce both a paradigmatic example of the shortcomings of the historical-critical school and a perfect litmus test for his own historical methodology. Why? Because no piece of information we have about him is solid:[46]

> [A]lmost all our information is derived from three writers living about five hundred years later [...]. Moreover, as far as we can descry, there is no possibility of testing any hypothesis. In such a case, we must renounce at the outset any attempt to reach anything approaching certainty. Yet we are not to aim at verisimilitudes, which are merits in romances, but not in scientific results. What, then, are we to do? We are to embody, or rather, to ensoul, all the pertinent facts, that is to say, the facts *that those writers make those statements*, in such a hypothesis as best unifies them, and will serve as a source of experiential predictions, whenever, in the future, it may be in our power to verify or refute any predictions on the subject.
>
> We produce our hypothesis. We shall not say that it is true; and it would be altogether aside from our purpose that it is likely. But it shall be simple and natural, shall explain all the facts we have by showing how the testimonies might probably come to be what they are, and it shall be definite enough to enable us to deduce consequences from it which can be tested experimentally.[47]

---

42 Peirce's chronology is in HP, p. 786–787.
43 One crucial source of Peirce's is Lutosławski 1897. See Liatsi 2006, p. 91–95.
44 HP, p. 789.
45 HP, p. 791–800. See Liatsi 2006, p. 98–112.
46 See W9, p. 148 (1892): "One thing which interests me particularly in regard to Pythagoras is that we are in possession of a great mass of testimony concerning him, which is extremely conflicting and all of it decidedly of an untrustworthy description, and it becomes a nice question for the scientific logician what can be concluded from this evidence." See also W9, p. 158–170 / HP, p. 216–226 (1892); HP, p. 1011–1021 (1903); HP, p. 997–1003 (1910).
47 HP, p. 791–792.

Hypothesis, Explanation, Truth

It is well known that one of the authors who exerted a decisive influence on the young Peirce was the logician Richard Whately. The latter's *Elements of Logic* (1826) may have been the very first book of logic Peirce ever held in his hands (see Chapter 1). Less well known is another circumstance, although Max H. Fisch pointed it out with his usual precision. Peirce was well acquainted with another book by Whately, namely the *Historic Doubts Relative to Napoleone Buonaparte* (1819). This book is a satire against precisely the kind of skepticism about historical truth that may derive from Hume's arguments about miracles. Whately pretended to doubt the very historical existence of Napoleon, thereby exposing the logical absurdities which radical skeptics incur. As Fisch put it, "[t]his was almost certainly the germ from which Peirce's theory of historical method developed."[48]

This circumstance supports the interpretation of Peirce's methodology of history as oriented toward the articulation of a realistic, non-skeptical approach to historical inquiry: an approach that makes it possible to speak about historical truths in the same sense in which we speak about other scientific truths. At the same time, Peirce's study of the life of Pythagoras shows better than anything else that it would be a mistake to interpret Peirce's historiographical realism as a form of positivism. In extreme cases such as the life of Pythagoras, Peirce was willing to open up historical inquiry to hypotheses that are not robustly supported by evidence (because, in that case, no hypothesis can), provided they fit the logical scheme of sound abductive reasoning.

Peirce took up this point in a 1903 lecture about logic. The life of Pythagoras is a perfect opportunity to study "Abduction under difficulties," because it is

> a case where the evidence is extremely slight and the testimonies are open to grave suspicion, so that we cannot make the most distant approach to certainty in any way. [...]. Here I can only make a conjecture which I predict that future discoveries will confirm in its main features as far as those discoveries shall go. This theory will make no pretension to being knowledge, but only to being a good guess, which we may strongly and confidently hope will be confirmed.[49]

---

[48] Fisch 1986a, p. 349. Cf. Liatsi 2006, p. 135. Fisch reports that a copy of Whately's book about Napoleon could be found in Peirce's private library. We should, however, keep in mind that Whately's satire was oriented to defending the revelation of the Bible and to criticizing the use of the historical-critical method to fuel skepticism about the Christian revelation.
[49] HP, p. 1011 (1903).

Even in these extreme cases, however, historical explanation retains the logical form of all other kinds of scientific explanation. We first perform an abduction or hypothesis; then we derive a number of consequences from that hypothesis by means of deductions; finally, we bring these consequences to a sort of experimental test that takes the form of an induction. Thus, a valid historical explanation is a hypothesis whose consequences can be confirmed independently by evidence. In this sense, the logic of induction and that of abduction – the two forms of ampliative inference – are the pivots of historical inquiry.

As regards induction, let me return for a moment to the role of archeology. Since no experimental procedures in the strict sense of the word can be performed on history, the inductive confirmation is primarily carried out by the analysis of archeological evidence. As I said before, Peirce was thereby taking inspiration from the great archeological discoveries of his times, with Schliemann's discovery of Troy playing center stage.

> [W]hen Schliemann entertained the hypothesis that there really had been a city of Troy and a Trojan War, this meant to his mind among other things that when he should come to make excavations at Hissarlik he would probably find remains of a city with evidences of a civilization more or less answering to the descriptions of the Iliad, and which would correspond with other probable finds at Mycenae, Ithaca, and elsewhere.[50]

The distinction between documents and monuments, so prominent in the 1901 treatise, helps us further articulate this idea. Depending on whether we give a heuristic primacy to documents or to monuments, Peirce argued, we end up with two main approaches to historical inquiry. The German historical school is based on the criticism of testimonies. Therefore, it gives prominence to documents.[51] On the contrary, the inferential-verificationist method sketched by Peirce himself is centered on using evidence of all kinds as a way to put historical hypotheses to the test. In this sense, it gives prominence to monuments. To

---

50 CP 5.597 (1903). In the lines that immediately follow, Peirce pits this conception of empirical verification against the narrower one advocated by Comte, which is conditional on the possibility of perceiving something directly. This shows from another angle the difference between a radical positivist position and Peirce's much more nuanced historical realism. "[I]t would be fair to infer that [Comte] would permit Mr. Schliemann to suppose he was going to find arms and utensils at Hissarlik, but would forbid him to suppose that they were either made or used by any human being, since no such beings could ever be detected by direct percept. [...] The same doctrine would forbid us to believe in our memory of what happened at dinnertime today. [...] Of course with memory would have to go all opinions about everything not at this moment before our senses."
51 Cf. Le Goff 1978, who insists on the role of Fustel de Coulanges in nineteenth-century historiography.

the best of my knowledge, only in one text did Peirce pronounce both approaches – the document-centered and the monument-centered – to be "sound and scientific," arguing that the choice of the one over the other is mainly a matter of "division of labor."[52] In all other cases, the second approach was clearly taken as the more valuable one.

In a late letter to Columbia sociologist Franklin Henry Giddins (1910), in particular, Peirce explained to his distinguished colleague that his approach consisted in treating everything, even written testimonies, as "monuments." Indeed, testimonies are "an important species of monuments."[53] What this means concretely is that we cannot be content with deciding whether a testimony is reliable or not. For even if we consider it unreliable or false, we have to explain how it is that it has come about. In this sense, false statements can be illuminating, indeed even "more illuminating than the true statement would have been."[54] But Peirce had already articulated a similar argument in 1892, this time with regard to the work of German historian and antiquarian August Boeckh. This is worth noting, given that some elements of Boeckh's methodology, like the attention not only to texts but to all kinds of historical evidence, might actually be seen to agree with Peirce's ideas. Peirce, however, was adamant: the "'school of Boeckh' […] attaches more importance to documents than to monuments. Now experience has shown that this method cannot lead to any fixed conclusion."[55]

---

52 CP 7.374 (1902): "[I]f there are two different methods, both of them sound and scientific, which are applicable to the same problem, they ought to be employed jointly; or if not, they at any rate are too closely associated to make different families of science. Nothing, for example, can be in stronger contrast than the method of investigating ancient history from monuments and from documents. But the only proper course is to use both methods conjointly. It is true that one man may not be strong enough to work in both ways to advantage; but still he will thoroughly know that his own work is only a result of the division of labour and that it has to be joined to another man's work by a third workman, before anything can be settled."
53 HP, p. 997. On the same page, however, Peirce seems to recognize that what he says applies particularly to ancient history, and that "what is called 'Modern History'" may need to rely more on the study of documents.
54 HP, p. 997.
55 HP, p. 430. In his influential *History of Classical Scholarship*, first published two years before Peirce's letter to Giddins, John E. Sandys pit the "historical and antiquarian" school of Boeckh against "the grammatical and critical school" of Gottfried Hermann. The first "investigated all the manifestations of the spirit of the old classical world," while the second focused on "questions of grammar and metre and style." (Sandys [1908] 2011, p. 89–101).

What about abduction, or hypothesis? The relevance of this concept to discussions about historical method has already received much attention.[56] Less obvious is the fact that the relation goes in the other direction as well. Indeed, it is not far-fetched to say that Peirce's reflections on the epistemic status of historical research influenced his thoughts about abduction throughout his career.[57] One of the strongest pieces of evidence thereof comes from "Deduction, Induction and Hypothesis," an essay from 1878. History, it is argued therein, is a paradigmatic example of hypothetical or abductive reasoning. In a possible allusion to Whately, Peirce brought up the example of Napoleon:

> It is an hypothesis that Napoleon Bonaparte once existed. How is that hypothesis ever to be replaced by an induction? It may be said that from the premiss that such facts as we have observed are as they would be if Napoleon existed, we are to infer by induction that *all* facts that are hereafter to be observed will be of the same character. There is no doubt that every hypothetic inference may be distorted into the appearance of an induction in this way. But the essence of an induction is that it infers from one set of facts another set of similar facts, whereas hypothesis infers from facts of one kind to facts of another. Now, [...] the facts which serve as ground for our belief in the historic reality of Napoleon are not by any means necessarily the only kind of facts which are explained by his existence. It may be that, at the time of his career, events were being recorded in some way not now dreamed of, that some ingenious creature on a neighboring planet was photographing the earth, and that these pictures on a sufficiently large scale may some time come into our possession [...].[58]

Two points are particularly worth mentioning here. First, abduction differs from induction in its linking "facts of one kind" with "facts of another." This property

---

56 See Eco/Sebeok 1983 for a link between abductive reasoning and a conception of historical inquiry modeled on what Ginzburg [1979] 1989 has called the "evidential paradigm" (*paradigma indiziario*). In that context, the comparison between abduction and the investigative mode of inquiry embodied by the literary figure of Sherlock Holmes plays a crucial role. We should not, however, forget a detail we touched upon in Ch. 6: for Peirce, a Sherlock Holmes-kind of reasoning does not exhaust the possibilities of our observation of the past. The more impressionist, artlike observation of biographers is another option.
57 As early as 1867, i.e., in the year in which he was articulating in a precise manner his concept of abduction, Peirce criticized positivism on the account of "the absurdities to which it gives rise when strictly applied to history, which is entirely hypothetical, and is absolute incapable of verification by direct observation." W2, p. 45.
58 W3, p. 336–337. Cf. p. 326, where some examples of hypothetical reasoning are brought up. One of them is the following: "Numberless documents and monuments refer to a conqueror called Napoleon Bonaparte. Though we have not seen the man, yet we cannot explain what we have seen, namely, all these documents and monuments, without supposing that he really existed." Another such example is the detective-like kind of inference we perform when we make a guess about the identity of a person.

comes in particularly handy when applied to historical knowledge because, in that case, we need to bridge two very different sets of objects: on the one hand, traces, which exist in the present; and on the other hand, historical facts, which belong to the past. With the second point worth mentioning, however, we introduce the third temporal dimension, namely the future. Perhaps influenced by his beloved analogy between history and astronomy, Peirce undertook the mental experiment of imagining that some extra-terrestrial creatures recorded some pictures of the earth at the time of Napoleon, which would give us some new evidence of his existence in an indefinite future time.

Peirce's mental experiment helps us cast light on yet another point. Although historical knowledge is knowledge of the past, the criteria of its verification are necessarily about the future. "History would not have the character of a true science if it were not permissible to hope that further evidences may be forthcoming in the future by which the hypotheses of the critics may be tested."[59] As with all other kinds of knowledge, historical knowledge is future-oriented. This helps us formulate an answer to a classical objection leveled against pragmatist epistemology, namely its alleged inability to take into account the specificities of historical knowledge, precisely because it is oriented toward the future.[60] Like Dewey, Peirce would answer this objection by pointing out that the past can only be known indirectly, as the result of abductive inferences that are based on present evidence and verified in the future.[61] These abductive inferences are, of course, by definition fallible. That is, they are liable to be disproved in the future by new evidence.

---

[59] CP 5.541 (c. 1902). The passage continues: "A theory which should be capable of being absolutely demonstrated in its entirety by future events, would be no scientific theory but a mere piece of fortune telling. On the other hand, a theory, which goes beyond what may be verified to any degree of approximation by future discoveries is, in so far, metaphysical gabble." In this sense, Peirce claims, all kinds of beliefs are "expectative."

[60] See in particular Lovejoy 1920, p. 63, who had mainly Dewey in mind: "The pragmatist [...] manifests a curious aversion from admitting that we have knowledge, and 'true' knowledge, about the past." See also Joas 2016, p. 73; Niklas 2016, and my discussion of Peirce's processualism in Ch. 3.

[61] Cf. Wiener 1949, p. 195: "Critics of pragmatism have argued that knowledge of the past confutes its experimental principle of verifiability, for we cannot verify or transform experimentally what is irretrievably past. The pragmatic reply to this argument refers us to the method of making historical propositions, namely, we use hypotheses and inferences based on *present* evidence [...] and on the continuity of processes *now* observable [...] with those of the past." Keep in mind that Wiener was a student of Lovejoy's. As regards Dewey's argument, see in particular Dewey [1938] 1986, p. 230–238, and Tamm 2014.

It may be worth relating this epistemological position to the metaphysical framework I have outlined in Chapter 3. As we know from that previous discussion, the mode of existence of the past is modeled on the category of Secondness. The past is simply and brutely there. We can experience it but we cannot change or refute it. To the contrary, the future is the modality of time that most closely aligns with Thirdness. It is the object of rational knowledge and it is open to changes. Now, historical knowledge refers to the past as its subject matter but is dependent on the future. It is a rational, continuously perfectible enterprise, which is nonetheless anchored to the 'brute' actuality of Secondness.

Unintentional Evidence: Betraying versus Parading

The 1901 treatise on ancient history, which has provided the guiding thread of my analysis until now, is concerned with one major epistemological and methodological question: how should we go about ascertaining the occurrence of a fact in the past? Its aim is to show the soundest logic to make conjectures about whether something has really happened. In order to answer that question, Peirce touched on other questions that are equally crucial for the historian. For instance: how should we interpret a historical source (whether a document or a monument)? How can we learn to extract information from that source about the period in which it was produced? These questions, however, tend to remain in the background of Peirce's writings about history. I would now like to push them into the foreground.

Let me start again with the distinction between documents and monuments. I have suggested that Peirce construed this distinction in quite an idiosyncratic way: documents are written testimonies about the past, while monuments are all artifacts (texts included) that can be used as evidence to confirm or disprove a given hypothesis. This way of construing the meaning of the two concepts should not be confused with an alternative way of defining them, which is the following. As the etymology of the word suggests, monuments can be defined as intentional or deliberate pieces of evidence: artifacts created with the explicit intention to convey the memory of a specific event, person, value, and so on. Documents, on the other hand, can be understood as unintentional pieces of evidence: artifacts that tell us something about the historical conditions of their production, over and above the intention of the producers.[62]

---

[62] See, e.g., Ceserani 2019, p. 15. The distinction between intentional and unintentional evi-

Here is a good reason not to conflate these two definitions: if we did conflate them, we would be led to think that Peirce's emphasis on the primacy of monuments over documents goes hand in hand with a strong emphasis on intentional over unintentional evidence. But this is not so. As we saw in Chapter 6, Peirce was eager to explore ways in which historical artifacts – Gothic churches, Egyptian pyramids, old scientific books – can be read as symptoms of more general intellectual tendencies, which go well beyond the intentions of their producers. In fact, his emphasis on monuments is perfectly consistent with the idea that the very existence of a given testimony is always potentially informative, whatever the truth value of its content, whatever the intention of its producers.

It is worth relating this problem to one of the central pieces of Peirce's epistemology, namely the doctrine of critical common-sensism (see Chapter 4). As we know, Peirce emphasized the role of historical inquiries in letting us appreciate that even the original beliefs of common sense are subject to changes over time.[63] But Peirce also added something more specific about the nature of that historical study. In a footnote to his 1905 "Issues of Pragmaticism," he made clear that the beliefs of past people only become accessible to historians if the latter make use of unintentional evidence.

> I wish I might hope, after finishing some more difficult work, to be able to resume this study and to go to the bottom of the subject, which needs the qualities of age and does not call upon the powers of youth. A great range of reading is necessary; for it is the belief men *betray* and not that which they *parade* which has to be studied.[64]

So, if we want to study the historical development of beliefs, it is necessary to look at what people unconsciously reveal about themselves rather than what they deliberately say. One crucial reason thereof should be sought in the relation between beliefs, habits, and consciousness. Beliefs are embodied in habits. They are habits of thought and action that we can control and deliberately approve of, but the full purport of which is not perfectly transparent to us. For we can never

---

dence has been most famously formulated by Bloch [1949] 1992, p. 74. See Ginzburg 2017 for a link between Bloch and the tradition of antiquarian research.

63 See, in particular, CP 5.444 (1905): "I made some studies preparatory to an investigation of the rapidity of these changes, but the matter was neglected, and it has been only during the last two years that I have completed a provisional inquiry which shows me that the changes are so slight from generation to generation, though not imperceptible even in that short period, that I thought to own my adhesion, under inevitable modification, to the opinion of that subtle but well-balanced intellect, Thomas Reid, in the matter of Common Sense (as well as in regard to immediate perception, along with Kant)."

64 CP 5.444n.

be entirely conscious of the general rules that govern our intellectual and practical conduct here and now; there will always be something that escapes our notice. (Recall a sentence I quoted in Chapter 4: "[T]he methods of thinking that are living activities in men are not objects of reflective consciousness. They baffle the student, because they are a part of himself.")[65]

This argument can be couched in semiotic terms as well. Human actions may have an explicit or intended meaning but they are also the interpretants of implicit beliefs. These implicit beliefs can be reconstructed abductively, starting from the very actions they give rise to. And the same applies to the tangible products of human action, such as artifacts.[66] As Peirce put it in 1908, "man's proper function" is to "embody general ideas in art creations, in utilities," and "theoretical cognitions[.]"[67]

The Journey of a Footnote

Peirce's mention of "art creations" and "utilities" as embodiments of general ideas remind us of a crucial aspect of Peirce's work as a historian (see Chapter 6), namely his interest in reconstructing the "spirit of the age" that breathes through the cultural expressions of a given historical period. The analogy between Gothic architecture and Scholasticism is the most important case in point. However, a similar attitude comes into view in many other cases. An Egyptian scribe, "having to suggest the idea of a god by means of a simple picture, draws a star [...].

---

[65] CP 3.404 (1892). The question of whether beliefs are conscious habits remains unsettled in Peirce's writings. In many passages, dating especially from the 1890s, Peirce insists that "[a] belief is a habit; but it is a habit of which we are conscious." (CP 4.53, c. 1893–1895). But from around 1902 on, Peirce started to write as though being able to deliberately approve of a belief is not the same as being perfectly conscious of it (see, e.g., NEM4, p. 39–40, 1902). In the same text in which he formulated the distinction between betraying and parading, he writes that "[b]elief is [...] a habit of mind essentially enduring for some time, and mostly (at least) unconscious" (CP 5.417, 1905). Cf. NEM4, p. 297–298 (1904): "A man does not necessarily believe what he thinks he believes. He only believes what he deliberately adopts and is ready to make a habit of conduct."

[66] For Peirce, the boundary between artifacts and the body is permeable. See CP 7.366 (1902): "A psychologist cuts out a lobe of my brain [...] and then, when I cannot express myself, he says, 'You see, your faculty of language was localized in that lobe.' No doubt it was; and so if he had filched my inkstand, I should not have been able to continue my discussion until I had got another. Yea, the very thoughts would not come to me. So my faculty of discussion is equally localized in my inkstand."

[67] CP 6.476 (1908).

What could better *betray* the Egyptian way of thinking?"⁶⁸ And again: "Every Greek seemed to be born a philosopher. Their architecture, their decoration, their sculpture, the construction of their dramas and of their prose writings *equally betray* this passion for unity."⁶⁹

It is worth noting that precisely the Peircean footnote about betraying and parading has been the object of a remarkable, if under-appreciated, reception.⁷⁰ Erwin Panofsky himself, the author of the best-known parallel between Gothic architecture and Scholastic philosophy, cited that footnote in a key passage of his influential book on *Meaning in the Visual Arts* (1955) in which he distinguished between the implicit content and the explicit subject matter of a work of art:

> Content, as opposed to subject matter, may be described in the words of Peirce as that which a work betrays but does not parade. It is the basic attitude of a nation, a period, a class, a religious or philosophical persuasion – all this unconsciously qualified by one personality, and condensed into one work.⁷¹

Panofsky was not citing Peirce firsthand, however; and I have already suggested that the parallel between the two authors on the topic of Gothic architecture is not due to any direct influence (see Chapter 1). The link is, rather, to be found in the work of the philosopher and art historian Edgar Wind, a pupil of both Panofsky and Ernst Cassirer, who had profound sympathies for pragmatism and cited precisely that Peircean footnote in a short paper on the methodology of history.⁷² Some years later, the French sociologist Pierre Bourdieu, drawing on the writings of Wind and Panofsky, dwelt on exactly the same distinction between betraying and parading. Though he failed to mention the name of Peirce, he used the latter's terminology to introduce one of the key ideas of his theory,

---

68 HP, p. 435 (1894). My emphasis.
69 W9, p. 143 / HP, p. 204 (1892). My emphasis.
70 I have dwelt on this reception much more at length in Viola 2012. See also Wagner 2012.
71 Panofsky 1955, p. 14. But see also Panofsky [1932] 1998, where the same sentence from a *geistvoller Amerikaner*, a "brilliant American," is cited; then Panofsky 1969, p. 204. On Gothic architecture, see Panofsky 1951.
72 Wind [1936] 1963, p. 258: "Whatever objections may be made to the current psychology of the unconscious, it is undeniable that men do not know themselves by immediate intuition and that they live and express themselves on several levels. Hence, the interpretation of historical documents requires a far more complex psychology than Dilthey's doctrine of immediate experience with its direct appeal to a state of feeling. Peirce wrote in a draft of a psychology of the development of ideas: 'it is the belief men *betray*, not that which they *parade*, which has to be studied.'" On Wind and pragmatism, see the essays collected in Bredekamp/Buschendorf/Hartung/Krois 1998. Niklas 2016 links Wind's paper on historical methodology to the debate between Lovejoy and Dewey that I have discussed above.

namely, the necessity of inquiring into the unintentional elements of human behavior as a means for sociological observation.⁷³

The remarkable journey of Peirce's footnote about betraying and parading runs in parallel with some theoretical analogies between Peirce and the other scholars I have just mentioned. A first such analogy is a shared interest in the social and cultural factors that influence individual thinking. A second analogy is a shared emphasis on the role of habits. Both Panofsky and Bourdieu related their emphasis on the unintentional layer of our conduct (on what we betray rather than parade) to a concept that was also relevant to Peirce, namely the Aristotelian-Scholastic concept of *habitus*. More specifically, they claimed that scholars' ability to reconstruct the unconscious beliefs of a given historical actor is dependent on the existence of a dispositional layer of human behavior. This *habitus* is durable but historically changeable. It is acquired through education and social interaction but remains largely implicit.

Still, these analogies should not mislead us into thinking that Peirce's concept of habit is merely the seat of our social or cultural unconscious, or that his historical methodology boils down to examining what documents and monuments betray about historical actors, looking, as it were, over their shoulders only. As I have already indicated, habits are, for Peirce, a necessary condition of consciousness, reflexivity, and self-control. Indeed, Peirce defined beliefs as habits that we can control and approve of, even when we are not entirely conscious of their scope and purport. In a similar spirit, Peirce's treatise on ancient history makes clear that we should begin our historical inquiries by taking witnesses and testimonies at face value. This means that the critical common-sensist's task of inquiring into what people betray as opposed to what they parade

---

73 Bourdieu 1969, p. 118: "To relate the works produced by an age to the educational practices of the time is [...] to provide oneself with one means of explaining not only what they say (*ce qu'elles proclament*) but also what they betray (*ce qu'elles trahissent*) in so far as they participate in the symbolic aspects of an age or society." For the French original, see Bourdieu 1966, p. 905. A few pages before (Bourdieu 1969, p. 112), Bourdieu explains: "What is *betrayed* by the eloquent silence of the work is precisely the culture (in the subjective sense) by means of which the creator participates in his class, his society and his age, and which he unwittingly introduces into the works he creates" (my emphasis). The same contrast between *proclamer* and *trahir* is highlighted in Bourdieu's early book on photography (Bourdieu 1965, p. 23–24). In the handbook on sociological method that he published in 1968 (Bourdieu/Chamboredon/Passeron [1968] 2005, p. 284), we find a French translation of Wind's text: "Peirce écrit dans un fragment sur la psychologie du développement des idées: 'ce qu'il nous faut étudier ce sont le croyances que les hommes nous livrent inconsciemment, et non pas celles dont ils font étalage.'" For Bourdieu's reliance on Panofsky's work on Gothic architecture, see Bourdieu [1967] 2005.

cannot turn into a condescending attitude that discards the viewpoint of witnesses and testimonies themselves.[74]

The complexity of Peirce's attitude to this methodological issue is reflected in his ideas about the role of historical interpretation in the articulation of our own position within history. On the one hand, the impossibility of getting an exhaustive grasp of our present habits of thought is tantamount to the idea that there is something about our conduct that necessarily escapes us. "Truly to paint the ground where we ourselves are standing is an impossible problem in historical perspective."[75] In this sense, future historians will be better positioned than we are to understand the purport of our own thoughts and actions. But on the other hand, the fact that we are rational agents means that we retain an ability to understand our own thoughts and actions in a non-delusional way.

Moreover, individual thought processes can be construed as an interiorized dialogue between a speaker and an interlocutor, with the latter acting as a sort of inner observer (see Chapter 5). In this sense, there is no watertight boundary between the interpretation we carry out while dialoguing with ourselves and the interpretation put forth by external observers.[76]

The Interpretation of Fellow Thinkers

The latter remark about dialogue and interpretation leads us to the final question of historical methodology that I would like to consider. This question falls within the remit of hermeneutics, or the general theory of interpretation. How did Peirce believe that we should go about interpreting and assessing the thought of other thinkers – scientists or philosophers?

---

[74] This argument displays some affinities with a defining tenet of pragmatist social inquiry, as formalized by Dewey in particular: sociologists or social philosophers need to take seriously the viewpoint of social actors. They have to look at actors' ability to articulate intelligently a problematic situation and to deal successfully with it. See, e.g., Dewey [1927] 1988. In France, this Deweyan idea triggered a reaction to Bourdieu's sociology that was labelled "pragmatic sociology." The pivotal figure of this movement is Bourdieu's former student, Luc Boltanski. See, e.g., Boltanski [2009] 2011. For an insightful transposition of pragmatic sociology onto the methodology of historical inquiry, see Cerutti 2004; Cerutti 1991. Cerutti and others speak of "pragmatic history," but in a different sense than the one I have considered in Ch. 2. For the relation between Bourdieu and pragmatism, see Dietz/Nungesser/Pettenkofer 2017.
[75] CP 4.32 (1893).
[76] Hoopes 1993 further notes that Peirce's emphasis on habits dovetails with his tendency to reject all clear-cut oppositions between the inner mental states of actors and their actions.

Let me start by noting an affinity between the issue of unintentional evidence and a concept I discussed in earlier chapters, namely the concept of *logica utens*. The historian of science and philosophy may want to look at the works of other thinkers with an eye to reconstructing the methods of thinking of which those thinkers were not fully aware, but which nevertheless governed their inferential procedures. This entails a decided effort at historical contextualization. Peirce signaled often the importance of understanding and assessing a specific intellectual tendency only against the background of history, without lapsing into anachronisms.[77]

A similar contextualist attitude is expressed in Peirce's insistence on the importance of anchoring the history of scientific and philosophical ideas to a study of non-intellectual facts. He programmatically envisaged his historical inquiries as a sort of progressive, concentric enlargement of focus. Starting from the ideas of a single author or a single epoch, the historian needs to take into account both the social and political context of those ideas and the broader historical processes that brought them about. "It is as with ordinary use of the eyes," He commented.[78] His interest in biography (see Chapter 6) can be read in the same way: "light may be thrown upon any doctrine from the life and personality of its author."[79]

How does this effort at contextualization play out at the level of a philosophical assessment of past thinkers' ideas? To answer this question, it is, I think, vital to keep in mind Peirce's processualism about ideas and his agapastic model of evolution (see Chapter 3). Ideas are processual entities. They are

---

[77] I find a particularly good example thereof in Peirce's discussion of Duns Scotus, CP 7.395 (c. 1893): "The great object of the metaphysics of Duns Scotus is to state the results of ordinary experience, that it shall not close any positive experimental inquiry, or pronounce anything possible observable to be a priori impossible. In Scotus, this naturally led to loyalty to Authority, then the recognized fountain of truth; in our day it will produce unfaltering faith in Observation."

[78] W9, p. 80 / HP, 150–151 (1892): To "really comprehend" a specific question in the history of science, "it is necessary to consider it in its relation to intellectual development as a whole. It is as with ordinary use of the eyes. When I open my eyes and look at something, there is but a very small area indeed, where things are seen sharply in focus; all the rest of the field of vision is ill-defined, but it is very necessary to enable me to see how the little thing that is in focus is situated with reference to other things. So we must not altogether neglect any part of the scientific history of the period in question. We must even go outside of that period, we must sketch vaguely the whole history of science before that period and its whole history since." Cf. the methodological observations of the 1870 Berkeley review, which I have considered in Ch. 1. The relation between the "history of thought" and "history in general" is also reflected upon in the "Minute Logic," though in a way that is more relevant to the philosophy of history than to actual historical practice. See CP 2.32–2.33, cited by Esposito 1983, p. 164–165.

[79] CN1, p. 164 (1892).

often born as "vague and shadowy" premonitions of what they will become and they are articulated through a process that turns their potencies into actualities. As a consequence, a major aspect of philosophical ingenuity and of hermeneutic subtlety is to be able to recognize whether ideas harbor something valuable – in Peirce's words, "whither they tend."[80]

In a 1909 letter to Victoria Welby, Peirce described himself as "*thorough* in penetrating the thoughts of his predecessors – not merely their ideas as they understood them, but the potencies that were in them."[81] Here, the viewpoint of actors ("their ideas as they understood them") is not measured against the study of an unintentional layer of meaning, as in the case I investigated above. Rather, it is put in opposition to the quintessentially philosophical task of further developing the implications of those ideas. This entails a distinct metaphysical commitment, which is indeed clearly displayed by the word "potencies."

It is often said that historians are more interested in giving a descriptive account of past ideas, while philosophers are more interested in exerting a normative judgment: in pronouncing those ideas valid or invalid, logical or illogical, true or false. But Peirce's approach to the history of philosophy, as is expressed in his letter to Welby, helps us make this contraposition a bit less rigid. Developing the "potencies" that are wrapped up in philosophical ideas is a kind of normative judgment, but one that straddles the divide between philosophers and historians. For we assess the validity of an idea insofar as we further develop it, by applying it to new cases and by making explicit new implications. But in order to do so, we need to be acquainted with its history.

In the same letter to John Dewey that I discussed in Chapter 4, in which Peirce criticized the younger colleague for his naturalization of logic, he added: "I should not write in such underscored terms to any man with whom I did not feel a very deep respect and sympathy. I am simply *projecting upon the horizon*, where distance gets magnified indefinitely, the *direction* of your standpoint as viewed from mine."[82] Although a genuine historical perspective is not predominant here (because Dewey was a contemporary of Peirce), we can recognize a similar attitude: normative judgment is about tracing out the "direction" of ideas, more than it is about carrying out a static analysis. Also, that Peirce made this remark to Dewey has a certain irony to it. For the conception of

---

[80] W8, p. 196 (1892), already discussed in Ch. 3.
[81] Quoted by Carolyn Eisele in HP, p. 37. The reference to the "potencies" of ideas is related to Peirce's view on the metaphysics of human personality, which we have examined in Ch. 3: "[I]t is what the man is destined to do, what of the future is wrapped up in him, that makes him what he is" (CP 7.666, 1903).
[82] CP 8.241 (1904).

philosophical judgment that I am attributing to him does bear some similarities to Dewey's understanding of moral judgment as being about "the direction in which [individuals or groups] are moving."[83] More generally, it belongs to a broad pragmatist family of reflections about what it means for a normative judgment to depend on historicity and change.[84]

Let me close the chapter by mentioning yet another methodological implication of Peirce's processualist take on ideas. This time, the point is not to articulate the relation between historical and normative interpretations but to reflect on two senses in which the study of ideas can contribute to a general theory of intellectual change. Peirce was convinced that the historical development of ideas could be studied from at least two different viewpoints, which he dubbed "public" and "private." The public viewpoint pays attention to the social arena of controversies and debates; the private one zeroes in on individual processes of thought.

In the late 1890s, for instance, Peirce wrote that "[t]he evolutionary theory in general throws great light upon history and especially upon the history of science – both its public history and the account of its development in an individual intellect."[85] But the same thought can be found in a much earlier text, namely the 1869 Harvard lecture on Whewell (see Chapter 1). Peirce observes therein that Whewell's focus on scientific controversies is "drawn from the public history of science." And without denying the value of this perspective, he adds a complementary one:

---

83 Dewey [1920] 1988, p. 180–181: "No individual or group will be judged by whether they come up to or fall short of some fixed result, but *by the direction in which they are moving.* The bad man is the man who no matter how good he *has* been is beginning to deteriorate, to grow less good. The good man is the man who no matter how morally unworthy he *has* been is moving to become better." (First emphasis mine.) Philip Wiener has suggested linking Peirce's respect for the history of philosophy to a statement of his friend and colleague, Chauncey Wright, which bears some similarities to Peirce's letter to Dewey. Wright said: "The most profitable discussion is, after all, a study of other minds, – seeing how others see, rather than the dissection of mere propositions. The re-statement of fundamental doctrines in new connections affords a parallax of their philosophical stand-points [...], which adds much to our knowledge of one another's thought." Cited in Wiener 1949, p. 30.
84 See Marshall 2013 for an analysis of another pivotal figures of American pragmatism, Robert Brandom, along similar lines.
85 CP 1.103 (1898). The passage continues: "As great a light is thrown upon the theory of evolution in general by the evolution of history, especially that of science – whether public or private."

> It is I have no doubt true that scientific conceptions have always first become clear in debates. And this is an important truth. But what was the mental process, what was the change and what the law of the change in the individual mind by which an obscure idea became clear? This Whewell tells us nothing of and indeed seems to have no conception of the question. A metaphysician's mind would have been wholly engrossed in *this* question to the entire exclusion of that one about the *public* process of controversy.[86]

Here, Peirce uses rather extreme, dichotomous language. As a practitioner of the public history of ideas, Whewell "tells us *nothing* of and indeed seems to have *no conception*" of the other question. Conversely, a practitioner of private history would have privileged the individual standpoint "to the *entire exclusion*" of the public one. In this sharp opposition, it is I think legitimate to recognize a sort of methodological counterpart to the predicament I have investigated in Chapter 5. On that occasion, we saw that Peirce was willing to recognize that controversies are an inescapable trait of scientific progress, but only to the extent that a termination of those controversies remains a viable task. Similarly, in the passage I have just brought up, Peirce seems to be claiming that controversies may well explain some important aspects of scientific progress but cannot tell us anything about the only question in which "a metaphysician's mind would have been wholly engrossed."

It would be a fruitful enterprise to ask whether this sharp opposition between private and public history could not be made more dynamic and permeable without leaving the ground of Peirce's philosophy. After all, just a few months before delivering his lecture on Whewell, Peirce had recognized that individual thought takes place in a dialogue and, therefore, cannot be fully private. This thesis, he claimed, would yield "immense consequences [...], quite unrecognized, I believe, hitherto."[87]

---

[86] W2, p. 342. Why Peirce speaks about the "metaphysician's mind" is not entirely clear to me. He may have wished to emphasize the stronger affinity between a philosophical approach to ideas and a non-sociological approach to intellectual development.
[87] W2, p. 172 (1868).

Conclusion: The Legacy of a Realist

1

In this book, I tried to give a comprehensive overview of the role of history in Peirce's philosophy. I examined both Peirce's work as a historian and his work as a philosopher with an eye to unearthing the many ways in which the one sheds light on the other. This project had to deal with a basic difficulty: the arguments explicitly used by Peirce to justify his interest in history do not seem entirely conclusive as a systematization of his ideas. Peirce often gives the impression of relying on a more complex and multi-layered interplay between historical and philosophical inquiries than he was ready to admit. I tried, however, to take this difficulty as an opportunity to show the richness of Peirce's thinking and its relevance to a whole range of problems.

In this conclusion, I would like to focus on three major themes that have emerged from my analysis. The first is Peirce's pluralism with regard to the uses of history. The second is the relation between Peirce's interest in history and his more general philosophical commitments. The third is the problem of realism.

2

From the beginning of his intellectual career, Peirce explored a plurality of ways in which history could become relevant to his philosophical and scientific inquiries. One such way was a speculative account of the course of human affairs. Already detectable in the early 1860s, this approach informs the argumentative strategy of "The Fixation of Belief" and reaches the *Monist* metaphysical series of 1892–93. A second approach is more meticulous and fact-based. It becomes visible, in particular, in Peirce's philological and archival inquiries. But in between these two approaches are the many compound strategies by which Peirce investigated the history of the disciplines he himself practiced, such as mathematics, natural science, and philosophy.

In parallel with the rise of his historical interests, Peirce began to be concerned with the place history should occupy within the broader framework of his philosophical system. His lifelong allegiance to the teaching of William Whewell is an important component of his reflections. But another, even more important component is Peirce's classification of the sciences: a project he started to develop almost in parallel with his first serious engagement with the history of science. Finally, Peirce also attempted to spell out explicitly the rationales for his work as a historian by describing in detail the "many ways in which the history of science is interesting."¹

I have suggested looking closely at three of these rationales in particular. First, history may help us recognize that some of the ideas and beliefs we take for granted are, in fact, the outcome of a contingent historical process. This has the consequence of relativizing our certainties, of "cut[ting] the rope that tie us to the here and now."² Second, the history of science provides "practical lessons" about scientific reasoning. Third, the history of science – and intellectual history at large – presents us with empirical material on the basis of which we can reconstruct the general laws of intellectual evolution.

In the central part of the book, however, we discovered a couple of additional, less explicit rationales that support Peirce's interest in history. One is related to what Peirce called "genealogy." This is the attempt to discover the real boundaries of "natural kinds," hence to classify them, by looking at their development over time. While this approach is, quite plainly, borrowed from natural history, Peirce applied it to cultural objects as well, such as archeological artifacts. But more importantly, he used it in his classification of the sciences. Sciences are natural kinds. Therefore, a genealogical method can prove very useful when it comes to defining and classifying them. Faithful to his pluralism, however, Peirce made it clear that his reliance on both genealogy and natural history was not unconditioned. On some occasions he remarked on the advantages of these approaches, as in his polemic against abstract definitions. On other occasions, he remarked on their shortcomings (as in his critique of Dewey's naturalism about logic).³

In Chapter 4 we encountered yet another, less explicit rationale for the history of science. Taking Whewell as a source of inspiration, Peirce addressed the question of whether the history of science may be relevant not only to the philosophy of science as broadly construed, but more specifically, to logic. His answer to this question was nuanced. Whereas logic in general is not dependent on the empirical sciences (such as psychology, history, or linguistics), there is one point related to the justification of ampliative reasoning where a recourse to the history of science proves beneficial. History strengthens our hypothesis that we may guess correctly about the causes of natural events. Since this hypothesis is *de facto* an abduction about our ability to make abductions, we

---

1 W9, p. 97 / HP, p. 143. See Ch. 2.
2 W8, p. 349 (1892).
3 See CP 1.222 (1902); CP 8.239–242 (1904); 4.8 (1906); 1.570–572 (1910). I examined these passages in Ch. 4.

may call it "meta-abduction" and claim that it is, in turn, inductively confirmed by the history of science.⁴

3

The plurality of rationales for Peirce's uses of history is, in turn, predicated on a small number of philosophical presuppositions, which I have investigated in the central part of the book.

On a foundational, metaphysical level, Peirce saw natural and mental phenomena through a processualist and evolutionary lens, and this made it not only possible but sometimes even necessary to resort to historical or diachronic explanations. The basic idea here is *growth*, by which Peirce meant a dynamic and "living" process that moves from a state of relative indeterminacy to a state of higher generality and precision. Growth, moreover, is governed by a *telos*, or final cause, but one that allows for chance and random variation. This concept stitches together the three dimensions of time – past, present and future – into an indecomposable unit. To understand a living, growing entity, we should be alert to its historical origins but also to the direction in which it will develop in the future. This applies to signs (and in particular to symbols, such as concepts and words); but also to habits, beliefs, ways of thinking, even laws of nature. The 1892–93 Lowell Lectures, for instance, apply this conception to logic: "the course of logic is itself progressive and progressive toward fuller thought. Logic, therefore, tends to back up the suggestion of biology that the whole of creation ought to be regarded as an evolution."⁵

On a second, epistemological level, to ask about the relation between philosophy and history is also to ask about how the activity of philosophizing can be modified or enriched by knowledge of contingent, empirical facts. I showed that Peirce was at pains to find a balance between two different ideas. On the one hand, philosophy should preserve its autonomy vis à vis the empirical sciences. But on the other hand, this should not have the consequence of making the empirical sciences irrelevant. This delicate balance is in part achieved by an emphasis on the common observational source of all scientific activitiy. Granted, different kinds of observation take place at different levels of abstraction and are directed at different objects. Still, all the sciences, from mathematics to history and astronomy, are about observing the outer world. "There is no reason why

---

4 As I say in Ch. 4, the concept of "meta-abduction" was put forth by Eco 1983 and more recently taken up by Bellucci 2018.
5 W9, p. 89 (1892).

'thought' [...] should be taken in that narrow sense in which silence and darkness are favorable to thought."[6]

This emphasis on observation as a common trait of science and philosophy is in turn related to another important epistemological insight. Peirce was not interested in the empirical sciences as a tool to curb philosophy's claims to validity. Since philosophy moves at a higher level of abstraction than the empirical sciences, the cogency of its arguments hardly depends on them. However, the scientific investigation of empirical facts (be they the facts of history or of other sciences) can fundamentally enrich our theory. It can make philosophical investigations more detailed, more concrete, and more sensitive to the infinite nuances that characterize human experience. By carrying out empirical inquiries, we may hope to capture that "little living mouse of a quasi exception,"[7] which has the power of shedding new light on theoretical notions.

Finally, a third level of the history-philosophy relation has to do with the role we are prepared to concede to intellectual exchanges with other people. The history of philosophy and science is also the history of how opinions different from ours have been articulated over time. Consequently, our willingness to resort to history increases in function of our willingness to take those opinions seriously.

Both Peirce's semiotics and his epistemology allot a crucial role to dialogue. "The Fixation of Belief" is premised on the idea that our encounter with conflicting opinions (that is, with disagreement) leads us to the discovery of a more rational, scientific method of inquiry. As I said before, history opens our minds: it casts doubt on what seems indubitable. At the same time, philosophy and science, as collective intellectual endeavors, are dependent not so much on disagreement as on the possibility of reaching consensus. In this sense, history provides us with a repository of opinions and ideas that we ought to take seriously, but only insofar as they help to reduce disagreement among competent researchers in the future.

This explains why one of the most traditional topoi of cumulative knowledge, that of scientists standing on the shoulders of their predecessors, is so prominent in Peirce's thinking. While carrying out our scientific and philosophical work, we seek consistency with the past. Science, philosophy and other intellectual enterprises are all social facts, institutions, and history is "the only sound basis for any human institution."[8] But the cultivation of such a historical perspective on human facts does not mean sacrificing originality and autonomy.

---

[6] EP2, p. 337 (1905).
[7] R 498 (1906). See Ch. 4.
[8] W2, p. 336 (1869). See Ch. 1.

In fact, the contrary is the case. As Peirce put it in his polemic against positivists,[9] to think for oneself *is* to remain alert to the facts of experience, among which are the facts of history.

4

Peirce's critique of positivism helps us appreciate why his emphasis on realism should not be interpreted as a lack of sensitivity toward the historical contingencies that affect science as a human activity.[10] Consistently with his realist epistemology, Peirce conceptualized the progress of science as a gradual but steady approximation toward the truth. Still, some elements of his epistemology counterbalance this reassuring picture. First of all, he did not rule out the existence of truly revolutionary turning points in history. But most importantly, he made his philosophy of science conditional on a robust fallibilism.

Scientific truths are never absolute. They contain errors and approximations that can only be overcome by the subsequent progress of science. This, however, does not prevent us from speaking about scientific propositions as true and sound. Peirce's fallibilism is subtly but fundamentally distinguished from skepticism.[11] An essential trait of science is, indeed, its ability to grow. Scientific ideas can be very imprecise and undetermined. They can contain a good degree of error, but still be genuinely scientific and, in this sense, true, because they allow for future developments that will contribute to minimizing that error. ("I have often remarked in the history of philosophy, that the reasonings which were somewhat dark and formally imperfect, often went the deepest."[12])

For this reason, a historical examination of the long series of scientific theories that are now considered obsolete fulfills a double epistemological function. On the one hand, it pessimistically reminds us that our own scientific theories will look equally obsolete in the future. On the other hand, since even an obsolete theory may appear perfectly sound if placed in the right historical context, it optimistically confirms that we have a faculty to know reality in an increasingly correct way.

Finally, Peirce's realism is a leading motif not only in his history *of* science, but also in his conception of history *as* a science – that is, in his theory of historiography. Here again, Peirce managed to defend realism without lapsing into

---

9 See CP 6.604, as discussed in Ch. 4.
10 On the history of science as a challenge to realism, see Psillos 2018.
11 See Hookway 1985, p. 73: "Peirce's fallibilism [...] escapes scepticism only by a crucial hair's breadth."
12 CP 2.333 (c. 1895).

absolute objectivism. Historiography aims at truth. It aims at objectively reconstructing the facts of the past. But objective reconstruction is not the same as perfect reproduction.

A good illustration of the difference I am trying to articulate between Peirce's striving for objectivity and absolute objectivism is what we saw in Chapter 7 about the biography of Pythagoras. To Peirce, this case study represented a situation in which the scarcity of sources allows us to say almost nothing that is certainly true. We can only put forth hypotheses that are sound on the basis of our logical principles, and accept those hypotheses on probation.[13] But this rather extreme case is in fact revelatory of a more general fact about historiography. Our awareness that there are questions about which we will never be able to establish an irrefutable truth is no reason to relax our logical and epistemological criteria about *what it is* to look for the truth.

Another way of spelling out the same point is to say that Peirce's realism is first of all a realism about what constrains our scientific or historiographical hypotheses. No theory can ever be taken as the entirely faithful reconstruction of a state of affairs. However, there are things that can absolutely disprove a given theory. We ask questions to nature; we ask questions to documents and monuments. They cannot answer in the affirmative, but they can answer in the negative. They can say: No, you are wrong. Look elsewhere. This negative answer takes on the form of an outward clash, of an external shock that has the power of invalidating a given hypothesis, in that it exercises a sort of veto power over that hypothesis.[14]

As a matter of fact, Peirce often talked about the past in a way that resembles what he said about the outward clash. The past, he argued, is simply and brutely there. It cannot be reformed. "If you complain to the Past that it is wrong and unreasonable, it laughs. It does not care a snap of the finger for Reason."[15] This realism gives Peirce's philosophy of history a peculiar position within the pragmatist family, whose members have, in general, been willing to up-

---

13 Cf. the letter to Giddins already discussed in Ch. 7, HP, p. 998 (1910): "Not that any positive hypothesis can be *absolutely* verified; but the verification requisite is that from the hypothetical state of things there should follow so many necessary, or almost necessary consequences that accord with highly probably, strongly supported, independent historical results, as to warrant our accepting the hypothesis, as having that degree of credibility that we are forced to content ourselves with unless we are to abandon the attempt to get at any history of the age in question."
14 I am intentionally resorting to a metaphor that has circulated in the philosophy of historiography thanks to Reinhart Koselleck. The latter spoke of the "veto right" of historical sources. See Koselleck 1977; Jordan 2010.
15 CP 2.84 (1902). See Ch. 3.

hold a moderately constructivist view of the past.¹⁶ It remains, however, a bit unclear how exactly the past may be said to influence us in Peirce's philosophy: whether directly (in virtue of "synechism" and the "law of mind"; see Chapter 3) or through the influence of documents and monuments (see Chapter 7). Also, it remains debatable whether Peirce's objectivism is consistent with his emphasis on the "practical lessons" of the history of science. Peirce's beloved analogy with astronomy is not very helpful in this respect, because astronomy observes things that are distant from us and hardly influence us.¹⁷

Finally, it might be asked whether the analogy between historiography and the natural sciences sufficiently takes into account the role of interpretation in historiography. Historians do not just aim to ascertain the occurrence of an event; they also want to explain and interpret that event.¹⁸ Peirce's emphasis on consensus as a condition of scientific rationality, as well as the kind of historical case studies that he chose to focus on, may lead us to think that he took the work of the historian to be more about discovery than about interpretation. Still, Peirce also gave us reasons to believe that discovery and interpretation need not necessarily be seen as separated by a qualitative divide. From the viewpoint of his semiotics, abduction is the production of a new interpretant. It is an act of interpretation of the data at hand. In this sense, it is worth remarking that Whewell's concept of *colligation*, which was pivotal to the genesis of Peirce's theory of scientific discovery, was revived in the twentieth-century philosophy of historiography as the name for that constructive and interpretive operation that historians perform when they group a series of historical events under a single concept.¹⁹

Peirce himself occasionally showed how the machinery of his logical theory may be applied not only to the discovery of new facts, but also to the interpretation of texts, documents and artifacts that have been handed down from the

---

16 See, e.g., Mead 1932. Joas 2016, p. 72 convincingly argues, however, that Mead's constructivist or relationist view about the past should not be equated with historical relativism. On objectivity and relativism in Peirce's philosophy of history, see also Hoopes 1993; Collins/Hoopes 1995.
17 But see what Peirce himself wrote in HP, p. 718 (1901): "History is as much more worthy than astronomy of being studied scientifically as mind is more worthy of our attention than matter. The use we would desire to make of ancient history is to learn from the study of it." On astronomy and pragmatic history cf. Hampe 2006, p. 152.
18 Yet another dimension of historical inquiry that Peirce does not dwell on much is its narrative structure. The role of narrative as a peculiar form of explanation only gained centre stage in the philosophy of historiography in the mid-twentieth century. See, e.g., Gallie 1964; Danto 1965. For a more recent account, see Roth 2020.
19 See Walsh 1942; Kuukkanen 2015, Ch. 6; Cristalli 2019.

past. In doing so, he indicated the path for a hermeneutic strategy that relies on a robust contextualism[20] as well as on a tight interaction between interpretation and discovery. This perspective remains faithful to one of the basic ideas of Peirce's realism, one concisely expressed in his list of practical lessons from the history of science:

"Lesson 24. Do not trifle with Facts."[21]

---

[20] According to Apel [1967–1970] 1981, p. 126, Peirce's emphasis on the indexical anchoring of propositions entails that language cannot be conceived as a sort of "uninterpreted calculus," the meaning of which can be determined abstractly, without reference to the non-linguistic context. Jung 2009, p. 286–192 defends a similar thesis. On this point see in particular CP 8.112 (1901).
[21] HP, p. 410 (1898).

Bibliography

Abbott, Andrew (2001): *Chaos of Disciplines*. Chicago, London: The University of Chicago Press.
Abbott, Andrew (2016): *Processual Sociology*. Chicago, London: The University of Chicago Press.
Ambrosio, Chiara (2016): "The Historicity of Peirce's Classification of the Sciences". In: *European Journal of Pragmatism and American Philosophy* 8. No. 2. DOI: 10.4000/ejpap.625, visited on 7 November 2019.
Anderson, Douglas (2008): "Peirce and Pragmatism: American Connections". In: Cheryl Misak (Ed.): *The Oxford Handbook of American Philosophy*. Oxford, New York: Oxford University Press.
Apel, Karl-Otto ([1967–1970] 1981): *Charles S. Peirce: From Pragmatism to Pragmaticism*. Transl. J.-M. Krois. Amherst: University of Massachusetts Press.
Aristotle (1938): *The Categories. On Interpretation. Prior Analytics*. Harold P. Cooke/Hugh Tredennick (Eds.). Cambridge/MA: Harvard University Press, London: William Heinemann (Loeb Classical Library).
Aron, Raymond (1950): "La philosophie de l'histoire". In: Marvin Farber (Ed.): *L'activité philosophique contemporaine en France et aux États-Unis*. Vol. 2. *La philosophie française*. Paris: Presses Universitaires de France.
Atkins, Richard K. (2006): "Restructuring the Sciences: Peirce's Categories and His Classifications of the Sciences". In: *Transactions of the Charles S. Peirce Society* 42. No. 4, pp. 483–500.
Atkins, Richard K. (2016): *Peirce on the Conduct of Life. Sentiment and Instinct in Ethics and Religion*. Cambridge: Cambridge University Press.
Atkins, Richard K. (2019): *Charles S. Peirce's Phenomenology. Analysis and Consciousness*. Oxford: Oxford University Press.
Bancroft, George (1854–1878): *History of the United States of America, from the Discovery of the American Continent*. Boston: Little, Brown, & Co.
Barnouw, Jeffrey (1988): "'Aesthetic' for Schiller and Peirce: A Neglected Origin of Pragmatism". In: *Journal of the History of Ideas* 49. No. 4, pp. 607–632.
Bellucci, Francesco (2017): *Peirce's Speculative Grammar. Logic as Semiotics*. New York, London: Routledge.
Bellucci, Francesco (2018): "Eco and Peirce on Abduction". In: *European Journal of Pragmatism and American Philosophy* 10. No. 1. DOI: 10.4000/ejpap.1122, visited on 18 March 2020.
Bellucci, Francesco (2019): "Aristotelian Abductions: A Reply to Flórez". In: *Transactions of the Charles S. Peirce Society* 55. No. 2, pp. 185–196.
Bellucci, Francesco/Pietarinen, Ahti-Veikko (2020): "Peirce on the Justification of Abduction". In: *Studies in History and Philosophy of Science*. DOI: 10.1016/j.shpsa.2020.04.003, visited on 7 July 2020.
Bentham Jeremy ([1816] 1843): *The Works of Jeremy Bentham*. Vol VIII: *Chrestomathia*. John Bowring (Ed.). Edinburgh: William Tait.
Bergman, Mats (2009): *Peirce's Philosophy of Communication*. London, New York: Continuum.
Bergman, Mats (2010): "Serving Two Masters: Peirce on Pure Science, Useless Things, and Practical Applications". In: Mats Bergman/Saami Paavola/Ahti-Veikko Pietarinen/Henry

Rydenfelt (Eds.): *Ideas in Action: Proceedings of the Applying Peirce Conference.* Helsinki: Nordic Pragmatism Network. http://www.nordprag.org/nsp/1/Bergman.pdf, visited on 27 February 2020.

Berkeley, George (1871): *The Works of George Berkeley.* 4 vols. Alexander C. Fraser (Ed.). Oxford: Clarendon.

Bernstein, Richard J. (1981): "Toward a More Rational Community". In: Edward C. More/ Richard S. Robin (Eds.): *Studies in the Philosophy of Charles S. Peirce. Second Series.* Amherst: University of Massachusets Press.

Bloch, Marc ([1949] 1992): *The Historian's Craft.* Transl. P. Putnam. Manchester: Manchester University Press.

Boler, John F. (1963): *Charles Peirce and Scholastic Realism. A Study of Peirce's Relation to John Duns Scotus.* Seattle: University of Washington Press.

Boltanski, Luc ([2009] 2011): *On Critique. A Sociology of Emancipation.* Transl. G. Elliot. Cambridge: Polity Press.

Bourdieu, Pierre (Ed.) (1965): *Un art moyen. Essai sur les usages sociaux de la photographie.* Paris: Les Éditions de Minuit.

Bourdieu, Pierre (1966): "Champ intellectuel et projet créateur". In: *Les Temps Modernes* 22. No. 246, pp. 865–906.

Bourdieu, Pierre ([1967] 2005): "Postface to Erwin Panofsky: *Gothic Architecture and Scholasticism*". Transl. L. Petit. In: Bruce Holsinger: *The Premodern Condition. Medievalism and the Making of Theory.* Chicago, London: The University of Chicago Press, pp. 221–242.

Bourdieu, Pierre (1969): "Intellectual field and creative project". Transl. S. France. In: *Social Science Information* 8. No. 2, pp. 89–119.

Bourdieu, Pierre/Chamboredon, Jean-Claude/Passeron, Jean-Claude ([1968] 2005): *Le métier de sociologue. Préalables épistémologiques.* 5th edition. Berlin, New York: Mouton De Gruyter.

Bouton, Christophe (2018): "Learning From History. The Transformations of the topos *historia magistra vitae* in Modernity". In: *Journal of the Philosophy of History* 13. No. 2, pp. 183–215.

Brandom, Robert (2002): *Tales of the Mighty Dead. Historical Essays in the Metaphysics of Intentionality.* Cambridge/MA, London: Harvard University Press.

Bredekamp, Horst (2001): "Gazing Hands and Blind Spots: Galileo as Draftsman". In: Jürgen Renn (Ed.): *Galileo in Context.* Cambridge, New York: Cambridge University Press, pp. 153–192.

Bredekamp, Horst/Buschendorf, Bernhard/Hartung, Freia/Krois, John-Michael (Eds.) (1998): *Edgar Wind. Kunsthistoriker und Philosoph.* Berlin: Akademie Verlag.

Brent, Joseph ([1993] 1998): *Charles Sanders Peirce. A Life.* Bloomington, Indianapolis: Indiana University Press.

Brock, Jarrett (1981): "The Origin and Structure of Peirce's Logic of Vagueness". In: Annemarie Lange-Seidl (Ed.). *Zeichenkonstitution: Akten des 2. semiotischen Kolloquiums. Regensburg: 1978.* Vol. 1. Berlin, New York: De Gruyter.

Browning, Douglas/Myers, William T. (1998): *Philosophers of Process.* New York: Fordham University Press.

Brunson, Daniel (2007): "Memory and Peirce's Pragmatism". In: *Cognitio-Estudos. Revista Eletrônica de Filosofia* 4. No. 2, pp. 71–80.

Brunson, Daniel (2010): *Pragmatism and the Past: Charles Peirce and the Conduct of Memory and History*. PhD dissertation. State College: The Pennsylvania State University.

Bulwer-Lytton, Edward (1835): *Rienzi, the Last of Tribunes*. 3 vols. London: Saunders and Otley.

Cannon, W. Faye (1976): "The Whewell-Darwin Controversy". In: *Journal of the Geological Society* 132. No. 4, pp. 377–84.

Carbonell, Charles-Olivier (1985): "L'espace et le temps dans l'œuvre d'Hérodote". In: *Storia della storiografia* 7, pp. 138–149.

Carlyle, Thomas ([1841] 2013): *On Heros, Hero-Worship, and the Heroic in History*. David R. Sorensen/Brent E. Kinser (Eds.). New Haven, London: Yale University Press.

Cerutti, Simona (1991): "Pragmatique et histoire: Ce dont les sociologues sont capables". In: *Annales. Économies, Sociétés, Civilisations* 46. No. 6, pp. 1437–1445.

Cerutti, Simona (2004): "Microhistory? Social Relations versus Cultural Models? Some Reflections on Stereotypes and Historical Practices". In: Anna-Maija Castrén/Markku Lonkila/Matti Peltonen (Eds.): *Between Sociology and History. Essays on Microhistory, Collective Action, and Nation Building*. Helsinki: SKS/Finnish Literature Society.

Ceserani, Remo (2019): "The Difference between Document and Monument". In: Carmen van den Bergh/Sarah Bonciarelli/Anne Reverseau (Eds.): *Literature as Document. Generic Boundaries in 1930s Western Literature*. Leiden, Boston: Brill-Rodopi, pp. 15–27.

Colapietro, Vincent (1998): "Transforming Philosophy into Science: A Debilitating Chimera, or a Realizable Desideratum?". In: *American Catholic Philosophical Quarterly* 72. No. 2, pp. 245–278.

Colapietro, Vincent (2003a): "Portrait of an Historicist: An Alternative Reading of Peircean Semiotic". In: *Semiotics 2003*, pp. 3–14.

Colapietro, Vincent (2003b): "The Space of Signs: C. S. Peirce's Critique of Psychologism". In: Dale Jacquette (Ed.): *Philosophy, Psychology, and Psychologism: Critical and Historical Readings of the Psychological Turn in Philosophy*. Dordrecht: Kluwer Academic Publishing, pp. 157–179.

Colapietro, Vincent (2007): "C. S. Peirce's Rhetorical Turn". In: *Transactions of the Charles S. Peirce Society* 43. No. 1, pp. 16–52.

Colapietro, Vincent (2016): "The Historical Past and the Dramatic Present. Toward a Pragmatic Clarification of Historical Consciousness". In: *European Journal of Pragmatism and American Philosophy* 8. No. 2. DOI: 10.4000/ejpap.627, visited on 7 November 2019.

Colapietro, Vincent (forthcoming): "An 'Historicist' Reading of Peirce's Pragmatist Semeiotic. A Pivotal Maxim and Evolving Practices". In: *Transactions of the Charles S. Peirce Society*.

Collins, Stephen/Hoopes, James (1995): "Anthony Giddens and Charles Sanders Peirce: History, Theory, and a Way Out of the Linguistic Cul-de-Sac". In: *Journal of the History of Ideas* 56. No. 4, pp. 625–50.

Cowles, Henry M. (2016): "The Age of Methods: William Whewell, Charles Peirce, and Scientific Kinds". In: *Isis* 107. No. 4, pp. 722–737.

Cristalli, Claudia (2017): "Experimental Psychology and the Practice of Logic. Charles S. Peirce and the Charge of Psychologism, 1869–1885". In: *European Journal of Pragmatism and American Philosophy* 9. No. 1. DOI:10.4000/ejpap.1006, visited on 21 February 2020.

Cristalli Claudia (2019): "Narrative explanations in integrated History and Philosophy of Science". In: Emily Herring/Kevin M. Jones/Konstantin S. Kiprijanov/Laura M. Sellers (Eds.): *The Past, the Present and the Future of Integrated History and Philosophy of Science*. London: Routledge.

Csiszar, Alex (2010): *Broken Pieces of Fact: The Scientific Periodical and the Politics of Search in Nineteenth-Century France and Britain*. PhD dissertation. Cambridge/MA: Harvard University.

Danto, Arthur (1965): *Analytical Philosophy of History*. Cambridge: Cambridge University Press.

Darwin, Charles (1859): *On the Origin of Species*, London: John Murray.

Dauben, Joseph W. (1995): "Peirce and History of Science". In: Kenneth L. Ketner (Ed.): *Peirce and Contemporary Thought. Philosophical Inquiries*. New York: Fordham University Press, pp. 146–195.

Deacon, Terrence (1998): *The Symbolic Species. The Co-Evolution of Language and Brain*. New York, London: W. W. Norton & Company.

De Lourdes Bacha, Maria/Vannucci, João (2014): "A 'Epistola de Magnete', de Petrus Peregrinus: experimento, técnica e tecnologia na construção de instrumentos magnéticos". In: *Anais Eletrônicos do 14o Seminário Nacional de História da Ciência e da Tecnologia*. https://www.14snhct.sbhc.org.br/#, visited on 3 March 2020.

De Maricourt, Petrus Peregrinus (1995): *Opera*. Loris Sturlese/Ron B. Thomson (Eds.). Pisa: Scuola Normale Superiore.

De Tienne, André (1989): "Peirce's Early Method of Finding the Categories". In: *Transactions of the Charles S. Peirce Society* 25. No. 4, pp. 385–406.

De Tienne, André (forthcoming): "Introduction". In: *Writings of Charles S. Peirce. A Chronological Edition*. Vol. 9. Bloomington, Indiana: Indiana University Press.

Dewey, John (Ed.) (1903): *Studies in Logical Theory*. Chicago: The University of Chicago Press.

Dewey, John ([1920] 1988): *Reconstruction in Philosophy*. In: *The Middle Works*. Vol. 12. Jo Ann Boydston (Ed.). Carbondale, Edwardsville: Southern Illinois University Press, pp. 77–201.

Dewey, John ([1927] 1988): *The Public and Its Problems*. In: *The Later Works*. Vol. 2. Jo Ann Boydston (Ed.). Carbondale, Edwardsville: Southern Illinois University Press, pp. 235–372.

Dewey, John ([1938] 1986): *Logic: The Theory of Inquiry*. In: *The Later Works*. Vol. 12. Jo Ann Boydston (Ed.). Carbondale, Edwardsville: Southern Illinois University Press.

Dickens, Charles ([1854] 2008): *Hard Times*. Paul Schlicke (Ed.). Oxford, New York: Oxford University Press.

Dierse, U. (1995): "Selbstdenken". In: Joachim Ritter (Ed.): *Historisches Wörterbuch der Philosophie*. Vol. 9. Basel: Schwabe, pp. 386–392.

Dietz, Hella/Nungesser, Frithjof/Pettenkofer, Andreas (Eds.) (2017): *Pragmatismus und Theorien sozialer Praktiken. Vom Nutzen einer Theoriedifferenz*. Frankfurt am Main: Campus.

Diodorus Siculus [Diodore De Sicile] (1993–2002): *Bibliothèque historique*. 14 Vols. Paris: Les Belles Lettres.

Dynes, Wayne (1973): "Concept of Gothic". In: Philip P. Wiener (Ed.): *Dictionary of the History of Ideas*. Vol. 2. New York: Charles Scribner's Sons, pp. 366–374.

Eco, Umberto (1983): "Horns, Hooves, Insteps: Some Hypotheses on Three Types of Abduction". In: Umberto Eco/Thomas A. Sebeok (Eds.): *The Sign of Three*. Bloomington: Indiana University Press, pp. 198–220.

Eco, Umberto/Sebeok, Thomas A. (Eds.) (1983): *The Sign of Three*. Bloomington: Indiana University Press.

Eisele, Carolyn (1979): *Studies in the Scientific and Mathematical Philosophy of Charles S. Peirce*. Richard M. Martin (Ed.). The Hague, Paris, New York: Mouton.

Eisele, Carolyn (1985a): "Introduction". In: Charles S. Peirce: *Historical Perspectives on Peirce's Logic of Science. A History of Science*. Berlin, New York, Amsterdam: Mouton, pp. 1–14.

Eisele, Carolyn (1985b): "Petrus Peregrinus the Scientist". In: Charles S. Peirce: *Historical Perspectives on Peirce's Logic of Science. A History of Science*. Berlin, New York, Amsterdam: Mouton, pp. 39–57.

Ellis, Alexander J. (1869): *On Early English Pronunciation, with Especial Reference to Shakspere and Chaucer*. Vol. 2. London: Asher & Co.

Emerson, Ralph W. ([1841] 1888): "The Sphinx". In: *Emerson's Complete Works*. Vol. 9. *Poems*. London: George Routledge and Sons.

Esposito, Joseph L. (1983): "Peirce and the Philosophy of History". In: *Transactions of the Charles S. Peirce Society* 19. No. 2, pp. 155–166.

Ferrarin, Alfredo (2015): *The Powers of Pure Reason. Kant and the Idea of Cosmic Philosophy*, Chicago: University of Chicago Press.

Fichte, Johann G. ([1794] 1982): *Foundations of the Entire Science of Knowledge*. Transl. P. Heath. In: J. G. Fichte: *The Science of Knowledge*. Peter Heath/John Lachs (Eds.). Cambridge: Cambridge University Press.

Fisch, Max H. (1982): "Introduction". In: *Writings of Charles S. Peirce. A Chronological Edition*. Vol. 1. Bloomington, Indiana University Press, pp. xv-xxxv.

Fisch, Max H. (1984): "The Decisive Year and Its Early Consequences". In: *Writings of Charles S. Peirce. A Chronological Edition*. Vol. 2. Bloomington, Indiana University Press, pp. xxi-xxxvi.

Fisch, Max H. (1986a): *Peirce, Semeiotic, and Pragmatism*. Kenneth L. Ketner/Christian J. W. Kloesel (Eds.). Bloomington: Indiana University Press.

Fisch, Max H. (1986b): "Introduction". In: *Writings of Charles S. Peirce. A Chronological Edition*. Vol. 3. Bloomington, Indiana University Press, pp. xxi-xxxvii.

Flórez, Jorge Alejandro (2014): "Peirce's Theory of the Origin of Abduction in Aristotle". In: *Transactions of the Charles S. Peirce Society* 50. No. 2, pp. 265–280.

Frankl, Paul (1960): *The Gothic. Literary Sources and Interpretations through Eight Centuries*. Princeton: Princeton University Press.

Freely, John (2013): *Before Galileo. The Birth of Modern Science in Medieval Europe*. New York, London: Overlook.

Frega, Roberto (2012): *Practice, Judgment, and the Challenge of Moral and Political Disagreement. A Pragmatist Account*. Lanham: Lexington Books.

Gallie, Walter B. (1952): *Peirce and Pragmatism*. Harmondsworth, Middlesex: Penguin.

Gallie, Walter B. (1956a): "Essentially Contested Concepts". In: *Proceedings of the Aristotelian Society* 56. No 1, pp. 167–198.

Gallie, Walter B. (1956b): "Art as an Essentially Contested Concept". In: *Philosophical Quarterly* 6. No. 23, pp. 97–114.

Gallie, Walter B. (1964): *Philosophy and Historical Understanding*. London: Chatto & Windus.
Galton, Francis ([1869] 1892): *Hereditary Genius. An Inquiry into its Laws and Consequences*. 2nd edition. London, New York: Macmillan & Co.
Gava, Gabriele (2014): *Peirce's Account of Purpryosefulness. A Kantian Perspective*. New York: Routledge.
Gebauer, Sascha (2015): "Babel-Bibel-Streit". In: *WiBiLex. Das wissenschaftliche Bibellexikon im Internet*. https://www.bibelwissenschaft.de/stichwort/14345/, visited on 29 February 2020.
Gerhardt, Volker (2000): *Individualität. Das Element der Welt*. München: Beck.
Ginzburg, Carlo ([1979] 1989): "Clues: Roots of an Evidential Paradigm". In: *Clues, Myths, and the Historical Method*. Transl. J. Tedeschi/A. C. Tedeschi. Baltimore: The Johns Hopkins University Press. Reprinted in (Eco/Sebeok 1983).
Ginzburg, Carlo (2004): "Family Resemblances and Family Trees: Two Cognitive Metaphors". In: *Critical Inquiry* 30. No. 3, pp. 537–556.
Ginzburg, Carlo (2017): "Unintentional Revelations. Reading History Against the Grain". In: *Exploring the Boundaries of Microhistory. The Fu Ssu-nien Memorial Lectures 2015*. Taipei: Academia Sinica.
Ginzburg, Carlo (2019): "Schemi, preconcetti, esperimenti a doppio cieco. Riflessioni di uno storico". In: *Occhiacci di legno. Dieci riflessioni sulla distanza*. 2nd edition. Macerata: Quodlibet.
Girel, Mathias (2003): "The Metaphysics and Logic of Psychology: Peirce's Reading of James's 'Principles'". In: *Transactions of the Charles S. Peirce Society* 39. No. 2, pp. 163–203.
Girel, Mathias (2011): "Peirce's Early Re-readings of his Illustrations: The Case of the 1885 Royce Review". In: *Cognitio* 12. No. 1, pp. 75–88.
Girel, Mathias (2017): "'Éclaircir les conceptions' : Peirce et Whewell, 1869". *Cahiers philosophiques* 150, pp. 35–44.
Gombrich, Ernst H. (1969): *In Search of Cultural History. The Philip Maurice Deneke Lecture 1967*. Oxford: Clarendon Press.
Gombrich, Ernst H. ([1974] 1979): "The Logic of Vanity Fair. Alternatives to Historicism in the Study of Fashion, Style, and Taste". In: *Ideals and Idols. Essays on Values in History and in Art*. Oxford, New York: Phaidon.
Grigoriev, Serge (2017): "Hypotheses, Generalizations, and Convergence: Some Peircean Themes in the Study of History". In: *History and Theory* 56. No. 3, pp. 339–361.
Grigoriev, Serge/Piercey, Robert (Eds.) (2019): *Pragmatism and the Philosophy of History*. Sperical Issue. In: *Journal of the Philosophy of History* 13. No. 3.
Gronda, Roberto/Viola, Tullio (Eds.) (2016): *Pragmatism and the Writing of History*. Special Issue. In: *European Journal of Pragmatism and American Philosophy* 8. No. 2. DOI: 10.4000/ejpap.623, visited on 5 February 2020.
Grupo de Estudios Peirceanos, (2008–2019): "Correspondencia Europea de C. S. Peirce: creatividad y cooperación cientifica". http://www.unav.es/gep/CorrespondenciaEuropeaCSP.html, visited on 5 February 2020.
Haack, Susan (1994): "How the Critical Common-Sensist Sees Things". In: *Histoire Épistemologie Langage* 16. No. 1, pp. 9–34.
Haack, Susan (2009): "The Growth of Meaning and the Limits of Formalism: In Science, in Law". In: *Análisis Filosófico* 29. No. 1, pp. 5–29.

Hacking, Ian. (1988): "Telepathy: Origins of Randomization in Experimental Designs". In: *Isis* 79. No. 3, pp. 427–451.
Hahn, M. (1974): "Geschichte, pragmatische", In: Joachim Ritter (Ed.): *Historisches Wörterbuch der Philosophie*. Vol. 3. Basel: Schwabe, pp. 401–402.
Hampe, Michael (2006): *Erkenntnis und Praxis. Zur Philosophie des Pragmatismus*. Frankfurt am Main: Suhrkamp.
Hanson, Norwood R. (1958): *Patterns of Discovery*. Cambridge: Cambridge University Press.
Hanson, Norwood R. (1967): "The Genetic Fallacy Revisited". In: *American Philosophical Quarterly* 4. No. 2, pp. 101–113.
Hegel, Georg W. F. ([1807] 1977): *Phenomenology of Spirit*. Transl. A. V. Miller. Oxford: Oxford University Press.
Hegel, Georg W. F. ([1812] 1984): "Philosophy in the Gymnasium. Hegel to Niethammer". In: Clark Butler/Christiane Seiler (Eds.): *Hegel: The letters*. Bloomington: Indiana University Press, pp. 275–282.
Hegel, Georg W. F. ([1820] 1975): *Lectures on the Philosophy of World History*. Hugh Barr Nisbet/Duncan Forbes (Eds.). Cambridge: Cambridge University Press.
Hegel, Georg W. F. ([1830] 2010): *Encyclopedia of the Philosophical Sciences in Basic Outline. Part I: Science of Logic*. 3rd edition. Klaus Brinkmann/Daniel O. Dahlstrom (Eds.). Cambridge: Cambridge University Press. (Cambridge Hegel Translations).
Hook, Sidney (1943): *The Hero in History. A Study in Limitation and Possibility*. New York: The John Day Company.
Hookway, Christopher (1985): *Peirce*. London, New York: Routledge.
Hoopes, James (1993): "Objectivity and Relativism Affirmed: Historical Knowledge and the Philosophy of Charles S. Peirce". In: *The American Historical Review* 98. No. 5, pp. 1545–55.
Houser, Nathan (1989): "Introduction". In: *Writings of Charles S. Peirce. A Chronological Edition*. Vol. 4. Bloomington, Indianapolis: Indiana University Press, pp. xix-lxx.
Houser, Nathan (1993): "Introduction". In: *Writings of Charles S. Peirce. A Chronological Edition*. Vol. 5. Bloomington, Indianapolis: Indiana University Press, pp. xix-xlviii.
Houser, Nathan (1998): "Introduction". In: *The Essential Peirce. Selected Philosophical Writings*. Vol. 2. Bloomington, Indianapolis: Indiana University Press, pp. xvii-xxxviii.
Houser, Nathan (2010): "Introduction". In: *Writings of Charles S. Peirce. A Chronological Edition*. Vol. 8. Bloomington, Indianapolis: Indiana University Press, pp. xxv-xcvii.
Huebner, Daniel R. (2019): "Histoire, enquête et responsabilité. Le trésor perdu des premières générations de pragmatistes". In: *Pragmata. Revue d'études pragmatistes* 2. https://revuepragmata.files.wordpress.com/2020/01/pragmata-2019-2-huebner.pdf, visited on 11 March 2020, pp. 14–61.
Humboldt, Wilhelm von ([1827] 1997): "On the Dual Form". Transl. J. Wieczorek/I. Roe. In: Theo Harden/D. Farrelly (Eds.): *Essays on Language*. Frankfurt am Main etc.: Peter Lang, pp. 111–136.
Humboldt, Wilhelm von ([1829] 1997): "On the Relationship between Adverbs of Place and Pronouns in some Languages". Transl. J. Wieczorek/I. Roe. In: Theo Harden/D. Farrelly (Eds.): *Essays on Language*. Frankfurt am Main etc.: Peter Lang, pp. 151–159.
Hume, David ([1748] 2000): *An Enquiry Concerning Human Understanding*. Tom L. Beauchamp (Ed.). Oxford: Clarendon Press.

Irmscher, Christoph (2013): *Louis Agassiz. Creator of American Science.* Boston, New York: Houghton Mifflin Harcourt.

Jakobson, Roman ([1961] 1971): "Implications of Language Universals for Linguistics". In: , *Selected Writings.* Vol. 2. The Hague, Paris: Mouton, pp. 580–592.

James, William ([1880] 1979): "Great Men and their Environment". In: *The Will to Believe and Other Essays in Popular Philosophy.* Frederick Burkhardt/Fredson Bowers/Ignas K. Skrupskelis (Eds.). Cambridge/MA: Harvard University Press. (The Works of William James).

James, William ([1890] 1981): *The Principles of Psychology.* 2 vols. Frederick Burkhardt/Gerald E. Myers (Eds.). Cambridge/MA: Harvard University Press. (The Works of William James).

Jastrow, Joseph (1914): "The Passing of a Master's Mind". In: *The Nation* 98. No. 2550, p. 571.

Jastrow, Joseph (1916): "Charles S. Peirce as a Teacher". In: *The Journal of Philosophy, Psychology and Scientific Methods* 13. No. 26, pp. 723–726.

Joas, Hans ([1992] 1996): *The Creativity of Action.* Transl. J. Gaines/P. Keast. Chicago: The University of Chicago Press.

Joas, Hans ([2011] 2013): *The Sacredness of the Person. A New Genealogy of Human Rights.* Transl. A. Skinner. Washington, D.C.: Georgetown University Press.

Joas, Hans (2016): "Pragmatism and Historicism: Mead's Philosophy of Temporality and the Logic of Historiography". In: Hans Joas/Daniel R. Huebner (Eds.): *The Timeliness of George Herbert Mead.* Chicago, London: Chicago University Press.

Jordan, David S. (1923): "Louis Agassiz, Teacher". In: *Scientific Monthly* 17. No. 5, pp. 401–411.

Jordan, Stefan (2010): "Vetorecht der Quellen". In: *Docupedia-Zeitgeschichte.* DOI: 10.14765/zzf.dok.2.570.v1, visited on 20 February 2020.

Jung, Matthias (2009): *Der Bewusste Ausdruck. Anthropologie der Artikulation.* Berlin, New York: De Gruyter.

Kammerzell, Frank/Lapčić, Aleksandra/Nöth, Winfried (2016): "Charles Sanders Peirce's Egyptological Studies". In: *Transactions of the Charles S. Peirce Society* 52. No. 4, pp. 483–538.

Kant, Immanuel ([1764] 2007): "Observations on the feeling of the beautiful and sublime". Transl. P. Guyer. In: *Anthropology, History, and Education.* Günter Zoller/Robert B. Louden (Eds.). Cambridge: Cambridge University Press, pp. 18–62. (The Cambridge Edition of the Works of Immanuel Kant in Translation).

Kant, Immanuel ([1781/1787] 1998): *Critique of Pure Reason.* Paul Guyer/Allen W. Wood (Eds.). Cambridge: Cambridge University Press. (The Cambridge Edition of the Works of Immanuel Kant in Translation).

Kant, Immanuel ([1784] 1996): "An answer to the question: What is enlightenment?". Transl. M. J. Gregor. In: *Practical philosophy.* Mary J. Gregor (Ed.). Cambridge: Cambridge University Press, pp. 11–22. (The Cambridge Edition of the Works of Immanuel Kant in Translation).

Kant, Immanuel ([1785] 1996): *Groundwork of The metaphysics of morals.* Transl. M. J. Gregor. In: *Practical philosophy.* Mary J. Gregor (Ed.). Cambridge: Cambridge University Press, pp. 37–108. (The Cambridge Edition of the Works of Immanuel Kant in Translation).

Kant, Immanuel ([1793–1804] 2002): "What real progress has metaphysics made in Germany since the time of Leibniz and Wolff?". Transl. H. Allison. In: *Theoretical Philosophy after*

1781. Henry Allison/Peter Heath (Eds.). Cambridge: Cambridge University Press, pp. 337–424. (The Cambridge Edition of the Works of Immanuel Kant in Translation).

Kant, Immanuel ([1798] 2007): *Anthropology from a pragmatic point of view*. Transl. R. B. Louden. In: *Anthropology, History, and Education*. Günter Zoller/Robert B. Louden (Eds.). Cambridge: Cambridge University Press, pp. 227–429. (The Cambridge Edition of the Works of Immanuel Kant in Translation).

Kant, Immanuel ([1800] 1992): *The Jäsche Logik*. Transl. J. M. Joung. In: *Lectures on Logic*. J. Michael Young (Ed.). Cambridge: Cambridge University Press, pp. 521–640. (The Cambridge Edition of the Work of Immanuel Kant in Translation).

Kemp, Martin (2004): *Leonardo*. Oxford, New York: Oxford University Press.

Kempski, Jürgen von ([1951] 1992): "Charles Sanders Peirce und die Apagôgê des Aristoteles". In: *Prinzipien der Wirklichkeit. Schriften 3*. Frankfurt am Main: Suhrkamp, pp. 310–319.

Kempski, Jürgen von ([1988] 1992): "Charles Sanders Peirce zu Aristoteles' Analytica Priora II 23, 25". In: *Prinzipien der Wirklichkeit. Schriften 3*. Frankfurt am Main: Suhrkamp, pp. 320–324.

Kent, Beverly (1987): *Charles S. Peirce: Logic and the Classification of the Sciences*. Montreal, Kingston: McGill-Queen's University Press.

Ketner, Kenneth L. (1982): "Carolyn Eisele's Place in Peirce studies". In: *Historia Mathematica* 8. No. 3, pp. 326–332.

Ketner, Kenneth L. (1986): *A Comprehensive Bibliography of the Published Works of Charles Sanders Peirce with a Bibliography of Secondary Studies*. With the assistance of Arthur Franklin Stewart and Claude V. Bridges. Bowling Green: Philosophy Documentation Center, Bowling Green State University.

Ketner, Kenneth L. (2009): "Charles Sanders Peirce: Interdisciplinary Scientist". In: Charles S. Peirce: *The Logic of Interdisciplinarity*. The Monist-Series. Elize Bisanz (Ed.). Berlin: Akademie Verlag, pp. 35–57.

Ketner, Kenneth L./Stewart, Arthur F. (1984): "The Early History of Computer Design: C. S. Peirce and Marquand's Logical Machines". In: *Princeton University Library Chronicle* 45. No. 3, pp. 187–211.

Kevelson, Roberta (1983): "Time as Method in Charles Sanders Peirce". In: *American Journal of Semiotics* 2. No. 1–2, pp. 85–107.

Kloppenberg, James T. (2004): "Pragmatism and the Practice of History: From Turner and Du Bois to Today". In: *Metaphilosophy* 35. No. 1–2, pp. 202–225.

Koopman, Colin (2009): *Pragmatism as Transition. Historicity and Hope in James, Dewey, and Rorty*. New York: Columbia University Press.

Koopman, Colin (2010): "Bernard Williams on Philosophy's Need for History". In: *The Review of Metaphysics* 64. No. 1, pp. 3–30.

Koselleck, Reinhart ([1967] 2004): "*Historia Magistra Vitae:* The Dissolution of the Topos into the Perspective of a Modernized Historical Process". In: *Futures Past: On the Semantics of Historical Time*. Transl. K. Tribe. New York: Columbia University Press, pp. 26–42.

Koselleck, Reinhart (1977): "Standortbindung und Zeitlichkeit. Ein Beitrag zur historiographischen Erschließung der geschichtlichen Welt". In: Reinhart Koselleck/Wolfgang J. Mommsen/Jörn Rüsen (Eds.): *Objektivität und Parteilichkeit in der Geschichtswissenschaft*. München: dtv.

Kusch, Martin (1995): *Psychologism. A Case Study in the Sociology of Philosophical Knowledge*. London, New York: Routledge.

Kuukkanen, Jouni-Matti (2015): *Postnarrativist Philosophy of Historiography*. London: Palgrave Macmillan.
Kuukkanen, Jouni-Matti (2017): "Moving Deeper into Rational Pragmatism: A Reply to My Reviewers". In: *Journal of the Philosophy of History* 11. No. 1, pp. 83–118.
Lane, Robert (2018): *Peirce on Realism and Idealism*. Cambridge: Cambridge University Press.
Laudan, Larry (1981): "A Confutation of Convergent Realism". In: *Philosophy of Science* 48, pp. 19–48.
Le Goff, Jaques (1978): "Documento/Monumento". In: Ruggiero Romano (Ed.): *Enciclopedia Einaudi*. Vol. 5. Torino: Einaudi, pp. 38–48.
Liatsi, Maria (2006): *Interpretation der Antike. Die pragmatistische Methode historischer Forschung. Ein Kommentar zur Abhandlung von Charles S. Peirce "On the Logic of Drawing History from Ancient Documents, Especially from Testimonies"*. Hildesheim, Zürich, New York: Georg Olms Verlag.
Libri, Guillaume [Guglielmo] (1838): *Histoire des sciences mathématiques en Italie*. Vol. 2. Paris: Jules Renouard.
Lindsay, Hugh (1997): "Strabo on Apellicon's Library". In: *Rheinisches Museum für Philologie* 140. No. 3–4, pp. 290–298.
Llull, Ramon ([1295] 2000): *Raimundi Lulli. Opera Latina. Arbor Scientiae*. 3 vols. Pere Villalba Varneda (Ed.). Turnhout: Brepols Publishers. (Corpus Christianorum 24–26).
Lovejoy, Arthur O. (1920): "Pragmatism Versus The Pragmatist". In: Durant Drake (Ed.): *Essays in Critical Realism. A Cooperative Study of the Problem of Knowledge* London: MacMillan and Co., pp. 35–81.
Lovejoy, Arthur O. (1963): *The Thirteen Pragmatisms and Other Essays*. Baltimore: The Johns Hopkins Press.
Lutosławski, Wincenty (1897): *The Origin and Growth of Plato's Logic. With an Account of Plato's Style and of the Chronology of his Writings*. London: Longmans, Green & Co.
Mach, Ernst ([1883] 1893): *The Science of Mechanics. A Critical and Historical Account of Its Development*. 2nd edition. Transl. T. J. McCormack. Chicago: The Open Court, London: Kegan Paul.
Maddalena, Giovanni (2015): *The Philosophy of Gesture. Completing Pragmatists' Incomplete Revolution*. Montreal & Kingston, London, Chicago: Mc Gill-Queen's University Press.
Mandeville, Bernard ([1714] 1924): *The Fable of the Bees. Or, Private Vices, Publick Benefits*. 2 vols. Frederick B. Kaye (Ed.). Oxford: Clarendon Press.
Marcuse, Herbert ([1932] 1987): *Hegel's Ontology and the Theory of Historicity*. Seyla Benhabib (Ed.). Cambridge/MA, London: The MIT Press.
Margolis, Joseph (2019): "Pragmatism and Historicity". In: *Journal of the Philosophy of History* 13. No. 3, pp. 302–324.
Markosian, Ned (2016): "Time". In: Edward N. Zalta (Ed.): *Stanford Encyclopedia of Philosophy* (Fall 2016 Edition). https://plato.stanford.edu/archives/fall2016/entries/time/, visited on 17 February 2020.
Marshall, David L. (2013): "The Implications of Robert Brandom's Inferentialism for Intellectual History". In: *History and Theory* 52. No. 1, pp 1–31.
Marshall, David L. (2016): "Historical and Philosophical Stances. Max Harold Fisch, A Paradigm for Intellectual Historians". In: *European Journal of Pragmatism and American Philosophy* 8. No. 2. DOI: 10.4000/ejpap.647, visited on 7 November 2019.
McTaggart, John M. E. (1908): "The Unreality of Time". In: *Mind* 17. No. 68, pp. 457–474.

Mead, George H. (1932): *The Philosophy of the Present*. Chicago: Open Court.
Menand, Louis (2001): *The Pragmatist Club. A Story of Ideas in America*. New York: Farrar, Straus and Giroux.
Merrill, Kenneth R. (1991): "Hume's 'Of Miracles', Peirce, and the Balancing of Likelihoods". In: *Journal of the History of Philosophy* 29. No. 1, pp. 85–113.
Merton, Robert K. ([1957] 1968): *On Theoretical Sociology. Five Essays, Old and New*. New York: The Free Press.
Merton, Robert K./Barber, Elinor (2004): *The Travels and Adventures of Serendipity. A Study in Sociological Semantics and the Sociology of Science*. Princeton, Oxford: Princeton University Press.
Miller, Willard M. (1971): "Peirce on the Use of History". In: *Transactions of the Charles S. Peirce Society* 7. No. 2, pp. 105–126.
Miller, Willard M. (1972): "Further Thoughts on Peirce's Use of History". In: *Transactions of the Charles S. Peirce Society* 8. No. 2, pp. 115–122.
Miller, Willard M. (1978): "Peirce on Pragmaticism and History". In: *Transactions of the Charles S. Peirce Society* 14. No. 1, pp. 42–52.
Misak, Cheryl (2000): *Truth, Morality, Politics*. London: Routledge.
Misak, Cheryl (2004): "Peirce on Vital Matters". In: Cheryl Misak (Ed.): *The Cambridge Companion to Peirce*. Cambridge, New York: Cambridge University Press, pp. 150–174.
Momigliano, Arnaldo (1950): "Ancient History and the Antiquarian". In: *Journal of the Warburg and Courtauld Institutes* 13. No. 3/4, pp. 285–315.
Moore, James A. (1984): "The Semiotic of Bishop Berkeley – A Prelude to Peirce?". In: *Transactions of the Charles S. Peirce Society* 20. No. 3, pp. 325–342.
Murphey, Murray G. ([1961] 1993): *The Development of Peirce's Philosophy*. Indianapolis, Cambridge: Hackett Publishing Company.
Murphey, Murray G. (1979): "Toward an Historicist History of American Philosophy". In: *Transactions of the Charles S. Peirce Society* 15. No. 1, pp. 3–18.
Murphey, Murray G. (1994): *Philosophical Foundations of Historical Knowledge*. Albany: State University of New York Press.
Murphey, Murray G. (2009): *Truth and History*. Albany: State University of New York Press.
Murphy, Joseph J. ([1869] 1879): *Habit and Intelligence A Series of Essays on the Laws of Life and Mind*. London: Macmillan.
Nietzsche, Friedrich ([1874] 1995): *On the Utility and Liability of History for Life*. Transl. R. T. Gray. In: *Unfashionable Observations*. Stanford: Stanford University Press.
Niiniluoto, Ilkka ([1978] 1984): "Notes on Popper as Follower of Whewell and Peirce." In: *Is Science Progressive?* Springer: Dordrecht, pp. 18–60.
Niklas, Stefan (2016): "The Anticipated Past in Historical Inquiry. A. O. Lovejoy, C. I. Lewis and E. Wind on Accounting for Knowledge of the Past Within a Pragmatist Theory". In: *European Journal of Pragmatism and American Philosophy* 8. No. 2. DOI: 10.4000/ejpap.630, visited on 7 November 2019.
Nubiola, Jaime (2009): "29 enero – 30 enero 1871 (C. S. Peirce y Zina Fay, MS 1614, p. 12)". http://www.unav.es/gep/Agenda29-30Enero.html, visited on 7 November 2019.
O'Donnell, C. Oliver (2016): "Reading Allan Marquand's 'On Scientific Method in the Study of Art'". In: *European Journal of Pragmatism and American Philosophy* 8. No. 2. DOI: 10.4000/ejpap.649, visited on 7 November 2019.

Oehler, Klaus (1984–1985): "Peirce als Interpret der aristotelischen Kategorien". In: *Semiosis* 36–37, pp. 24–32.

O'Hara, David L. (2008): "Peirce, Plato and Miracles: On the Mature Peirce's Re-discovery of Plato and the Overcoming of Nominalistic Prejudice in History". In: *Transactions of the Charles S. Peirce Society* 44. No. 1, pp. 26–39.

Oppenheim, Frank M., S.J. (2005): *Reverence for the Relations of Life. Re-imagining Pragmatism via Josiah Royce's Interactions with Peirce, James, and Dewey*, Notre Dame: Notre Dame Press.

Panofsky, Erwin ([1932] 1998): "Zum Problem der Beschreibung und Inhaltsdeutung von Werken der bildenden Kunst". In: *Deutschsprachige Aufsätze*. Vol. 1. Karen Michels/ Martin Warnke (Eds.). Berlin: Akademie Verlag, pp. 1064–1077.

Panofsky, Erwin (1951): *Gothic Architecture and Scholasticism*. Latrobe: Archabbey Press.

Panofsky, Erwin (1955): *Meaning in the Visual Arts: Papers in and on Art History*. Garden City, Doubleday.

Panofsky, Erwin (1969): "Erasmus and the Visual Arts". In: *Journal of the Warburg and Courtauld Institutes* 32, pp. 200–227.

Parravicini, Andrea (2012): *Il pensiero in evoluzione. Chauncey Wright tra darwinismo e pragmatismo*. Pisa: ETS.

Pasquali, Giorgio ([1934] 1952): *Storia della tradizione e critica del testo*. 2nd edition. Firenze: Le Monnier.

Peirce, Charles S. (1878): *Photometric Researches. Made in the Years 1872–1875*. Leipzig: Wilhelm Engelmann.

Peirce, Charles S. (Ed.) (1883): *Studies in Logic by Members of the Johns Hopkins University*. Boston: Little, Brown, and Company.

Peirce, Charles S. (1931–1958): *Collected Papers of Charles S. Peirce*. 8 vols. Charles Hartshorne/Paul Weiss /Arthur W. Burks (Eds.). Cambridge/MA: The Belknap Press.

Peirce, Charles S. (1975–1987): *Charles S. Peirce: Contributions to The Nation*. 4 vols. Kenneth L. Ketner/James E. Cook (Eds.). Lubbock: Texas Tech Press.

Peirce, Charles S. (1976): *The New Elements of Mathematics*. 4 vols. Carolyn Eisele (Ed.). The Hague, Paris: Mouton.

Peirce, Charles S. (1977): *Semiotics and Significs. The Correspondence between Charles S. Peirce and Victoria Lady Welby*. Charles S. Hardwick/James Cook (Eds.). Bloomington, London: Indiana University Press.

Peirce, Charles S. (1982–): *Writings of Charles S. Peirce: A Chronological Edition*. Peirce Edition Project (Ed.). Bloomington, Indianapolis: Indiana University Press.

Peirce, Charles S. (1985): *Historical Perspectives on Peirce's Logic of Science. A History of Science*. 2 vols. Carolyn Eisele (Ed.). Berlin, New York, Amsterdam: Mouton.

Peirce, Charles S. (1992): *Reasoning and the Logic of Things. The Cambridge Conferences Lectures of 1898*. Kenneth L. Ketner (Ed.). Cambridge/MA, London: Harvard University Press.

Peirce, Charles S. (1992–1998): *The Essential Peirce: Selected Philosophical Writings*. 2 vols. Nathan Houser/Christian Kloesel/Peirce Edition Project (Eds.). Bloomington, Indianapolis: Indiana University Press.

Pencak, William (1991): "Charles S. Peirce, Historian and Semiotician". In: *Semiotica* 83. No. 3–4, pp. 311–332.

Peterson, Sven R. (1955): "Benjamin Peirce. Mathematician and Philosopher". In: *Journal of the History of Ideas* 16. No. 1, pp. 89–112.
Pfeifer, David E. (2017): "Josiah Royce Influenced Charles Peirce". In: *European Journal of Pragmatism and American Philosophy* 8. No. 2. DOI: 10.4000/ejpap.659, visited on 20 February 2020.
Pietarinen, Ahti-Veikko (2005): "Cultivating Habits of Reason: Peirce and the *logica utens* versus *logica docens* Distinction". In: *History of Philosophy Quarterly* 22. No. 4, pp. 357–372.
Pietarinen, Ahti-Veikko (2015): "Two Papers on Existential Graphs by Charles Peirce". In: *Synthese* 192. No. 4, pp. 881–922.
Pillsbury, Walter B. (1944): "Joseph Jastrow, 1863–1944". In: *The Psychological Review* 51. No. 5, pp. 261–265.
Podro, Michael (1982): *The Critical Historians of Art*. New Haven: Yale University Press.
Principe, Lawrence M. (2013): *The Secrets of Alchemy*. Chicago, London: The University of Chicago Press.
Psillos, Stathis (2018): "Realism and Theory Change in Science". Edward N. Zalta (Ed.): *The Stanford Encyclopedia of Philosophy* (Summer 2018 edition). https://plato.stanford.edu/archives/sum2018/entries/realism-theory-change/, visited on 20 March 2020.
Queloz, Matthieu (2019): "Nietzsches affirmative Genealogien". In: *Deutsche Zeitschrift für Philosophie* 67. No. 3, pp. 429–439.
Quine, Willard V. O. ([1951] 1953): "Two Dogmas of Empiricism". In: *From a Logical Point of View*. Cambridge/MA: Harvard University Press.
Quinn, Aleta (2016): "William Whewell's philosophy of architecture and the historicization of biology". In: *Studies in History and Philosophy of Science Part C: Studies in History and Philosophy of Biological and Biomedical Sciences* 59, pp. 11–19.
Robins, Gay/Shute, Charles (1987): *The Rhind Mathematical Papyrus: An Ancient Egyptian Text*. London: British Museum Publications.
Roth, Paul A. (2020): *The Philosophical Structure of Historical Explanation*. Evanston: Northwestern University Press.
Royce, Josiah (1885): *The Religious Aspect of Philosophy*. Boston: Houghton Mifflin.
Royce, Josiah (1899–1901): *The World and the Individual*. 2 vols. London: The Macmillan Company.
Ruse, Michael (1975): "Darwin's debt to philosophy: An examination of the influence of the philosophical ideas of John F.W. Herschel and William Whewell on the development of Charles Darwin's theory of evolution". In: *Studies in History and Philosophy of Science* 4. No. 2, pp. 159–181.
Sandys, John E. ([1908] 2011): *A History of Classical Scholarship. The Eighteenth Century in Germany and the Nineteenth Century in Europe and the United States of America*. Vol. 3. Cambridge: Cambridge University Press.
Schiller, Friedrich ([1795] 1998): *Letters on the Aesthetic Education of Man*, Transl. E. M. Wilkinson/L. A. Willoughby. In: *Essays*. Daniel O. Dahlstrom/Walter Hinderer (Eds.). New York: Continuum.
Schnädelbach, Herbert (1984): *Philosophy in Germany. 1831–1933*. Transl. E. Matthews. Cambridge: Cambridge University Press.
Segre, Michael (1991): *In the Wake of Galileo*. New Brunswick: Rutgers University Press.

Shakespeare, William (2016): *The New Oxford Shakespeare. The Complete Works. Modern Critical Edition*. Gary Taylor/John Jowett/Terri Bourus/Gabriel Egan (Eds.). 2 vols. Oxford: Oxford University Press.

Shapiro, Michael (1991): *The Sense of Change. Language as History*. Bloomington, Indianapolis: Indiana University Press.

Short, Thomas L. (1980): "Peirce and the Incommensurability of Theories", *The Monist* 63. No. 3, pp. 316–328.

Short, Thomas L. (2001): "The Conservative Pragmatism of Charles S. Peirce". In: *Modern Age* 43. No. 4, pp. 295–303.

Short, Thomas L. (2007): *Peirce's Theory of Signs*. Cambridge: Cambridge University Press.

Shusterman, Richard (1992): *Pragmatist Aesthetics. Living Beauty, Rethinking Art*. Oxford: Blackwell.

Skagestad, Peter (1995): "Discussion: Peirce and the History of Science." In: Kenneth L. Ketner (Ed.): *Peirce and Contemporary Thought. Philosophical Inquiries*. New York: Fordham University Press, pp. 196–201.

Snyder, Laura J. (2006): *Reforming Philosophy: A Victorian Debate on Science and Society*. Chicago, London: University of Chicago Press.

Snyder, Laura J. (2019): "William Whewell". In: Edward N. Zalta (Ed.): *The Stanford Encyclopedia of Philosophy* (Spring 2019 Edition). https://plato.stanford.edu/archives/spr2019/entries/whewell/, visited on 7 November 2019.

Spencer, Herbert ([1873] 1966): *The Study of Sociology*. In: *The Works of Herbert Spencer*. Vol. 12. Osnabrück: Otto Zeller.

Steger, Stewart A. (1913): *American Dictionaries*. Baltimore: J. H. Furst.

Stern, Robert (2009): *Hegelian Metaphysics*. Oxford, New York: Oxford University Press.

Stjernfelt, Frederik (2014): *Natural Propositions. The Actuality of Peirce's Doctrine of Dicisigns*. Boston: Docent Press.

Strabo (1917–1932): *Geography*. Transl. H. L. Jones. 8 Vols. Cambridge, Mass: Harvard University Press. (Loeb Classical Library).

Strong, E. W. (1955): "William Whewell and John Stuart Mill: Their Controversy about Scientific Knowledge". In: *Journal of the History of Ideas* 16. No. 2, pp. 209–231.

Talon, Philippe (2013): "Enūma Eliš". In: Constance M. Furey/Steven L. McKenzie/Thomas C. Römer/Jens Schröter/Barry Dov Walfish/Eric Ziolkowski (Eds.): *Encyclopedia of the Bible and its Reception*. Vol. 7. Berlin, New York: De Gruyter, pp. 970–972.

Tamm, Marek (2014): "Truth, Objectivity and Evidence in History Writing". In: *Journal of the Philosophy of History* 8. No. 2, pp. 265–90.

Tiercelin, Claudine (1992): "Vagueness and the Unity of C. S. Peirce's Realism". In: *Transactions of the Charles S. Peirce Society* 28. No. 1, pp. 51–82.

Timpanaro, Sebastiano ([1981] 2005): *The Genesis of Lachmann's Method*. Glenn W. Most (Ed.). Chicago, London: The University of Chicago Press.

Tonelli, Giorgio (1962): "Qu'est-ce que l'histoire de la philosophie?". In: *Revue philosophique de la France et de l'Étranger* 152, pp. 289–306.

Topa, Alessandro (2007): *Die Genese der Peirce'schen Semiotik. Teil I: Das Kategorienproblem (1857–1865)*. Würzburg: Königshausen & Neumann.

Topa, Alessandro (2016): "'I Have To Confess I Cannot Read History So,' On the Origins and Development of Peirce's Philosophy of History". In: *European Journal of Pragmatism and American Philosophy* 8. No. 2. DOI: 10.4000/ejpap.628, visited on 5 February 2020.

Topa, Alessandro (2019): "'In Memory of these Concrete Living Gests': C. S. Peirce on Science of Review". In: *Transactions of the Charles S. Peirce Society* 55. No 3, pp. 273–303.
Trabant, Jürgen (2000): "Le courant humboldtien". In: Sylvain Auroux (Ed.): *Histoire des idées linguistiques*. Vol. 3. Sprimont: Mardaga, pp. 311–322.
Trabant, Jürgen (forthcoming): "Das Gespräch. Wilhelm von Humboldt über den unabänderlichen Dualismus des Denkens und Sprechens – mit Blick auf Levinas". In: Burkhard Liebsch (Ed.): *Emmanuel Levinas: Dialog. Ein kooperativer Kommentar*. Freiburg, München: Alber.
Turrisi, Patricia A. (1997): "Commentary". In: Charles S. Peirce. *Pragmatism as a Principle and Method of Right Thinking. The 1903 Harvard Lectures on Pragmatism*. Patricia A. Turrisi (Ed.). Albany: State University of New York Press.
Turrisi, Patricia A. (2014): "Peirce's Method of Work". In: Torkild Thellefsen/Bent Sorensen (Eds.): *Charles Sanders Peirce in His Own Words. 100 Years of Semiotics, Communication and Cognition*. Berlin, New York: De Gruyter, pp. 385–392.
Viola, Tullio (2011): "Philosophy and the Second Person. Peirce, Wilhelm von Humboldt, Benveniste, and Personal Pronouns as Universals of Language". In: *Transactions of the Charles S. Peirce Society* 47. No. 4, pp. 389–420.
Viola, Tullio (2012): "Peirce and Iconology. Habitus, Embodiment, and the Analogy between Philosophy and Architecture". In: *European Journal of Pragmatism and American Philosophy* 4. No. 1. DOI: 10.4000/ejpap.764, visited on 5 February 2020.
Viola, Tullio (2019): "From Vague Symbols to Contested Concepts: Peirce, W. B. Gallie, and History". In: *History and Theory* 58. No. 2, pp. 233–251.
von Renthe-Fink, Ludwig (1974): "Geschichtlichkeit". In: Joachim Ritter (Ed.): *Historisches Wörterbuch der Philosophie*. Vol. 3. Basel: Schwabe, pp. 404–408.
Wagner, David (2012): "Peirce, Panofsky, and the Gothic". In: *Transactions of the Charles S. Peirce Society* 48. No. 4, pp. 436–455.
Walsh, William H. (1942): "The Intelligibility of History". *Philosophy* 17. No. 66, pp. 128–143.
Werner, Petra (2004): *Himmel und Erde. Alexander von Humboldt und sein Kosmos*. Berlin: Akademie Verlag.
Whately, Richard (1819): *Historic Doubts Relative to Napoleon Buonaparte*. London: Hatchard.
Whately, Richard (1826): *Elements of Logic*. London: Mawman.
Whewell, William ([1835] 1842): *Architectural Notes on German Churches. With Notes Written during an Architectural Tour in Picardy and Normandy*. 3rd edition. London: John W. Parker.
Whewell, William (1837): *History of the Inductive Sciences. From the Earliest to the Present Times*. 3 vols. London: John W. Parker.
Whewell, William (1840): *The Philosophy of the Inductive Sciences, Founded Upon Their History*. 2 vols. London: John W. Parker.
Whewell, William (1858a): *The History of Scientific Ideas*. 2 vols. London: John W. Parker.
Whewell, William (1858b): *Novum Organum Renovatum*. London: John W. Parker.
Whewell, Willam (1860): *On the Philosophy of Discovery: Chapters Historical and Critical*. London: John W. Parker.
White, Morton ([1950] 2005): "The Analytic and the Synthetic: An Untenable Dualism". In: *From a Philosophical Point of View*. Princeton, Oxford: Princeton University Press.

Whitney William Dwight (Ed.) (1889–1891): *Century Dictionary. An Encyclopedic Lexicon of the English Language*. Edited with assistance from Benjamin Eli Smith, New York: The Century Co. http://www.global-language.com/century/, visited on 5 February 2020.

Wiener, Philip P. (1946): "The Evolutionism and Pragmaticism of Peirce". In: *Journal of the History of Ideas* 7. No. 3, pp. 321–350.

Wiener, Philip P. (1947): "The Peirce-Langley Correspondence and Peirce's Manuscript on Hume and the Laws of Nature". In: *Proceedings of the American Philosophical Society* 91. No. 2, pp. 201–228.

Wiener, Philip P. (1949): *Evolution and the Founders of Pragmatism*, Cambridge, MA: Harvard University Press.

Wiener, Philip P. (1952): "Peirce's Evolutionary Interpretation of the History of Science". In: Philip P. Wiener/Frederic H. Young (Eds.): *Studies in the Philosophy of Charles S. Peirce*. Cambridge/MA: Harvard University Press.

Wiener, Philip P. (1971): "W. M. Miller on Peirce's Interpretation of the History of Science". In: *Transactions of the Charles S. Peirce Society* 7. No. 4, pp. 233–236.

Wiener, Philip P. (1972): "More Thoughts about Miller's 'Further Thoughts on Peirce's Use of History'". In: *Transactions of the Charles S. Peirce Society* 8. No. 3, pp. 187–195.

Willis, Robert (1845): *Architectural History of Canterbury Cathedral*, London: Longman.

Wimsatt, James I. (1996): "John Duns Scotus, Charles Sanders Peirce, and Chaucer's Portrayal of the Canterbury Pilgrims". In: *Speculum* 71. No. 3, pp. 633–645.

Wind, Edgar ([1936] 1963): "Some Points of Contact between History and Natural Science". In: Raymond Klibansky/Herbert J. Paton (Eds.): *Philosophy and History. Essays Presented to Ernst Cassirer*. Oxford: Clarendon Press.

Wölfflin, Heinrich ([1888] 1964). Renaissance and Baroque. Transl. K. Simon. Ithaca: Cornell University Press.

Woods, Frederick A. (1913): *The Influence of Monarchs. Steps in a New Science of History*. New York: The Macmillan Company.

Wray, K. Brad (2015): "Pessimistic Inductions: Four Varieties". In: *International Studies in the Philosophy of Science* 29. No. 1, pp. 61–73.

Index of names

Abbot, Francis E.   30
Abbott, Andrew   66
Agassiz, Louis   12, 15f., 61f., 128, 130
Ambrosio, Chiara   53, 59
Anderson, Douglas   102
Andronicus of Rhodes   200f.
Apellicon   200–202
Aristotle   42, 134, 147, 169, 177, 192, 195, 198–203, 213
Aron, Raymond   71

Bacon, Francis   183
Bacon, Roger   181f.
Baldwin, James   121
Bancroft, George   18
Bascom, John   42
Basilius Valentinus   41, 199
Bellucci, Francesco   89, 125
Benhabib, Seyla   71
Bentham, Jeremy   57
Bentley, Richard   196
Berkeley, George   25f., 29
Bloch, Marc   175, 210
Boeckh, August   206
Boltanski, Luc   214
Bourdieu, Pierre   212–214
Bulwer-Lytton, Edward   188
Burt, Benjamin Chapman   42

Cajori, Florian   173
Carlyle, Thomas   186
Cassirer, Ernst   212
Cayley, Arthur   65
Cerutti, Simona   214
Chaucer, Geoffrey   179
Cola di Rienzo   188
Colapietro, Vincent   143
Collier, Arthur   42
Comte, Auguste   19, 56–58, 61, 64, 112, 120, 187, 189, 205
Constantine (*Roman emperor*)   169

Copernicus, Nicolaus   43, 142, 162, 175, 187
Cuvier, Georges   84

Darwin, Charles   3, 11f., 19, 35, 78, 83–85, 119, 129, 152, 162, 170, 172f., 186
De Tienne, André   40
Deacon, Terrence   90
Descartes, René   23, 42, 100, 105, 196
Dewey, John   3, 35, 49, 127–129, 141, 151, 208, 212, 214, 216f., 220
Dickens, Charles   153
Dickson White, Andrew   42
Dilthey, Wilhelm   71, 212
Diodorus Siculus   18
Duns Scotus   22f., 215
Dwight Whitney, William   37

Eisele, Carolyn   6, 42 181, 216
Ellis, Alexander John   17
Emerson, Ralph Waldo   11, 81, 88, 107
Esposito, Joseph L.   4, 6, 53, 193
Euclid   126

Falckenberg, Richard   42
Faraday, Michael   162
Fay, Melusina   14, 29
Fechner, Gustav Theodor   118
Ferrarin, Alfredo   101
Fichte, Johann G.   50f.
Fisch, Max H.   5, 39, 204
Flinders Petrie, William M.   61, 194
Franklin, Benjamin   76, 189
Fraser, Alexander   25
Frege, Gottlob   118

Galilei, Galileo   171, 177
Gallie, Walter B.   5, 150, 152
Galton, Francis   186f.
Gava, Gabriele   93, 110, 149
Gauss, Johann C. F.   116
Giddins, Franklin H.   39, 206, 224
Gilbert, William   181

Ginzburg, Carlo 207
Gombrich, Ernst H. 175
Green, Nicholas St. John 30
Grosseteste, Robert 182

Haack, Susan 114
Hanson, Norwood R. 119
Harris, William T. 23
Hegel, Georg W. F. 2f., 22, 24, 32, 50, 71f., 86f., 90f., 101, 103, 109f., 124, 126, 142, 147, 168, 191
Heidegger, Martin 71
Hermann, Gottfried 206
Herodotus 67
Hipparchus 141
Holmes, Oliver Wendell 30
Houser, Nathan 137, 186
Huber, François 190
Humboldt, Alexander von 16–18, 61
Humboldt, Wilhelm von 18, 133, 135
Hume, David 105, 192, 195, 204
Husserl, Edmund 118
Huxley, Thomas 153, 155

Jakobson, Roman 133
James, William 30, 75, 79, 96, 144, 153, 186f.
Jaspers, Karl 71
Jastrow, Joseph 35, 118
Jesus 152, 189
Joas, Hans 43, 143, 225

Kant, Immanuel 11, 14, 16, 19, 28, 31, 42, 50–52, 61, 77, 93, 100–103, 105f., 110, 115, 117f., 133f., 144f., 210
Kepler, Johannes 142, 177
Koselleck, Reinhart 50, 224
Kuhn, Thomas 170f.

La Bruyère, Jean de 189
Ladd-Franklin, Christine 36
Lamarck, Jean-Baptiste 84, 170
Langley, Samuel P. 192
Lathrop, Francis 132
Laudan, Larry 143
Lavater, Johann Kaspar 189f.
Libri, Guglielmo 181

Lobachevsky, Nikolai 126
Locke, John 103, 105, 117, 187
Lockyer, J. Norman 166
Lombroso, Cesare 187
Lovejoy, Arthur O. 6, 71f., 208, 212

Mach, Ernst 39
Maricourt, Petrus Peregrinus de 36, 39f., 140, 181–184, 199
Marquand, Allan 36
Maupassant, Guy de 189
Mead, George H. 3, 225
Mendeleev, Dmitri 162, 177
Merton, Robert K. 112
Michelangelo Buonarroti 171
Michelet, Jules 28
Mill, James 24, 113
Mill, John Stuart 19f., 27, 48, 126, 177
Miller, Willard M. 5, 40
Misak, Cheryl 151, 153
Mitchell, Oscar H. 36
Murphey, Murray G. 5
Murphy, Joseph J. 79

Napoleon Bonaparte 188, 204, 207f.
Neleus of Scepsis 199
Newton, Isaac 43, 162, 177, 187
Nietzsche, Friedrich 43, 67
Noyes, John B. 17
Numa Pompilius 33

Ockham, William of 23

Panofsky, Erwin 28, 212f.
Parker, Samuel 42
Pasquali, Giorgio 202
Patterson, Carlile P. 31
Paul, St. 7, 88
Peirce, Benjamin 11f., 14, 22, 30, 38
Peirce, Charles S. *Passim*
Peirce, James 181, 183
Pietarinen, Ahti-Veikko 125
Pius IX 33
Plato 59, 109, 134, 177, 195, 198f., 202f.
Plimpton, George A. 40, 199
Plutarch 187, 190
Podro, Michael 179

Index of names

Polybius 18
Prantl, Karl von 169
Ptolemy, Claudius 31, 137, 141f.
Putnam, G. 47
Putnam, Hilary 114
Pythagoras 111, 177, 189, 195, 198f., 203f., 224

Quine, Willard V. O. 113

Reid, Thomas 210
Rosmini, Antonio 42
Rousseau, Jean-Jacques 153
Royce, Josiah 109f., 119, 137, 144, 149, 153, 186
Russell, F. C. 93

Saint-Beuve, Charles-Augustin 190
Sandys, John E. 206
Sayce, Archibald 136
Schelling, Friedrich W. J. 16, 79, 83
Schiller, Friedrich 11, 14, 16
Schliemann, Heinrich 194, 205
Schnaase, Karl 179
Semper, Gottfried 28
Senebier, Jean 42
Shakespeare, William 17, 38, 93, 98
Sherlock Holmes 190, 207
Shapiro, Michael 91, 93
Short, T. L. 92, 114
Spencer, Herbert 170, 186
Spinoza, Baruch 189
Steinthal, Heymann 136

Stjernfelt, Frederik 90
Strabo 199, 201
Sulla, Lucius Cornelius 200
Swedenborg, Emanuel 11

Teophrastus 189, 199
Tetens, Johannes Nikolaus 42
Thales 175
Thucydides 58
Toland, John 42
Topa, Alessandro 2, 16, 51
Trendelenburg, Friedrich A. 134

Veblen, Thorstein 35
Vico, Giambattista 5
Viviani, Vincenzo 171

Wagner, Richard 188
Washington, George 189
Welby, Victoria 59, 94, 154, 157, 216
Whately, Richard 11, 204, 207
Whewell, William 18–22, 24, 27, 29f., 35, 47f., 52, 58f., 61, 66, 102, 124–126, 148, 163, 169, 173f., 179, 184, 217–220, 225
Wiener, Philip P. 5f., 46, 51, 175, 208, 217
Willis, Robert 29
Wind, Edgar 212f.
Windelband, Wilhelm 42
Wölfflin, Heinrich 28
Woods, Frederick A. 186
Wright, Chauncey 30, 217

Zeller, Eduard 194

Index of terms

a priori/a posteriori   13, 20, 64, 112, 115–118, 130
– a priori method. *See* fixation of belief
abduction   6, 49, 112, 123, 125 f., 177, 184, 197–199, 201, 204 f., 207 f., 211, 225
– meta-abduction   125, 143, 220 f.
Ahmes Papyrus   166, 180 f.
American Academy of Arts and Sciences   22 f.
American Historical Review   40, 42, 142
analytic/synthetic   112 f., 115 f., 118, 123
ampliative reasoning   115, 117, 123, 143, 162, 205, 220
antiquarianism   2, 193, 206, 210
Arabs   30
architectonic   52, 54, 61, 101–103, 143–147
architecture   27–30, 33, 144, 174, 178 f., 185, 211–213
autonomy   7, 12, 67, 71, 100, 102 f., 111, 120, 131 f., 145, 157, 161, 167, 221 f.

Babylonia   162, 165 f., 199
– *Enûma Eliš*   166
Bible   28, 84, 166, 196, 204
– Gospel   84, 107, 153
Bibliothèque Nationale   36
biography   36–39, 54, 56, 177, 185, 187–191, 195, 199, 202 f., 207, 215, 224
– autobiography   146

Century Dictionary   37, 53, 56, 58 f., 135, 153
Civil War   11
cenoscopy/idioscopy   56–58, 111 f., 118, 121, 144, 156
chance. *See* determinism
China   162, 165
civilization   16, 36, 38, 153, 162–165, 171, 177, 188, 205
clear and distinct ideas   113
colligation   19 f., 48, 184, 225

common sense   92, 97, 99, 104–108, 126, 131, 144, 147, 156, 162, 210, 213
conservatism   27, 33, 131 f., 151–158, 172
contingency. *See* determinism
continuity   43, 46, 74 f., 79 f., 83, 87, 98, 173 f., 183, 202, 208, 225, 227
controversy. *See* disagreement
conversion   88
creativity   19, 67, 82, 84 f., 87, 102

determinism   43, 72, 80, 82–87, 94 f., 99, 164 f., 168–170, 175, 186, 221
diagrammatic reasoning   89, 93, 116 f., 129 f., 135
dialogue   31, 68, 131–137, 140, 214, 218, 222
disagreement   21, 25 f., 34, 45, 66, 131, 134 f., 147–151, 217 f., 222
document/monument   193–195, 198, 205–210, 213, 224 f.

Egypt   61, 89, 162, 165–167, 172, 179–181, 185, 194, 196 f., 199, 210 f., 212
– Great Pyramid of Giza   180
embodiment   27, 80, 92–94, 203, 210 f.
empirical knowledge   103 f., 109, 112, 118
empiricism   19 f., 103, 110, 116
Enlightenment   50 f., 100, 103
essentially contested concept   5, 152, 154
ethics of terminology   37, 89, 132, 155 f.
evolution/evolutionism   2 f., 5–7, 12, 40, 44–47, 49, 52 f., 71 f., 82–90, 116, 128–130, 135, 142, 155, 162, 164 f., 167–173, 183, 189, 215, 217, 220 f.
experiment   1 f., 30, 35, 48, 51, 116–118, 121, 140, 182–184, 190, 197, 203, 205, 208, 215

fallibilism   104, 138, 144, 148, 151, 223
feeling   75, 79–82, 88, 119, 139, 188, 190, 212
final cause. *See* teleology

Firstness, Secondness, Thirdness. *See* metaphysical categories
fixation of belief   31, 33f., 38, 67, 109f., 148f., 151, 163, 165, 222
French Revolution   153, 165, 169

genealogy   32, 39, 43, 58, 60, 62f., 92, 96, 115, 128–130, 220
generality   56, 78–80, 94, 103, 111, 121, 221
genetic method. *See* genealogy
genetic fallacy   119
Gothic architecture   27–30, 33, 174, 178–180, 185, 210–213
great men   36f., 38f., 54, 176f., 185–191, 197, 203
Greece   36f., 67, 135, 162, 164f., 171, 175, 197, 199f., 212
growth   40, 45, 47–49, 57–59, 65f., 72f., 75–78, 82, 88–92, 94–96, 114, 132, 137, 141f., 151, 157, 162, 167, 170–174, 183, 221, 223

habit   71–73, 77–85, 87, 92, 94f., 104, 107, 114, 120, 149, 154, 170f., 184f., 210f., 213f., 221
– *habitus*   213
Harvard College Observatory   22, 31
Harvard University   17f., 20, 30, 38
hermeneutics   72, 136, 214, 216, 226
higher criticism   125, 193f., 197, 201, 203
historicism   3, 72, 90, 124, 126, 132
historicity   7, 53, 58–60, 63, 67, 71, 73, 78, 81, 88, 96, 99f., 131, 141, 145f., 161, 217
history
– ancient   164, 177, 192–195, 197, 199, 206, 225
– of art and architecture   16, 27–30, 33f., 36, 111, 164f., 169, 171f., 174, 178–180, 212–214
– of concepts   23f., 37, 43
– historical periodization   175f.
– of ideas   5f., 137, 218
– intellectual   6, 85f., 168f., 171, 176, 183, 220
– of logic   22, 24
– metaphysical   25–28, 36
– of philosophy   16, 24, 34, 36, 42, 48, 101f., 108, 150, 162, 195, 216f., 222f.
– political   16, 26, 45, 162
– pragmatic   48–51, 214, 225
– public   21, 46, 217f.
– of science   1, 6f., 15, 20f., 29, 36f., 39–42, 44–54, 57–59, 62, 71, 83, 102, 111, 123–128, 137–140, 142f., 161f., 167–170, 174, 177f., 183f., 187f., 215, 217, 219–221, 223, 225f.
– of thought   46, 90f., 124, 127, 129, 175, 215

iconology   28
idealism   2, 6, 13, 17, 79, 109f.
indeterminacy   82f., 91, 93, 95f., 99, 221
India   162
individualism   27, 84f., 140, 144f., 154, 168, 173
Indo-European languages   122f.
induction   13, 19f., 47f., 116, 123, 125f., 157, 162, 183f., 188, 197f., 201, 205, 207, 221
– meta-induction   143
instinct   59, 117, 131, 136, 152–155, 163–165, 196
institution   25, 32f., 45, 132, 152, 154–156, 191, 222
introspection   81
intuition   23, 73, 75, 110, 134, 212

Johns Hopkins University   30, 36f., 38f., 65, 187
Journal of Speculative Philosophy   22

law of mind   46, 77, 79–81, 85, 92, 188, 225
laws of nature   49, 71f., 83, 192, 221
learning   4, 76, 78, 91, 101f., 104, 109, 113, 117, 131, 139–141, 151, 182, 225
lectio difficilior   196, 202
lexicography   37, 156
liberalism   84, 155

life
- as a philosophical concept   63, 71–73, 76, 82, 85, 87, 90 f., 94 f., 98 f., 141, 157, 221
- life-history   72, 116 f., 124, 139
- mode of life. *See* science, definition of
- study of lives. *See* biography
logica utens   107 f., 138, 173, 215
logic of relatives   44, 115
love   83–85, 98, 152
Lowell Institute   18, 40, 199
lume naturale   154

magnetism   181, 184
memory   76, 98, 137, 139, 158, 205, 209
Metaphysical Club   30, 35
metaphysics   2, 7, 11–17, 20–22, 24–26, 34, 37 f., 43, 54–56, 71, 73, 77, 80, 83, 86, 89, 97 f., 111, 122 f., 128, 131–134, 147, 151, 164, 168, 172, 175, 179, 209, 215 f., 218, 221
- metaphysical categories (Firstness, Secondness, Thirdness)   14–17, 22, 71 f., 76 f., 80, 82, 87, 94, 98 f., 110, 133, 139 f., 147, 172, 209
- metaphysical history. *See under* history
Middle Ages   20, 26, 29, 162, 169, 171, 179, 181
Monist   39 f., 79, 91, 101, 146
morphology   58

narrative   5, 32, 127, 188 f., 196, 225
Nation   22, 39, 181
natural class/natural classification   59–65, 96, 114 f., 128 f.
natural history   12, 45, 60 f., 63, 83, 121, 127–130, 190, 220
nominalism   13, 20, 22 f., 25–27, 96, 142, 177
normativity   49, 120, 128 f., 151, 163, 216 f.
- normative sciences. *See* sciences, classification of
North American Review   17, 25

objectivity/objectivism   4, 14, 34, 61, 110, 175, 194, 224 f.

observation (its cognitive role)   13, 19 f., 31, 48 f., 57, 102, 109, 111–113, 117, 118–122, 129, 144, 146, 172 f., 182, 184–186, 180–190, 207, 215, 221 f.
Office of Weights and Measures   156
Open Court   40
organicism   72, 76, 85, 93
outward clash   109 f., 112, 119, 149, 224
Oxford English Dictionary   37, 58

personality   99, 189, 212, 215 f.
personal pronouns   14–17, 133–135
phenomenology   56, 60, 64, 71, 76, 97, 121, 129, 146 f., 190
philosophy of history/of historiography   3–5, 16, 19, 36, 39, 50, 54, 67, 98, 111, 150, 155, 192 f., 215, 224 f.
phlogiston   142
positivism   24, 102, 146, 204, 205, 207, 223
pragmatic maxim   78, 91, 96, 114, 120
prejudice   13, 100, 104 f.
probable reasoning   123 f.
processualism   7, 23, 71–73, 75–81, 83, 88, 96 f., 100, 115 f., 124, 131 f., 168, 170, 208, 215, 217, 221
psychologism   3, 18, 76, 103, 115, 118–123, 128 f., 146
Putnam's Sons   41

racism   12, 18, 165, 180
rationalism   13, 105, 115, 154 f., 157 f.
realism   2, 4, 6, 13, 20, 22 f., 25–27, 34, 109 f., 151, 193, 204 f., 219, 223 f., 226
- Scholastic (*see* Scholasticism)
relativism   3, 175, 225
religion   11 f., 14, 17, 45, 151, 172
- Catholic   27, 33
- Christianity   14, 16, 84, 132, 151, 153, 169, 204
- Episcopal Church   14
- Trinitarianism   14
- Unitarianism   11, 14
Renaissance   165, 171

Index of terms — 249

Scholasticism   22–25, 27–29, 107, 156, 169, 179, 211–213
– scholastic vs. cosmic philosophy (in Kant)   101
Science   40
science, definition of   43, 59f., 137–143, 166
sciences
– archeology   61f., 166, 193f., 197, 199, 205, 220
– astronomy   15, 30f., 37, 55f., 137, 141, 165, 177, 208, 221, 225
– biology   29, 35, 55–57, 61, 64f., 221
– chemistry   15, 55f., 61, 116, 172
– classification of the sciences   7, 41, 48, 52–65, 67, 71, 111, 118, 146, 163, 219f.
– geodesy   15, 30
– linguistics   56, 122f., 128, 220
– logic   11, 13, 15, 18, 22, 30f., 35f., 44, 55f., 60, 76f., 87, 90, 107f., 112, 118–130, 135f., 184, 192–194, 204f., 220f., 225 and *passim*
– mathematics   1, 11, 15, 22, 36f., 40, 42, 55f., 60, 63–65, 107, 116f., 119, 121, 129, 137, 147, 185f., 197, 219, 221
– medicine   172
– natural science   11, 15, 21, 25, 38f., 50, 132, 190, 197, 220, 225
– philology   2, 17, 31, 36f., 38, 181, 183, 194, 196, 199, 202, 219
– physics   11, 55–57, 59, 64, 107, 116, 141f., 147, 163, 184f.
– psychology   35, 55f., 81, 115, 117, 118–123, 128f., 135, 147, 211–213, 220
– scientific method   27, 32f., 35, 47–49, 57, 138f., 148f., 181, 185, 222
– semiotics   7, 18, 22f., 60, 73, 77, 91–93, 122, 133–136, 156f., 168, 172, 211, 222, 225
– sociology   39, 55, 64, 66, 147, 206, 212–214
– tree of science   64–66
– zoology   62
Scottish philosophy. *See* common-sensism
Selbstdenken. See autonomy
Self-control   95, 105, 120f., 128, 163, 213
sentimentalism   151–154, 158
serendipity   112
sign   22f., 71, 73–77, 83, 88–93, 122, 129, 131, 135f., 156, 221
– icon   89f., 122, 172
– index   110, 122, 149, 226
– interpretant   73, 76, 88, 93, 156, 211, 225
– symbol   72, 76–78, 81, 88–93, 95–97, 114, 122, 124, 156f., 172, 221
skepticism   13, 16f., 34, 138, 143, 193f., 196, 204, 223
Smithsonian Institution   192
socialism   135, 153
solipsism   102, 131, 136
spirit of an age   13, 168, 173–175, 178, 180, 211
Stone Age   163
stream of thought   75, 79f., 97, 100, 105
subjectivism   194, 196
synechism. *See* continuity

teleology   62f., 72, 78, 82–87, 92–96, 99, 114f., 129, 164, 168, 175, 221
time (past, present, future)   4, 6f., 63, 67, 71f., 75f., 78f., 80f., 93, 95–100, 114, 131, 137–140, 155, 158, 167, 208f., 221, 224f.
testimony   41, 134, 180, 192, 194–198, 203–206, 209f., 213f. *See also* document/monument
theology   27, 33, 55, 144, 151, 164
tradition   16, 34, 103–108, 131, 155, 157, 167
transcendentalism   11
Troy   194, 205
truth   8, 20, 27, 42f., 45, 51, 66, 137f., 140f., 143, 149, 151, 162, 166, 168, 170, 182, 192, 204, 223f.
tuism. *See* personal pronouns
tychasm/anancasm/agapasm   46, 84–88, 91, 95, 127, 141f., 164, 167–170, 173–174, 189, 215
tychism   82, 84

unconscious   19, 35, 104, 107, 210–213
unintended consequences   94, 111
unintentional evidence   21, 209f., 213, 215f.

United States Coast Survey 15, 22, 30, 38, 156

vagueness 64, 91f., 106, 136, 142, 176

www.ingramcontent.com/pod-product-compliance
Lightning Source LLC
Chambersburg PA
CBHW030536230426
43665CB00010B/916